BEST of the BEST
from

Michigan

Selected Recipes from Michigan's
FAVORITE COOKBOOKS

BEST of the BEST
from
Michigan

Selected Recipes from Michigan's
FAVORITE COOKBOOKS

Edited by
GWEN McKEE
and
Barbara Moseley

Illustrated by Tupper England

QUAIL RIDGE PRESS

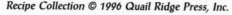
Library of Congress Cataloging-in-Publication Data

Best of the best from Michigan: selected recipes from Michigan's
    favorite cookbooks / edited by Gwen McKee and Barbara Moseley;
    illustrated by Tupper England.
        p. cm.
    Includes index
    ISBN 0-937552-69-0
        1. Cookery, American.   2. Cookery—Michigan.
    I. McKee, Gwen. II. Moseley, Barbara.
    TX715.B485639   1996
    641.59774–dc20

                                                        96-43779
                                                        CIP

First printing, October 1996 • Second, March 1998 • Third, January 2000
Fourth, January 2001 • Fifth, November 2002

Manufactured in the United States of America

Front cover photo: Nickless-Hubinger Flour Mill, courtesy of Frankenmuth Convention and Visitors Bureau. Back cover photo by Gordon Denman. Chapter opening photos courtesy of: Bay Area Convention & Visitors Bureau; Flint Area Convention & Visitors Bureau; Greater Battle Creek/Calhoun County Visitor & Convention Bureau; Greater Lansing Convention & Visitors Bureau; Jackson Convention & Tourist Bureau; Joel Spykerman/Photographic Concepts; Kenny Darwin/Midwest Outdoors; Mackinac Island Chamber of Commerce; Michigan Travel Bureau; Philip W. Stephens/Chippewa Nature Center/Midland County Convention & Visitors Bureau; Steve and Pattie Constable; Traverse City Convention & Visitors Bureau

QUAIL RIDGE PRESS
P. O. Box 123 • Brandon MS 39043 • 1-800-343-1583
Email: info@quailridge.com • www.quailridge.com

CONTENTS

An authentic working Dutch windmill at Windmill Island. Holland.

PREFACE

Michigan, the Great Lakes State, is a cornucopia of wonderful things. One can find ice fishing, snowboarding, skiing, swimming, sailing, golfing, boating, biking, hiking, and hunting, along with wine tasting, fruit picking, art, music, history, and fun festivals.

From the Upper Peninsula to Kalamazoo, there is bounty and beauty everywhere. The straits separating the Upper and Lower Peninsulas have a charm like no other; Mackinac Island is a true paradise. Traverse City, the Cherry Capital of the World, offers everything from cherry pie to cherry hamburgers. And the village of Frankenmuth, with its alpine-style buildings, Bavarian atmosphere, and Christmas-all-year-trimmings, is like walking into a storybook. Detroit offers everything from big city culture to skyscraper views, and motor car and Motown history. And Holland's windmills and tulips are indeed a magical sight to behold.

We discovered that people throughout Michigan, whether in the fast-paced big cities, or farm lands brimming with lush vegetation, to Gingerbread-trimmed cottages along the bay, love to talk about their state and their heritage. They take great pride in their bountiful harvests of sugar beets, maple syrup, apples, blueberries, mushrooms, asparagus, corn, peaches...the list goes on and on. The lakes temper the climate for a perfect mix to create the abundant harvests.

Want to know how Michigan cooks prepare Applesauce Bread Baked in a Jar? What about Big Bear's Deep Woods Chili? Or Traverse City Cherry Berry Pie? How about "wild" recipes like Stuffed Michigan Morels or Curried Caribou? And who wouldn't want to come to an Open Fire Walleye Fish Fry? These are but a few of the outstanding Michigan recipes in store for you throughout this twenty-first edition of our Best of the Best State Cookbook Series. So many of these recipes were created to take advantage of the abundance of fresh fish, fruits, vegetables, and wild game. And some were concocted simply out of love, like "I Need A Hug" Peanut Butter Cookies.

Talking with the many people involved in producing this collection of recipes from sixty-two contributing cookbooks throughout the Great Lakes State is one of the highlights of the work involved. We are grateful to each and every one of our Michigan contributing cookbook chairpersons (see catalog listing beginning on page 265), and though we feel we have garnered the very best cookbooks available in Michigan, we do beg forgiveness from any we may have inadvertently overlooked. Getting to know about the state and its people made it a joy to taste our way through Michigan. Come and join us, enjoy the facts scattered throughout, as well as illustrations and pictures that enhance the wide array of recipes we have gathered.

Thanks always to our "Best" artist, Tupper England; to the many newspaper editors across the state who helped in our search for Michigan cookbooks; to the many helpful personnel at tourist bureaus, chambers of commerce, and bookstores all across the state; our office staff who diligently dug for more information and kept up with loads of paperwork; and to the cooks, chefs, authors and committees who provided us with these wonderful recipes to make this one of the finest sources of Michigan cookery available.

From the land of the Great Lakes, we offer you great eating. Enjoy!

Gwen McKee and Barbara Moseley

Contributing Cookbooks

Allen Park Garden Club Recipe Book
The Bell Tower Cookbook
Blissfield Preschool Cookbook
The Bountiful Arbor
Bringing Grand Tastes to Grand Traverse
Centennial Cookbook
A Century of Recipes Through the Windows of Time
Chelsea Cooks
Come and Dine
Cook Book: The Best of Michigan
Cookies and Bars
Country Cookbook
Country Life Vegetarian Cookbook
Cranbrook Reflections: A Culinary Collection
Crystal Clear Cooking
Dad's Cook Book
Dawn to Dusk
The Dexter Cider Mill Apple Cookbook
Ferndale Friends Cook Book
Fish & Game Menu Cookbook
Four Seasons Cookbook
From Our Home to Yours
From Our Kitchens with Love
The Fruit of Her Hands
Good Food From Michigan
Great Lakes Cookery
Halvorson-Johnson Family Reunion Cookbook
Heavenly Helpings
Herbal Favorites
High Fit - Low Fat
High Fit - Low Fat Vegetarian
Historically Delicious

Contributing Cookbooks

Hollyhocks & Radishes
Home Cookin': Almont Elementary PTA
Home Cookin': First Congregational United Church of Christ
How to Make A Steamship Float and Other Great Lakes
Recipes
In the Dough
The Junior League of Grand Rapids Cookbook I
Just Inn Time for Breakfast
"Life Tastes Better Than Steak" Cookbook
Michigan Gourmet Cookbook
Mrs. Boone's Wild Game Cookbook
Mucky Duck Mustard Cookbook
Northcountry Kitchens Cookbook
Of These Ye May Freely Eat
Opaa! Greek Cooking Detroit Style
Our Best Home Cooking
Pleasures from the Good Earth
Recipes and Memories - A Taste of Yesterday for Today
Recipes & Remembrances II
Renaissance Cuisine
Seasoned Cooks II
Sharing Our Best Volume II
The Simply Great II Cookbook
Simply Sensational
Smart Snacks
Some Enchanted Eating
Something Special
Tasteful Art
Trendfully Cookin'
What's Cookin'
Woman's National Farm and Garden
Association - Rochester Cookbook Volume II

Appetizers and Beverages

Visiting Mackinac Island is like stepping back into the Victorian era. No cars are allowed on this peaceful three-mile-long island.

Rosemary Punch for a Bunch

2 cups water
1/2 cup dried rosemary
1 (46-ounce) can unsweetened
  pineapple juice

2 quarts 7-Up
1 quart ginger ale

Rosemary infusion: heat the water and rosemary to a boil. Steep for 15 minutes. Strain. Pour pineapple juice into punch bowl. Stir in the strained rosemary infusion. Add 7-Up and ginger ale. Float a rosemary sprig on top. Freeze additional 7-Up in an ice ring.

Herbal Favorites

Homemade Powdered Cocoa
(Fat free)

1 pound Nestles Quick
1 (25.6-ounce) package nonfat
  dried skim milk powder

1³/4 cups + 2 tablespoons
  light coffeemate
1 cup powdered sugar

Thoroughly combine all ingredients and store in an airtight container. To make one cup hot cocoa: add 6 ounces water to 1/4 cup powdered cocoa. Stir well and microwave on HIGH for 100 seconds. Yield: approximately 55 cups.

From Our Home to Yours

Jay's Orange Julius

1 (6-ounce) can frozen orange
  juice
1 (6-ounce) can frozen
  lemonade

5 juice cans water
2 cups French vanilla ice
  cream

Combine orange juice, lemonade, and water. Put ice cream into blender, add 3 cups juice mixture, and blend on medium speed until mixed and foamy. Makes 5 servings.

The Junior League of Grand Rapids Cookbook I

Hot Buttered Rum

A Michigan cold weather drink.

1 pound brown sugar
1/2 cup butter or oleo
1/4 teaspoon nutmeg

1/2 teaspoon cinnamon
1/2 teaspoon cloves
Rum

Cream sugar and butter. Add spices to make base. In a 6-ounce mug, put one jigger rum and one heaping tablespoon of base mixture. Fill with boiling water. Base keeps in refrigerator for months. Make a batch of the recipe and place in attractive wine glass or mug; include recipe and give as a gift. Makes 32 servings.

The Junior League of Grand Rapids Cookbook I

Hot Pecan Dip

Like rabbits in the lettuce patch, your guests won't leave this alone.

3/4 cup chopped pecans
2 tablespoons butter, melted
1/2 teaspoon salt
1 (8-ounce) package cream
  cheese, softened
2 tablespoons milk
2 1/2 ounces dried beef,
  chopped

1/4 cup finely chopped green
  pepper
1/2 small onion, grated
1/2 teaspoon garlic powder
Freshly ground pepper to
  taste
1/2 cup sour cream

Preheat oven to 350°. Combine pecans, butter, and salt, and spread out in a pie plate. Bake 15 minutes. Cool several minutes. Combine remaining ingredients in given order. Pour into an ungreased, shallow 8- or 9-inch baking dish. Cover with prepared nuts. At this point, the dip may be set aside or refrigerated until baking time. Bake 20 minutes. Serve hot with crackers or pumpernickel bread for dipping. Yield: 3 cups.

Hollyhocks & Radishes

 Michigan ranks fifth nationally in wine production.

Warm Artichoke Dip

An excellent sandwich spread, good with a grilled veggie sandwich; on baked potatoes instead of sour cream; or in grilled mushroom caps.

1 teaspoon olive oil
1 medium onion, diced
3 cloves garlic, minced
1 (9-ounce) package frozen
  artichoke hearts, or 2
  (15-ounce) cans
1 (8-ounce) package fat-free
  cream cheese

1/3 cup Parmesan cheese,
  freshly grated
Dash hot sauce
1/4 teaspoon salt, or to taste
1/4 cup fresh basil, chopped
Dash paprika

Heat oil in skillet. Add onion and garlic and sauté over medium heat until soft (about 3 minutes). Add artichoke hearts and cover. Reduce heat to low and cook 5 minutes. Transfer mixture to food processor. Add cream cheese and Parmesan; pulse ingredients to combine. Add hot sauce, salt and basil. Pulse to combine ingredients. Serve warm, sprinkled lightly with paprika, accompanied by wedges of Crispy Pita Triangles or your favorite fat-free cracker. Makes 10 servings.

Nutrient calculations per serving (1/4 cup) (not including pita triangles or crackers): Cal 58; Total Fat 2g (Sat 0.7g); Chol 3mg; Carb 5g; Dietary Fiber 1.5g; Prot 6g; Sod 275mg; Cal 143mg; Iron 0.4mg. Exchanges: 1 Vegetable, 1/2 Very lean meat.

High Fit - Low Fat Vegetarian

Broccoli Cheese Dip

2 packages chopped broccoli
1 stick oleo
1/2 medium onion, chopped
1 large can mushrooms

1 can mushroom soup
12 ounces Velveeta cheese
Lipton Onion Dry Soup Mix

Cook broccoli and drain. Sauté onion and mushrooms with oleo in large frypan until onion is soft. Melt mushroom soup and Velveeta cheese in onion and mushroom mixture. Mix broccoli, cheese mixture and onion soup mixture in crock-pot on low. Use large dipping corn chips.

Heavenly Helpings

Italian Crab Meat Dip

1 (8-ounce) and 1 (3-ounce)
    package cream cheese
2 tablespoons mayonnaise
Dash of garlic powder
Dash of Worcestershire sauce

Dash of lemon juice
1 (12-ounce) jar chili sauce
Diced onion to taste
6 ounces crab meat, drained
Green parsley for garnish

Blend in blender cream cheese, mayonnaise, garlic powder, Worcestershire sauce, and lemon juice. Spread onto a 13- to 14-inch pizza pan. Spread chili sauce on top of cream cheese mixture. Top with diced onion, crab meat, and parsley. Serve with assorted crackers.

Just Inn Time for Breakfast

Shanty Creek's Hot Crab Dip

Serve hot or cold....Delicious!!!

2 (8-ounce) packages cream
    cheese
3/4 cup mayonnaise
2 (6-ounce) cans crabmeat

1/4 cup white wine
1 teaspoon mustard
Dash of seasoning salt

Melt in double boiler the cream cheese and mayonnaise; then add other ingredients.

Our Best Home Cooking

Chocolate Raspberry Dip

Scored an A+ with the adults who tested it.

1 cup water	2 tablespoons margarine
1 cup sugar	1¹/₂ teaspoons vanilla
²/₃ cup cocoa	¹/₂ cup wheat germ
¹/₄ cup flour	3 (8-ounce) containers low-fat
¹/₂ teaspoon salt	raspberry yogurt

In a large saucepan, boil the water. In a medium bowl, blend the sugar, cocoa, flour, and salt. Add this mixture to the boiling water; stir constantly. Cook until thick. Remove from heat. Blend in the margarine and vanilla. Cool 5 minutes. In a large bowl, combine the wheat germ and raspberry yogurt. Pour the slightly cooled chocolate mixture over this and whisk together well. Refrigerate several hours or overnight. Stir again before serving.

Dipper suggestions: Strawberries, banana chunks, large marshmallows, vanilla wafers.

Nutrition per serving: Cal 93; Fat 2g; Prot 2g; Carb 17g; Chol 1mg; Fiber 0g; Vit A 54IU; Sod 93mg; Iron 0mg; Vit C 0mg.

Smart Snacks

Venison Dip

1 can refried beans	3 cups grated cheese (colby,
2 pounds ground venison	co-jack, muenster)
1 envelope dry taco mix	¹/₂ cup sour cream
1 can enchilada sauce	Nacho chips
1 jar taco sauce	

Spread refried beans in bottom of 9x13-inch pan. Brown meat and remove from heat. Add taco mix, enchilada sauce and taco sauce. Mix well and pour over beans. Spread grated cheese on top. Heat in 400° oven 15-20 minutes or until bubbly. Spread sour cream over cheese and return to oven for 5 minutes. Use teaspoon to dip and serve with nacho chips.

Blissfield Preschool Cookbook

Beverly Boos' Meatballs

3 pounds pork sausage
3 (8-ounce) cans sliced water
   chestnuts, drained, chopped
3/4 cup Mucky Duck* mustard

1 - 1¹/₂ cups commercial
   barbecue sauce

Combine sausage, water chestnuts, and mustard in large bowl; mix well by hand. Shape into walnut-sized balls. Place on greased rack in roasting pan. Bake at 375° for 40 minutes or until browned. Remove meatballs to chafing dish, electric wok or electric frying pan. Add barbecue sauce. Cook until heated through, stirring gently. Serve hot. After baking, meatballs can be frozen in plastic container, with or without sauce. Makes about 75 meatballs.

*Sweet-tangy mustard.

Mucky Duck Mustard Cookbook

Ham Meatballs

1 pound ham, ground
1 pound veal or pork, ground
2 cups soft bread crumbs (8
   slices)
1 cup milk
2 eggs

1/4 cup onion, minced
1 teaspoon dry mustard
1/3 - 1/2 cup almonds or
   walnuts, ground
1/2 teaspoon garlic powder

Mix well and roll into small balls (about 1/2 inch). Brown in pan or oven at 350° for 20 minutes. Shake pan from time to time to keep balls round. Put into Cranberry Glaze.

CRANBERRY GLAZE:
1 (16-ounce) can jellied
   cranberry sauce
3 tablespoons wine vinegar
3 tablespoons apricot
   preserves
2 tablespoons brown sugar
1 teaspoon lemon juice

2 tablespoons currants
1/2 teaspoon Worcestershire
   sauce
1/4 cup water (optional)
1 teaspoon orange juice
1 teaspoon dry mustard
8 teaspoons cinnamon

Heat and stir till blended. Put meatballs into Glaze. Makes 100 meatballs.

Allen Park Garden Club Recipe Book

Taco Tartlets

MEAT SHELLS:

1 pound ground beef
2 tablespoons taco seasoning
 mix

2 tablespoons ice water

To make meat shells, combine ingredients; mix well. Press meat mixture into bottom and sides of tiny tart pans and set aside.

FILLING:

1 cup dairy sour cream
2 tablespoons red taco sauce
2 ounces chopped black
 olives

1 cup coarsely crushed tortilla
 chips, divided
1/2 cup shredded Cheddar
 cheese

Combine sour cream, taco sauce, olives, and 3/4 cup tortilla chips. Spoon filling into each shell, mounding slightly. Combine remaining chips and cheese; sprinkle over each tartlet. Bake at 375° for 10 minutes. Garnish with taco sauce if desired. Yield: 32 tartlets.

Home Cookin': First Congregational United Church of Christ

Easy Appetizer

1 package bologna
1 package cream cheese,
 whipped

Horseradish, to taste

Spread each piece of bologna with cream cheese that has been mixed with horseradish, if desired. Layer the bologna until all pieces are used. Wrap stack of layered bologna and place in refrigerator. When ready to serve, cut into bite-sized triangular wedges.

Note: This is much easier to cut when cold.

Crystal Clear Cooking

Crispy Pita Triangles

Delicious with savory dips and spreads as an alternative to fat-free crackers.

5 pita bread pockets,
  whole-wheat
Vegetable cooking spray

1/4 cup shredded Parmesan
  cheese, freshly grated

Preheat oven to 375°. Separate each pita pocket into 2 equal pieces (insert small sharp knife into the edge of the pita pocket; gently cut around outer edge to separate the 2 halves.) Stack the pieces on top of each other and cut in half, then cut each half into 4 to make 16 wedges altogether. Separate wedges and place on a cookie sheet (lightly sprayed with vegetable cooking spray) in a single layer. Lightly spray the pita wedges with vegetable cooking spray, then sprinkle with the Parmesan cheese.

Place in a preheated oven to bake until crispy and lightly golden in color. This usually takes from 7-10 minutes. Watch carefully to avoid burning. Allow to cool and store, unrefrigerated, in heavy-duty zip-lock bags. Will keep fresh for several weeks. Makes 20 servings (4 triangles each).

Nutrient calculations per 4-piece serving: Cal 50; Total Fat 1g (trace Sat); Chol 1mg; Carb 9g; Dietary Fiber 1g; Prot 2g; Sod 108mg; Cal 20mg; Iron trace. Exchanges: 1/2 starch.

High Fit - Low Fat Vegetarian

Bourbon Sausage Slices

2 pounds smoked Polish
  sausage, cut in 1/4-inch slices
2 cups catsup
3/4 cup brown sugar

3/4 cup bourbon
1 tablespoon grated onion
1/2 cup water

In a large saucepan, combine all ingredients except sausage. Add sausage; simmer for 25 minutes. Serve warm. Can be refrigerated for several days and reheated. Yield: 8-10 appetizer servings.

Something Special

Chicken Dijon

This appetizer is delicious right from the oven or at room temperature.

8 chicken breasts, boned and
  halved
1/2 cup oil
1/2 cup (1 stick) butter or
  margarine, melted
6 tablespoons Dijon-style
  mustard

1/2 teaspoon dried basil
Dash black pepper
Dash red (cayenne) pepper
6 tablespoons chopped fresh
  chives or green onion tops
2 cups fine bread crumbs

Preheat oven to 350°. Use a cookie sheet or large baking dish sprayed with nonstick cooking spray.

Cut each breast half into about 4 strips. Mix the oil and melted margarine, mustard, basil, peppers, and chives and whisk until mixture is thoroughly blended. Dip chicken pieces into mustard mixture and roll in bread crumbs until coated. Place in baking pan and bake for 25-30 minutes.

Historically Delicious

Shrimp Mousse

1 (8-ounce) package cream
  cheese, softened
1 cup real mayonnaise
2 envelopes Knox gelatin
1/2 cup cold water
1 can tomato soup

Dash or 2 of Tabasco
1/4 teaspoon lime juice (or to
  taste)
1 medium red onion, chopped
2-3 ribs celery, chopped
1 pound small shrimp, cooked

Whip cream cheese and mayonnaise together in electric mixer until smooth. Soften Knox gelatin in cold water. Bring tomato soup just to a boil. Add gelatin mixture and stir to dissolve. While whipping cream cheese mixture on low, slowly add tomato soup mixture, Tabasco, and lime juice. Fold in remaining ingredients. Pour into lightly greased mold and chill until set (at least several hours).

Unmold and serve with crackers. Leftovers can be served by mixing together as a spread.

The Bell Tower Cookbook

Crabmeat Quesadillas

1¹/₂ cups shredded Cheddar cheese	2 tablespoons finely chopped green onion
¹/₄ cup mayonnaise	2 tablespoons chopped chilies, drained
¹/₃ cup sour cream	10 (8-inch) flour tortillas
8 ounces cooked crabmeat, chopped	2 tablespoons butter, melted

In large mixing bowl, combine all ingredients, except tortillas and butter. Refrigerate until ready to complete. Spread about 3 tablespoons filling on each tortilla. Fold in half. Brush both sides of tortillas with butter. Place on baking sheet. Bake at 375° for 10-15 minutes or until heated through. Cut each quesadilla into 3 wedges. Yield: 30 appetizers.

Something Special

Rounds of Crab

1 (6-ounce) can crab meat, rinsed, well drained	1 cup shredded sharp cheese
1 cup mayonnaise	2 tablespoons Mucky Duck* mustard
¹/₂ cup grated onion	1 baguette French bread

Combine crab meat, mayonnaise, onion, cheese, and mustard in medium bowl; mix well. Slice baguette into 3-4 dozen ¹/₂-inch rounds. Spoon one tablespoon crab meat mixture on each. Place on baking sheet. Broil until golden. Serve hot.

*Sweet-tangy mustard.

Mucky Duck Mustard Cookbook

Greek Mini Pizzas

4 pita breads, split
1/4 cup olive oil
4 cloves garlic, minced
2 tomatoes, chopped
1 bunch scallions, chopped

3/4 cup chopped Greek olives
11/2 teaspoons oregano
1 cup feta cheese, crumbled
1 cup shredded provolone
   cheese

Brush pita with olive oil. Sprinkle with garlic, tomatoes, scallions, and olives. Add oregano, feta, and top with shredded provolone. Can refrigerate several hours. Bake at 350° for 10-12 minutes. Cut each round in fourths and serve warm. Yield: 32 appetizers.

Something Special

Puff Pastry Prosciutto Pinwheels

Impressive looking and not hard to make!

1 sheet puff pastry
  (approximately 1/2 pound)
3 tablespoons honey mustard
1/4 pound thinly sliced
  prosciutto, chopped

1 cup grated Parmesan cheese
1 egg
Water
Parchment paper
Pam cooking Spray

Preheat oven to 400°. Place puff pastry on lightly floured surface and roll out to 12x18 inches; spread mustard on top of pastry. Arrange prosciutto evenly to cover all the pastry; sprinkle with cheese. Lightly press cheese into prosciutto with a rolling pin.

Starting at one long edge, roll up the pastry like a jelly roll just to the middle of the dough (approximately 3 times); roll up the other side in the same way. Where the 2 rolls meet in the center, use a small amount of water to seal seam.

Cut the rolls into 1/2-inch slices using a serrated knife. Place slices on cookie sheet lined with parchment sprayed with Pam; flatten slightly with spatula. Refrigerate at least 15 minutes or until ready to bake.

Beat egg with 2 tablespoons water; brush each pinwheel with egg wash. Bake 10 minutes, until lightly golden. Turn pinwheels over; bake 5 minutes more. Serve warm. Makes 2 dozen.

The Bountiful Arbor

Pepperoni & Cheese Appetizer Bread

2 packages yeast
2¹/₂ cups warm water
1 tablespoon sugar
1 tablespoon salt
1 tablespoon margarine,
softened

6¹/₂ cups all-purpose flour
(approximately)
18 thin slices provolone
cheese
1¹/₂ cups chopped pepperoni
1 egg, beaten

Sprinkle yeast over warm water in large bowl, stir. (May use food processor.) Add sugar, salt, margarine, and 3 cups flour. Beat until smooth. Add additional flour to make soft dough. On floured board (or in processor), knead until smooth and elastic. Place in greased bowl. Turn to grease top. Cover. Let rise in warm, draft-free place until doubled, about one hour.

Punch dough down. Divide into 3 pieces. Roll each piece to 12x8-inch rectangle. Place 6 slices provolone and ¹/₂ cup pepperoni on each rectangle. Roll up from long side as for jelly roll. Seal. Place on greased baking sheets. Cover and let rise until doubled, about one hour.

Slash tops, brush loaves with egg. Bake at 400° for 25-30 minutes, or until done. Cool slightly. Serve warm. Refrigerate leftovers; reheat to serve. Yields 3 loaves.

A Century of Recipes Through the Windows of Time

Mini Quiches

1/2 cup margarine or butter
1 (3-ounce) package cream
  cheese, softened
1 2/3 cups unsifted flour
1 1/2 cups sour cream
3/4 cup shredded Swiss cheese

2 eggs, beaten
3 tablespoons finely chopped
  onion
2 teaspoons chicken bouillon
2 slices bacon, crumbled

Preheat oven to 400°. In mixer bowl beat margarine and cream cheese until fluffy; stir in flour. Divide dough into 24 balls. Place in 2-inch tart pans or muffin cups; press evenly on bottom and up sides. Combine remaining ingredients except bacon; mix well. Spoon one tablespoon mixture into each pan. Sprinkle with bacon. Bake 20 minutes or until golden. Serve warm.

Simply Sensational

Toast Cups with Mushroom Filling

Lovely "finger food" for a special occasion. Or, if you're pressed for time, the mushroom filling alone makes a great spread for crackers. Place in an ovenproof dish and heat before serving.

TOAST CUPS:

2 loaves of bread, thin sliced   1 cup butter or margarine, melted

Cut the crust from the bread. Roll slices thin with a rolling pin and cut with a 3-inch round cutter. Brush both sides of rounds with melted butter and press into mini muffin pan cups. Bake the cups in a 450° oven for 5 minutes or until golden brown.

MUSHROOM FILLING:

1 large onion, finely chopped
1 tablespoon butter
1 pound fresh mushrooms,
  washed and chopped
1/2 teaspoon garlic powder

12 ounces cream cheese
Dash of Worcestershire sauce
Salt
Pepper

Sauté the onion in the butter, add mushrooms and garlic powder and sauté for several minutes. Remove from heat and add cream cheese and Worcestershire. Salt and pepper to taste, then blend with spoon or fork until smooth. Fill toast cups with filling. Reheat in oven at 375° for about 8 minutes. Makes about 4 dozen.

Historically Delicious

Pesto Cheese Layered Torte

Shaped in clay pot.

CHEESE LAYER:

3/4 cup cream cheese

3/4 cup butter

PESTO LAYER:

2 1/2 cups basil*

1/4 cup pine nuts

3 cloves garlic

3/4 cup fresh Parmesan
   cheese

3/4 cup olive oil

1/4 cup fines herbs (chives,
   parsley, thyme, tarragon and
   chervil)

Line clean clay pot with foil and cheese cloth. Blend cream cheese and butter. In food processor, mix basil, nuts, garlic, Parmesan cheese, olive oil, and herbs. Layer cream cheese/butter mixture and pesto until pot is full. Refrigerate up to 5 days.

*If basil is unavailable, substitute 2 cups spinach and 1/2 cup parsley.

Herbal Favorites

Appetizer Roll-Ups

1 (8-ounce) package cream
   cheese

1/2 cup sour cream

Chopped onion

1 cucumber, peeled and
   chopped

Black olives, chopped

Garlic salt

Large soft flour tortillas

Mix cream cheese and sour cream. Add more or less of the sour cream to have a good spreading consistency. Add chopped onion, cucumber, black olives and garlic salt to taste. Spread on tortillas. Spread to all but one of the edges. Roll up, starting on the side opposite this edge. Place rolls in covered container several hours or overnight. Slice chilled rolls in 1/2 - 1-inch slices. Can use chopped ham or corned beef and leave out cucumbers. Experiment with combinations.

Centennial Cookbook

Stuffed Michigan Morels

Michiganians are fortunate to have access to 3 native varieties of fresh morels in early May each year.

25 large morels	1/2 teaspoon paprika
1/2 cup butter	5 cups dry bread crumbs
1 cup chopped onion	11/2 cups coarsely chopped
1 cup chopped celery	pecans
1 teaspoon salt	Beaten eggs
1/2 teaspoon black pepper	1/2 - 1 cup melted butter

Select large (preferably white) morels. Rinse thoroughly; trim off stems; set morels aside and chop stems. Heat butter in large, heavy skillet and sauté onion, celery, and chopped mushroom stems until tender and transparent. Stir in seasonings, bread crumbs, and pecans. Stir in enough beaten eggs to moisten mixture. Spoon filling in pastry bag fitted with a serrated metal tip, and stuff morels. Set stuffed morels, points up, on a buttered baking sheet. Drizzle with melted butter and bake at 350° for 20-30 minutes. Serve upright on chopped parsley or other greens. Serves 10-12.

Cranbrook Reflections

Starboard Stuffed Mushrooms

1 pound medium mushrooms
1/4 pound butter or margarine,
   melted
1/4 cup green onions, minced

1/4 cup water, white wine or
   sherry
1 cup herb-seasoned stuffing

Wash mushrooms; remove stems. Dip caps in melted butter and place upside-down on baking pan. Finely chop 1/4 of stems and sauté with green onions in remaining butter. Add water or wine. Stir in stuffing. Spoon in mushroom caps. Bake in 350° oven about 10 minutes. Makes about 18 hors d'oeuvres.

How to Make A Steamship Float

Eggroll

1/2 cup dry black mushrooms
1 bunch glass noodles
1 small onion
2 stalks celery
2 carrots
1 pound ground beef, chicken,
   or pork

1 teaspoon salt
1 teaspoon garlic powder
1 teaspoon pepper
1 package eggroll wrap

Soak black mushrooms and glass noodles in warm water in two separate bowls. Take both of them out when you think they are soft enough, then chop them into little pieces. Chop onion, celery, and carrots into small pieces. Put everything together in large mixing bowl: ground meat, salt, garlic powder, pepper, glass noodles, black mushrooms, chopped onion, celery, and carrots. Use your hands to mix them good and roll them into eggroll wrappers. Deep fry in a frying pan. Keep watching until eggrolls turn brown, then take out and serve. Serves 15-20.

A Century of Recipes Through the Windows of Time

 Celery was first commercially grown in the US in the Kalamazoo area.

Artichoke Squares

2 (6-ounce) jars marinated
artichokes
1 small onion, finely chopped
4 eggs
6 soda crackers, crushed
1/4 teaspoon salt

1/8 teaspoon each pepper,
oregano
1/2 pound sharp Cheddar
cheese, grated (2 cups)
2 tablespoons minced parsley

Preheat oven to 325°. Drain artichokes and pat dry. Use some of the drained oil to sauté onion in frypan. Chop artichokes. (May be chopped in food processor.) Beat eggs; add crushed crackers and seasonings. Stir in cheese, artichokes and onion. Pour into greased 7x11-inch pan. Bake at 325° for 30 minutes or until set. Cool and cut into squares and serve as finger food.

Renaissance Cuisine

Onion Pâté

This is an especially tasty mixture. The recipe calls for sliced French bread, but it is just as good on crackers or melba toast.

1/2 cup chopped onion
1 (8-ounce) package fresh
mushrooms, cleaned and
chopped
1 tablespoon vegetable oil
2 (3-ounce) packages cream
cheese, quartered

1/4 cup grated Parmesan
cheese
1/4 cup minced fresh parsley
2 tablespoons soy sauce
French bread, thinly sliced

Sauté onion and mushrooms in hot oil in large skillet over medium heat 2 minutes; remove from heat. Stir in cream cheese until blended. Add Parmesan cheese, parsley, and soy sauce, stirring to combine. Refrigerate, covered, 3 hours, or until thoroughly chilled. Serve with French bread slices. Yield: approximately 1²/₃ cups pâté.

Good Food From Michigan

Betty's Bread and Butter Pickles

5-8 pounds sliced medium
    cucumbers, unpeeled
6 medium white onions, sliced
3 cloves garlic
1/3 cup coarse salt

5 cups sugar
1 1/2 teaspoons turmeric
1 1/2 teaspoons celery seed
2 tablespoons mustard seed
3 cups cider vinegar

Slice unpeeled, washed cucumbers thinly. Mix together with sliced onions, garlic cloves and the coarse salt. Cover with cracked ice. Mix thoroughly. Cover and let stand at least 3 hours at room temperature, or as long as 2 days refrigerated. Drain thoroughly.

Combine sugar, spices, and vinegar. Pour over cucumber mixture in large kettle and heat just to a boil. Seal in hot sterilized jars. Makes about 8 pints. Serve chilled.

Our Best Home Cooking

Mango Chutney

2 pounds green mangoes,
    sliced (ripe ones work, too)
1 pound dried apricots (soak
    in boiled water at least 1/2
    hour), chopped
2 pounds dark brown sugar
1 cup malt vinegar
4 cloves garlic, chopped
2 teaspoons heaping grated
    ginger

1/2 pound raisins or currants
1 teaspoon whole cloves (may
    use less and/or powdered,
    depending on the strength
    desired, or whether you like
    finding things in your food
    that you can't eat)
1/2 teaspoon cayenne

Bring all ingredients to a boil in a large pot. Turn down to simmer till thick and brown and mangoes are tender. Be careful not to let it stick and burn or get too thick. It will be a little thicker when it's refrigerated.

This makes enough to give some away and have enough left for yourself. It's good on fresh bread and cheese, or homemade mayonnaise. Keeps several months.

Tasteful Art

Fresh Tomato Salsa

2 medium tomatoes, chopped
  (2 cups)
1/2 cup onion, chopped
1/2 cup green bell pepper,
  chopped
1/2 cup fresh cilantro, chopped

2 tablespoons lemon juice
1 tablespoon lime juice
1 jalapeño pepper, seeded,
  chopped (or 2 tablespoons)

In small non-metal bowl, combine all ingredients; mix well. Cover; refrigerate 1-2 hours to blend flavors. Store covered in refrigerator up to 5 days. Makes 3 1/2 cups.

Trendfully Cookin'

Dr. John Kellogg and Charles W. Post made Battle Creek the "Cereal Capital of the World." In the 1840s, seventh-day Adventists had come there, and their emphasis on health led to Kellogg's establishing a sanitarium. Post came for treatment, and stayed on to become Kellogg's greatest competitor. Once a year 40,000 revelers congregate around "the world's longest breakfast table" to savor cornflakes and other fare.

Bread
and
Breakfast

The "World's Longest Breakfast Table" in the "Cereal Capital of the World."
Battle Creek is the home of Kellogg's and Post.

Almond Poppy Seed Bread

3 eggs
1¹/₂ cups milk
1¹/₈ cups oil
2¹/₂ cups sugar
1¹/₂ teaspoons salt

3 cups flour
1¹/₂ teaspoons baking powder
1¹/₂ tablespoons poppy seed
1¹/₂ teaaspoons each of vanilla,
    butter, and almond flavorings

GLAZE:
¹/₄ cup orange juice
³/₄ cup powdered sugar

¹/₂ teaspoon each of vanilla,
    butter, and almond flavoring

Combine eggs, milk, oil, sugar, and salt. Sift flour with baking powder and add to egg mixture gradually. Add poppy seed and flavorings. Mix well. Pour into 2 greased and floured loaf pans. Bake at 350° for one hour. Combine and mix Glaze ingredients. While bread is still warm, poke holes into top of bread with fork and drizzle Glaze slowly over top so it runs into the bread. This bread can be frozen for up to several months.

Blissfield Preschool Cookbook

Applesauce Bread Baked in a Jar

²/₃ cup shortening
2²/₃ cups sugar
4 eggs
²/₃ cup sugar
2 cups applesauce
3¹/₃ cups flour

2 teaspoons baking soda
1 teaspoon cinnamon
²/₃ cup chopped nuts
¹/₂ teaspoon baking powder
1¹/₂ teaspoons salt
1 teaspoon cloves

Cream the shortening and 2²/₃ cups sugar together. Beat in eggs, ²/₃ cup sugar and applesauce. Sift together and blend into first mixture the remaining ingredients. Mix well. Pour into well-greased pint jars (wide mouth with no neck), filling half full. Bake at 325° for about 45 minutes. Remove one jar at a time from oven; wipe the sealing edge clean. Put on lid and ring and screw tight. Jar will seal as bread cools. Store as you would regular canned goods. Delicious! Enjoy!

Centennial Cookbook

Banana Bread

1³/₄ cups flour
1 cup sugar
2¹/₂ teaspoons baking
   powder
1 teaspoon salt
³/₄ cup Grape Nuts cereal

1 cup mashed ripe banana
¹/₂ cup milk
1 egg, well beaten
2 tablespoons oil or melted
   shortening

Mix flour with sugar, baking powder, and salt; stir in cereal. Combine banana, milk, egg, and shortening; add flour mixture, stirring until all flour is moistened. Pour into greased 9x5-inch loaf pan. Bake at 350° one hour, until cake tester inserted into center comes out clean. Cool in pan 10 minutes. Remove from pan; finish cooling on rack.

Great Lakes Cookery

Lemon Tea Bread

³/₄ cup milk
1 tablespoon finely chopped
   lemon balm
1 tablespoon finely chopped
   lemon thyme
2 cups all-purpose flour
1¹/₂ teaspoons baking
   powder

¹/₄ teaspoon salt
6 tablespoons butter (at room
   temperature)
1 cup sugar
2 eggs, beaten
1 tablespoon grated lemon
   rind

Butter a loaf pan. Heat the milk with the chopped herbs and let steep until cool. Mix flour, baking powder, and salt together. In another bowl, cream butter and gradually add sugar. Continue beating until light and fluffy. Beat in eggs, one at a time. Beat in lemon. Add flour mixture alternately with herbed milk. Mix until just blended. Pour into pan. Cook 50 minutes at 325°. Makes 1 loaf. Glaze while hot.

GLAZE:

Juice of 2 lemons   Confectioners' sugar

Combine juice of lemons and confectioners' sugar. Stir until thick, but still pourable, paste forms. Pour over hot bread.

Herbal Favorites

Tart Cherry Almond Bread

3 cups all-purpose flour
2 teaspoons baking powder
1 teaspoon baking soda
1/2 teaspoon salt
1/4 cup butter or margarine,
  softened
1 cup sugar

2 eggs
1 cup buttermilk
2 teaspoons almond extract
1 cup pitted tart cherries,
  drained
1 teaspoon sugar
3 tablespoons sliced almonds

Preheat oven to 350°. Combine flour, baking powder, baking soda, and salt. Set aside. In a large bowl, beat together butter and one cup sugar. Add eggs and mix well. Stir in buttermilk and almond extract. Stir in flour mixture. Chop drained cherries; stir into batter. Spread batter in greased 9x5-inch loaf pan. Sprinkle one teaspoon sugar and sliced almonds over batter. Bake at 350° for 70 minutes, or until toothpick inserted in center comes out clean. Cool 10 minutes, then turn out of pan onto cooling rack. Yield: 1 loaf.

Good Food From Michigan

Soy-Pumpkin Bread

This unique bread is a real crowd pleaser.

3/4 cup sifted soy flour
1 1/2 cups sifted all-purpose
  flour
1/3 teaspoon baking powder
1 teaspoon baking soda
1 3/4 teaspoons ground
  cinnamon
1/2 teaspoon ground nutmeg

1 teaspoon salt
1/3 cup soybean oil
3/4 pound Michigan beet
  sugar
2-3 eggs, well beaten
7 ounces canned pumpkin
1 1/4 ounces water

Preheat oven to 350°. Sift flours together. Combine dry ingredients except sugar. Sift. Cream soy oil and sugar together. Add eggs and beat until light. Blend in pumpkin and water. Add dry ingredients in two portions, blending well after each addition. Pour batter into greased loaf pan. Bake 65-70 minutes. Remove loaf from pan immediately and cool on a wire rack. Serve with margarine or butter. Serves 12.

Michigan Gourmet Cookbook

Dana's Pumpkin Bread

3 cups sugar
1 cup oil
4 eggs
1 (16-ounce) can pumpkin
3 1/2 cups flour
2 teaspoons salt

1 teaspoon baking powder
1 teaspoon nutmeg
1 teaspoon allspice
1 teaspoon cinnamon
1/2 teaspoon cloves
3/4 cup water

Mix sugar and oil together at high speed. Add eggs one at a time, beating after each. Add pumpkin and mix well. Mix dry ingredients together and add to pumpkin mixture alternating with additions of water until all is well blended. Pour into 2 greased loaf pans. Bake at 350° for one hour.

Recipes and Memories

House Bread

Although the recipe can also be mixed by hand, an electric mixer with paddle attachment, or a food processor with plastic dough blade is recommended.

1 package dry yeast
1¹/₂ cups water
1 tablespoon sugar
1 tablespoon salt
2 tablespoons olive oil

4 cups high gluten bread flour
¹/₄ cup kosher salt
2 tablespoons poppy seed
Chef Larry's Blessing

In a bowl, sprinkle yeast on top of warm water (110°). When yeast has dissolved and starts to form bubbles, add sugar, salt, and oil. Mix well. Using an electric mixer or food processor on low speed, slowly mix in the 4 cups bread flour. As the ingredients combine, the dough should become soft. If it is sticky, add a little more flour. Knead dough at medium speed for 5 minutes. The dough should be smooth and elastic. Remove dough from machine and knead by hand for 2-3 minutes. Place dough in a lightly oiled bowl and cover with clear plastic wrap or a clean towel. Set bowl in a warm place and allow dough to rise until doubled in size, about 25-35 minutes.

Mix kosher salt and poppy seeds. Set aside. When the dough has risen, separate it into 4 equal pieces. Sprinkle your work surface with the salt-seed mixture. Form each dough piece into a long loaf and roll through the salt-seed mixture to lightly coat each piece.

Place loaves on a baking sheet lined with parchment paper. With kitchen scissors, cut loaves into 5 sections, leaving the sections still attached. Brush loaves completely with Chef Larry's Blessing. Let the loaves rise for 30 minutes before baking. (At this point, they may be refrigerated for up to 8 hours before baking.) Bake at 450° for 10 minutes. Then lower oven temperature to 400° and continue baking another 10 minutes or until golden brown. Serve immediately. Yield: 4 loaves.

Recipe by Chef Larry Pagliara.

Note: Tasty ways to enjoy rolls tomorrow: 1. Slice bread in half, top with tomato sauce and Mozzarella cheese, sprinkle with Parmesan cheese and broil. 2. Slice bread rolls in finger-size pieces, bake at 350° until golden brown. Mix softened cream cheese and dry onion soup base to use as a dip for baked bread fingers.

The Simply Great II Cookbook

Chef Larry's Blessing
(Olive Oil Marinade)

Chef Larry would perform this final act over an already good thing to make it even more wonderful.

1 large garlic clove, peeled
1 cup olive oil

2 tablespoons dried oregano
1/8 teaspoon salt

In a blender, emulsify garlic and olive oil. Add spices, then turn blender on and off intermittently to mix thoroughly. Store covered at room temperature until ready to use. The marinade will keep for about one week. Yield: 1 1/4 cups.

Note: Use Larry's Blessing to: Marinate meats, fish or fowl before grilling, baste grilled vegetables, toss with salad greens and croutons, and brush on breads and pizza crusts.

The Simply Great II Cookbook

Easy Monkey Bread

1 package J. B. Dough
    Classic White Bread mix
1/2 cup sugar
1 teaspoon cinnamon

Sugar
1 teaspoon cinnamon
1/2 cup melted butter or
    margarine

Prepare bread mix following package instructions. Set your machine on the dough mode or on the manual setting. Remove dough from bread machine. Divide dough into 16 portions on lightly floured surface. Shape each into a ball. Roll in mixture of 1/2 cup sugar and one teaspoon cinnamon. Place in greased Bundt pan.

Pour any remaining cinnamon-sugar mixture into 2-cup measure. Add enough additional sugar to bring mixture to 1-cup level. Stir in one teaspoon cinnamon and melted butter. Spoon over dough balls.

Let rise for one hour. Bake at 350° for 30 minutes. Let stand for 10 minutes. Invert onto serving plate. Serve warm. Makes 16 servings.

Note: After spooning melted butter over dough balls, you may place in refrigerator overnight and bake in the morning.

In the Dough

Mom's Teddy Bear

Tie thin red ribbon around Teddy Bear neck for giving. Teddy Bear makes a great gift for parents of newborn baby. Place in a basket with a jar of Honey Butter (¹/₂ cup softened butter mixed with 2 tablespoons honey) and a baby gift. The parents will be delighted.

1 package J. B. Dough Whole
   Earth Bread mix
1 tablespoon honey
¹/₄ cup slivered almonds
   (optional)

4 raisins
1 egg, beaten
2 teaspoons water
Vanilla Sugar

Prepare bread mix following package instructions. Add honey with liquid. Add almonds if desired. Set your machine on the dough mode or on the manual setting. Remove dough from bread machine. Divide dough into 2 equal portions on lightly floured surface.

Shape one portion into a ball; place on greased baking sheet. Divide remaining dough into 2 portions. Shape one portion into a ball; position on baking sheet for head. Divide remaining dough into 5 pieces. Shape 4 of the pieces for hands and feet, flattening slightly and snipping with scissors to make fingers and toes. Position ears and nose on head; press firmly. Press 2 raisins into head to make eyes, one raisin for the nose and remaining raisin into body for belly button.

Brush with mixture of egg and water. Sprinkle with Vanilla Sugar. Let rise in warm place for one hour or until doubled in bulk. Bake at 350° for 25-30 minutes or until golden. Makes one Teddy Bear.

VANILLA SUGAR:
1 vanilla bean
1 quart jar

Sugar

Place vanilla bean in clean quart jar. Fill jar to the top with sugar. Place jar lid on tightly. Place in dark warm place for 3 weeks.

In the Dough

Spinach-Cheese Bread

1 package J. B. Dough
  Classic White Bread mix
2 tablespoons butter
1 clove of garlic, finely
  chopped
1 (10-ounce) package frozen
  spinach, cooked, drained

1/3 cup grated Parmesan
  cheese
1/2 teaspoon onion powder
1/4 teaspoon basil
1 egg, beaten
1 tablespoon water
Grated Parmesan cheese to taste

Prepare bread mix following package instructions. Set your machine on the dough mode or on the manual setting. Remove dough from bread machine. Roll into rectangle on lightly floured surface.

Microwave butter and garlic in microwave-safe dish for 30 seconds or until butter melts. Drizzle butter mixture over dough. Spread with mixture of spinach and Parmesan cheese; sprinkle with onion powder and basil. Roll as for jelly roll, sealing edge. Cut roll lengthwise with sharp knife or scissors forming 2 strips; turn filling-side-up. Twist strips together loosely.

Coil strip into circle, turning end under. Transfer with spatula to greased springform pan; dough does not touch edge of pan. Brush with mixture of egg and water; sprinkle with Parmesan cheese. Let rise in warm place for one hour. Bake at 350° for 30 minutes or until brown. Makes one loaf.

In the Dough

Sausage Bread

Tastes great when served with a homemade soup.

1 loaf frozen white bread,
  thawed
1 pound cooked, ground
  Italian sausage

2 eggs, beaten separately
2-3 cups Mozzarella cheese,
  shredded
Parmesan cheese

Roll bread into a rectangle. Mix Italian sausage with one beaten egg. Spread mixture on bread. Add shredded Mozzarella cheese. Roll up bread, jelly-roll style, and put into the shape of a horseshoe. Brush beaten egg on top and sprinkle with Parmesan cheese. Bake at 350° for 20 minutes.

Home Cookin': Almont Elementary PTA

Beer Nut Rolls

DOUGH:

3 sticks oleo
4 cups all-purpose flour
4 egg yolks

²/₃ cup beer
Ground walnuts

Mix oleo and flour together (as for pie crust) with fork until small beads form. Mix egg yolks and beer with fork and pour into flour mixture, mixing until everything is worked in. Roll out each ball of dough on floured pastry cloth (will make 3 large or 6 small balls of dough). Spread filling on dough and sprinkle with ground walnuts. Roll up (as a jelly roll) on greased cookie sheet. Bake in 375° oven for 25 minutes, or until golden brown, or when cake springs back when touched lightly with finger.

FILLING:

4 egg whites
1 cup granulated sugar

1 teaspoon vanilla

Beat egg whites until stiff. Gradually add sugar and beat. Add vanilla and beat.

FROSTING:

1 cup powdered sugar
2 tablespoons butter

1¹/₂ tablespoons milk
Chopped nuts

Beat first 3 ingredients until smooth. Frost each cake when cool, and cover with chopped nuts.

Simply Sensational

Detroit Corn Bread

1 cup white flour
³/₄ cup cornmeal
3 tablespoons sugar
1 tablespoon baking powder

1 teaspoon salt
1 egg
²/₃ cup milk
6 tablespoons butter, melted

Grease 8x8-inch baking pan. In a bowl, mix first 5 ingredients. In a small bowl, beat egg, milk, and melted butter. Stir egg mixture into flour mixture just until blended. Spread batter in pan. Bake at 425° 25 minutes until inserted toothpick comes out clean. Cut into squares; serve warm. Per serving: 200 calories. Makes 9 servings.

Cook Book: The Best of Michigan

Yogurt Muffins

2 cups flour
1/4 cup sugar
1 tablespoon baking powder
1/2 teaspoon baking soda
1/2 teaspoon salt

1/4 cup melted butter
1 container plain yogurt
1/4 cup milk
1 egg
1/2 teaspoon vanilla

Combine dry ingredients; combine liquid ingredients. Mix the two together until moistened. Bake at 425° for 25 minutes.

Home Cookin': First Congregational United Church of Christ

Chocolate Cheesecake Muffins

1 (3-ounce) package cream
  cheese
2 tablespoons sugar
1 cup flour
1/2 cup sugar
3 tablespoons cocoa powder

2 teaspoons baking powder
1/2 teaspoon salt
1 egg, slightly beaten
3/4 cup milk
1/3 cup vegetable oil
Powdered sugar

In small bowl, beat cream cheese and 2 tablespoons sugar until light and fluffy. Set aside. In large bowl, combine flour, 1/2 cup sugar, cocoa, baking powder, and salt. In another small bowl, combine egg, milk, and oil. Add wet mixture to flour mixture. Stir with fork only until flour is moistened. Mixture will be lumpy. Spoon about 2 tablespoons batter into greased muffin cups. Drop one teaspoon of cheese mixture on batter; then add more chocolate batter to fill cups 2/3 full. Bake at 375° for 20 minutes. Dust with powdered sugar. Can be prepared up to 24 hours ahead and reheated in foil. Yield: Approximately 1 dozen.

Something Special

Michigan Blueberry Muffins

Holland has acres and acres of blueberry fields.

3/4 cup sugar
1/4 cup margarine, softened
2 eggs
2 cups flour
2 teaspoons baking powder
1/4 teaspoon salt

1/2 cup milk
2 cups fresh blueberries
1/4 cup margarine, softened
1/2 cup sugar
1/3 cup flour
1/2 teaspoon cinnamon

Cream 3/4 cup sugar and 1/4 cup margarine in a mixer bowl until light and fluffy. Beat in the eggs one at a time. Mix 2 cups flour, baking powder, and salt together. Add to the creamed mixture alternately with the milk, beating well after each addition. Fold in blueberries. Line the muffin cups with paper liners. Fill the muffin cups 3/4 full.

Mix the 1/4 cup margarine, 1/2 cup sugar, 1/3 cup flour, and the cinnamon together in a bowl. Sprinkle over the muffin batter. Bake at 350° for 18-20 minutes or until the muffins test done. Serve warm. Yield: 12 muffins.

Dawn to Dusk

Scottish Scones

Made "famous" at Shannon's Lil' Cafe.

3 cups flour
1 1/2 cups oatmeal
1/2 cup brown sugar
2 teaspoons baking powder

2 teaspoons cinnamon
1 cup butter
1/2 cup currants
1 cup milk

GLAZE:
1 cup powdered sugar

2 tablespoons hot water

Mix dry ingredients together in large bowl. Cut in butter until mixture resembles coarse meal. Toss in currants. Add milk. Toss just until mixture is evenly moist. Divide and shape dough into 12 rounded mounds. Place on greased cookie sheet. "Push" an X shape into top of each scone with a blunt-edged knife. Bake 20-25 minutes at 350°. Will be slightly brown on top and edges when done. Remove from oven and cool. Mix powdered sugar with water to form thick glaze. Drizzle over top of scones. Makes 1 dozen.

Recipes and Memories

Fruit Oat Scones

1 1/2 cups all-purpose flour
1 1/4 cups quick old-fashioned
 oats, uncooked
1/4 cups sugar
1 tablespoon baking powder
1/4 teaspoon salt
1/3 cup margarine

1 (6-ounce) package diced
 dried mixed fruit (1 1/3 cups)
1/2 cup milk
1 egg, lightly beaten
1 teaspoon sugar
1/8 teaspoon cinnamon

Heat oven to 375°. Combine flour, oats, sugar, baking powder, and salt. Cut in margarine until mixture resembles coarse crumbs; stir in fruit. Add milk and egg, mixing just until dry ingredients are moistened. Shape to form a ball. Turn out onto lightly floured surface; knead gently 6 times. On lightly greased cookie sheet, roll out dough to an 8-inch circle. With sharp knife, score 12 wedges; sprinkle with combined 1 teaspoon sugar and 1/8 teaspoon cinnamon. Bake about 30 minutes or till golden brown. Break apart and serve warm. Makes 12 scones.

Allen Park Garden Club Recipe Book

Listy

A Czech/Bohemian pastry.

4 egg yolks
1 tablespoon sugar
1 tablespoon brandy
3 tablespoons cream

Few drops vanilla
Flour
Oil for deep frying

Blend egg yolks with sugar. Add brandy, cream, vanilla, and enough flour to make a stiff dough. Mix well, turn out onto floured board and roll very thin, as for noodles. Cut into square or diamond shapes. Cut a slit in the middle and deep fry until lightly golden. Drain on paper towels and dust with powdered sugar.

Historically Delicious

Polish Paczki
(Jelly Doughnuts)

6 egg yolks
1/4 cup sugar
2 small cakes yeast
1/2 pint cream
3 or 4 cups flour

1 teaspoon salt
3 tablespoons melted butter
Lemon rind or vanilla
Jam

Beat egg yolks well and add sugar. Dissolve yeast in warm cream. Add yolks, flour, salt, gradually, then melted butter and lemon rind or vanilla, then more flour. Beat well until dough no longer clings to spoon. Set aside and let rise for 2 hours. Take small piece and flatten it out in palm of hand. Put a teaspoon of jam in center and fold edges of dough until a ball is formed. Fry balls in deep fat at 350° about 5 minutes. Cool on absorbent paper. Sprinkle with powdered sugar.

Simply Sensational

Angel Wings
(Chrusciki)

6 cups sifted flour
1 1/2 cups powdered sugar
1/2 cup (1 stick) butter
12 egg yolks

1 cup sour cream
1 teaspoon salt
1 teaspoon baking powder
1 jigger clear whiskey

With pastry blender, cut in flour, sugar, and butter. Beat together egg yolks and sour cream. To flour and butter mixture, add salt, baking powder, and whiskey. Add egg mixture and blend well. Transfer to a well-floured board and knead until the dough blisters. Cut in halves, roll very thin and cut into strips about 4 inches long. Slit each piece in center and pull one end through the slit. Fry in hot oil until lightly browned. Drain on absorbent paper and sprinkle with powdered sugar.

Simply Sensational

 Ernest Hemingway immortalized Michigan in his "Up in Michigan" stories.

Sticky Buns

3/4 cup milk
1/2 cup sugar
1 1/4 teaspoons salt
1/2 cup margarine
1/3 cup warm water
2 packages dry yeast
3 eggs (beaten)

4 2/3 cups flour (about, sifted)
3/4 cup soft margarine
2 cups dark brown sugar
1 cup pecans (coarsely
    chopped)
3/4 cup maple-blended syrup

Scald milk, stir in sugar, salt, and 1/2 cup margarine, cool to luke-warm. Measure warm water into large bowl, sprinkle yeast and dissolve. Add lukewarm milk mixture, eggs, and half of flour. Beat well. Stir in remaining flour with spoon to make a soft dough. On a floured board, knead until smooth and elastic, about 8 minutes. Place in greased bowl, and grease top. Cover and let rise until double in bulk.

While dough is rising, prepare pans. Use 3 deep 9-inch pie plates or 8x8x2-inch pans. Spread 2 tablespoons soft margarine in each pan. Sprinkle 1/2 cup brown sugar and 1/3 cup pecans in each pan.

Punch dough down and turn on floured board. Divide into 3 parts. Roll each part into rectangle 9 inches long and 1/2-inch thick. Spread each with some of the remaining soft margarine, sprinkle with remaining brown sugar. Roll each up from long side and cut into 9 slices. Arrange 9 rolls in each pan, cut-side-up. Cover, let rise in warm place about 1/2 hour or until double in bulk. Pour 1/2 cup syrup over rolls in each pan. Bake in hot oven, 400°, about 20-25 minutes or until done. Cool in pans 10 minutes, invert into plates to finish cooling. Makes 27 rolls.

Northcountry Kitchens Cookbook

Bubble Bread Coffee Cake

1 loaf frozen bread dough	1/2 package instant
1 cup chopped nuts	butterscotch pudding
6-ounces butterscotch chips	1/2 cup packed brown sugar
1 stick melted margarine	1 1/2 teaspoons cinnamon

Thaw bread dough for one hour, then cut into pieces. Place chopped nuts and butterscotch chips in a buttered Bundt pan. Then add pieces of bread. Pour melted margarine over dough. Mix dry pudding, brown sugar, and cinnamon and sprinkle on top. Cover with foil. Let rise for one hour, and place in refrigerator overnight. In the morning, bake at 350° for 30 minutes.

Just Inn Time for Breakfast

Red Dog Treats

2 cans Pillsbury crescent rolls	1 teaspoon vanilla
2 (8-ounce) packages cream	Brown sugar
cheese	Cinnamon
1 cup sugar	Walnuts
1 egg yolk	

Line bottom of a 9x13-inch pan with one can of crescent rolls. Mix together cream cheese, sugar, egg yolk, and vanilla. Spread over crescent rolls. Top mixture with second can of crescent rolls. Top with a mixture of brown sugar, cinnamon, and walnuts. Bake in 350° oven for 45 minutes.

Pleasures from the Good Earth

French Breakfast Puffs

1/3 cup margarine
1/2 cup sugar
1 egg
1 1/2 cups flour
1 1/2 teaspoons baking
  powder

1/2 teaspoon salt
1/4 teaspoon nutmeg
1/2 cup milk (sour cream,
  buttermilk, or yogurt may
  be used)

COATING:
1/2 cup sugar
1 teaspoon cinnamon

1/2 cup margarine, melted

Cream margarine, sugar, and egg until light and fluffy. Stir in flour, baking powder, salt, and nutmeg alternately with milk. Fill greased muffin tins 2/3 full. Bake at 350° for 20-25 minutes. Mix cinnamon and sugar. Roll puffs in margarine and then in the sugar mixture. Serve warm.

Pleasures from the Good Earth

Kuchen
(Coffee Cake)

From the early 1900s, The Inn at Watervale has been serving this coffee cake every summer Sunday morning.

1 cup butter
1/2 cup sugar
3 eggs
1 teaspoon salt

1 cake of yeast (dissolved in
  1 1/4 cups lukewarm milk)
5 1/2 cups flour

Cream butter and sugar. Add eggs one at a time. Add salt, dissolved yeast, and flour gradually. Cover and let rise in warm place until double in size. Toss on board and form into desired shape. Place in 9x13-inch pan and let rise again. Preheat oven to 350°. Place pats of butter every inch or so across top. Press pats of butter down in to make "butter holes." Sprinkle top with cinnamon and sugar. Bake until done (about 20 minutes or until golden brown).

Recipes and Memories

Overnight Coffee Cake

Do ahead. Low fat.

2 cups all-purpose flour
1 cup granulated sugar
1 cup firmly packed brown
   sugar, divided
1 teaspoon baking soda
1 teaspoon baking powder
$1/2$ teaspoon salt

2 teaspoons cinnamon, divided
1 cup low fat buttermilk (1
   gram fat per cup)
$2/3$ cup Butter Buds liquid
$1/2$ cup egg substitute
$1/2$ cup pecans, chopped
   (optional)

Preheat the oven to 350°. In a mixing bowl, combine the flour, granulated sugar, $1/2$ cup brown sugar, baking soda, baking powder, salt, and one teaspoon cinnamon. Add the buttermilk, Butter Buds, and egg substitute. Beat on low speed until the mixture is moistened, then beat on medium speed for 3 minutes.

Spoon into an oil-sprayed and floured 9x13x2-inch baking pan. Combine the remaining $1/2$ cup brown sugar, pecans, and one teaspoon cinnamon. Sprinkle over the batter. Cover and refrigerate 8-12 hours. Uncover and bake for 30-35 minutes or until a toothpick inserted in the center comes out clean. Serve warm.

Come and Dine

Breakfast Bundt Cake

BATTER:
1 package yellow cake mix
1 (3-ounce) package instant
   vanilla pudding
$3/4$ cup corn oil

$3/4$ cup water
4 eggs
1 teaspoon vanilla
1 teaspoon butter flavoring

Mix first 4 ingredients well. Then mix in next 3 ingredients, one at a time. Grease and flour tube pan, then alternate batter and filler. Bake for 45-50 minutes at 350°.

FILLER:
$1/3$ cup sugar

$2 1/2$ teaspoons cinnamon

GLAZE:
1 cup powdered sugar
3 teaspoons milk

$1/2$ teaspoon vanilla
1 teaspoon butter flavoring

Mix. Spread over hot cake.

Pleasures from the Good Earth

Hearty Whole Wheat Banana Waffles

2 cups whole-wheat flour
1/2 cup oat bran
2 teaspoons baking powder
2 teaspoons cinnamon
2 tablespoons brown sugar
1/8 teaspoon salt, optional

2 cups skim milk, divided
1 ripe banana, mashed
2 tablespoons canola oil
3 egg whites, lightly whisked
Vegetable cooking spray

Preheat waffle iron. Combine dry ingredients, mix well. Combine 1 1/2 cups of the milk with the banana, oil, and egg whites. Stir the milk/banana mixture into the dry ingredients. Add more milk if necessary to achieve a thick custard consistency. Spray heated waffle iron with vegetable cooking spray. Ladle approximately 1/3 of the mixture (enough to cover the surface) onto your waffle iron. Cook until lightly golden and firm to the touch. Serve immediately. Makes 10 servings.

Note: Good to drizzle with warmed honey or maple syrup and top with a large dollop of nonfat vanilla yogurt. Garnish with fresh fruit in season.

Nutrient calculations per one Belgian-Style waffle: Cal 166; Total Fat 3.9g (Sat 0.4g); Chol 1mg; Carb 25g; Dietary Fiber 3.8g; Prot 7g; Sod 168mg; Cal 134mg; Iron .5mg. Exchanges: 2 starch, 1/2 fat.

High Fit - Low Fat Vegetarian

Waffled French Toast

The kids love these...everyone does; and any leftovers can be reheated in the toaster.

1/2 cup milk	1/2 teaspoon salt
4 eggs	2 tablespoons butter, melted
1 tablespoon sugar	8-10 slices bread

Preheat waffle iron. If the iron is well-seasoned (in other words, had its share of waffles baked in it without being abused by soap!), there should be no need to oil it. In a shallow bowl, with a flat whisk, combine milk, eggs, sugar, and salt, then melted butter. Dip bread slices, one at a time, in egg mixture, and drain. Bake in waffle iron 2-3 minutes, until brown. Serve with bacon or sausage and maple syrup or Strawberry Butter. Yield: 8-10 slices.

STRAWBERRY BUTTER:
Just wonderful over pancakes, waffles, and French toast.

1/2 pound butter, softened	10 ounces frozen strawberries,
1/2 cup powdered sugar	thawed and drained

Combine all in a mixer or food processor until smooth and creamy. It's best served at room temperature, but can be stored in fridge for several weeks. Yield: 2 1/2 cups.

Hollyhocks & Radishes

French Toast Casserole

1 loaf day old French or	1 teaspoon vanilla
Italian bread, sliced	1/2 teaspoon nutmeg
1 cup sweet cream	1 cup butter
1 cup milk	1 cup brown sugar
8 eggs	1 cup finely chopped pecans
1 tablespoon sugar	

Layer bread in a 9x12-inch buttered pan. Mix the cream, milk, eggs, sugar, vanilla, and nutmeg and pour over the toast. Mix the butter, brown sugar, and pecans. Dot this mixture over the egg/bread. Cover with foil. Refrigerate overnight. Bake at 350° for 45 minutes, covered.

Sharing Our Best Volume II

Stuffed French Toast

4 large eggs
1 cup half-and-half
1 teaspoon cinnamon
1/4 teaspoon salt
1 teaspoon nutmeg
1 teaspoon vanilla extract
1 (8-ounce) package cream
   cheese, softened

1/4 cup milk
8 (1/2-inch thick) slices egg
   bread, divided
4 tablespoons orange
   marmalade, divided

In a pie plate or shallow dish, mix together eggs, half-and-half, cinnamon, salt, nutmeg, and vanilla extract. Set aside. In a medium bowl, beat together cream cheese and milk. Start on low speed and increase to high; beat until lump free.

Spread cream cheese mixture evenly on 4 bread slices. Top and spread each with one tablespoon orange marmalade. Top each with remaining bread slice. Preheat grill or griddle. Quickly dip both top and bottom sides of bread in the egg mixture and place on grill or griddle. Cook 4 minutes, turn once, and cook 4 minutes on second side. Serves 4.

The Fruit of Her Hands

Pigs in the Blankets
(Saucijzenbroodjes)

This recipe is a Tulip Time tradition.

2³/₄ - 3 pounds sausage	1 teaspoon salt
3 cups flour	1 cup margarine
3 tablespoons baking powder	1 cup milk

Shape the sausage by hand or with a fork into 30-36 portions. Sift the flour, baking powder and salt into a bowl. Cut in the margarine until crumbly. Stir in the milk. Shape the dough into a smooth ball. Roll ¹/₄-inch thick on a floured surface. Cut into strips about 3¹/₂ inches wide. Wrap each sausage portion loosely in a strip of dough.

Place sausage rolls seam-side-down on an ungreased baking sheet. Pierce the top of each sausage roll with a fork. Bake at 400° for 15 minutes. Reduce the oven temperature to 350°. Bake for 15 minutes or until brown. Yield: 30-36 servings.

Note: May freeze for up to 4 months.

Dawn to Dusk

Dutch Omelet

2 extra-large eggs	2 tablespoons butter
Salt to taste	2 ounces Gouda cheese,
Freshly ground pepper to taste	sliced
1 tablespoon snipped fresh chives	

Whisk the eggs, salt, pepper, and chives in a small bowl. Melt the butter in a 7-inch ovenproof skillet, swirling the butter to coat the skillet. Pour the egg mixture in the skillet when the butter begins to bubble. Place the cheese in the center of the egg mixture. Cook over low heat for a few seconds or until the egg mixture begins to set.

Place the skillet in the oven under a preheated broiler. Broil just until the cheese melts. Remove from the oven. Fold the omelet in half carefully, using a spatula. Serve immediately. Yield: 1 serving.

Note: May substitute finely chopped scallions for the chives.

Dawn to Dusk

Greek Omelette for Two
(Omeletta)

When you think of Greek cooking, omelettes don't even enter your mind—but after reading this egg omelette recipe, you may alter your thinking. This can be made with ingredients that you probably have on hand. So if you're having unexpected guests, this is a good problem-solver.

$^1/_2$ (10-ounce) package frozen chopped spinach
$^1/_4$ cup crumbled feta cheese (1 ounce)
$^1/_4$ cup cream-style cottage cheese
2 teaspoons minced dried onion

$^1/_4$ teaspoon dried mint leaves, crushed
Dash pepper
3 or 4 eggs
Salt and pepper to taste
1 tablespoon butter

In a medium saucepan, cook spinach according to package directions; drain well. In same pan, combine spinach, cheeses, onion, mint, and pepper. Heat thoroughly over low heat, stirring occasionally. Meanwhile, beat eggs; season with salt and pepper. Melt butter in an 8- or 10-inch skillet. (For a 3-egg omelette, use 8-inch skillet; for a 4-egg omelette, 10-inch pan.) Add eggs; cook slowly, running spatula around edge and lifting egg mixture to allow uncooked portion to flow underneath. Spoon spinach mixture onto one-half of omelette; fold other side over filling. Slice onto serving platter. Makes 2 servings.

Opaa! Greek Cooking Detroit Style

Potato/Sausage Casserole

1 (32-ounce) package hash
  browns (thawed)
1 package brown and serve
  sausage, smoky links, or
  smoked sausage, cut into
  bite-size pieces
1/2 cup melted margarine

1 teaspoon salt
1/8 teaspoon pepper
1 can cream of celery soup
1 soup can warm water
1 (31/2-ounce) can Durkee
  onion rings
1 cup Parmesan cheese

Mix together potatoes, sausage, margarine, salt and pepper. In separate bowl mix together soup and one can warm water. Add 3/4 of soup mixture to other ingredients and blend. Place in 9x13-inch pan (sprayed with Pam) or several smaller bowls (ramekins). Pour remainder of soup across top. On top of soup spread onion rings and Parmesan cheese. Bake at 350° about 30 minutes (until bubbly). Serve hot. This can be refrigerated or frozen until the day it's needed. Can also be rewarmed in microwave. Makes 10-12 servings.

Just Inn Time for Breakfast

Country Breakfast Hash

A side dish for breakfast or a main course.

1 teaspoon canola oil
4 cups potatoes, diced*
1/2 cup onion, diced
1 cup mushrooms, diced
1 cup red or green bell
  peppers, diced

1/2 teaspoon dry thyme, or 1
  teaspoon fresh leaves
1/2 teaspoon salt
Black pepper, freshly ground

Preheat canola oil in a nonstick pan. Add potatoes and sauté until tender, approximately 15 minutes. Reduce the time to 5 minutes if using leftover baked potatoes. Add remaining ingredients and cook an additional 10 minutes. Serve hot. Leftovers reheat well. Makes 4 servings.

*Leftover baked potatoes, diced 1/4-inch thick may be used.

Nutrient calculations per one cup serving: Cal 229; Total Fat 2g; (Sat 0.2g); Chol 0mg; Carb 50g; Dietary Fiber 5g; Prot 6g; Sod 284mg; Cal 34mg; Iron 2.7mg. Exchanges: 3 starch, 1 vegetable.

High Fit - Low Fat Vegetarian

Morning Pizza

1/4 cup milk
5 eggs
1 package pizza crust mix
1 pound sausage, cooked and
    drained
2 cups frozen hash browns
1/4 cup Parmesan cheese

1 1/2 cups shredded cheese (a
    variety may be used if
    desired)
Mushrooms, peppers, etc.
    (optional)
Picante sauce

Add milk to eggs and scramble in skillet. Prepare pizza dough as directed on package, and pat into 13-inch greased pizza pan. Spread crumbled sausage on dough. Cover with hash browns, Parmesan cheese, scrambled eggs, and shredded cheese, in that order. Bake at 375° for 25-30 minutes. Serve with picante sauce. Excellent recipe. Makes 8 or more servings.

Just Inn Time for Breakfast

Sunshine Casserole

1 (20-ounce) package frozen
    hash brown potatoes
1/2 pound sausage links,
    cooked and cut into 1/2-inch
    slices
1 1/2 cups shredded
    Monterey Jack or Cheddar
    cheese
6 eggs, lightly beaten

4 cups milk
4 tablespoons finely chopped
    onion
2 teaspoons Dijon-style
    mustard
Paprika
2 medium tomatoes, sliced
    (for garnish)

Grease a 13x9-inch baking pan. Cook the hash browns according to the package directions. Spread them in a single layer in the prepared pan. Spread the sausage and cheese evenly over the potatoes. Combine the eggs, milk, onion, and mustard in a large bowl; pour the mixture over the top. Sprinkle with paprika. Cover and refrigerate for at least one hour or overnight. When ready to cook, heat oven to 325°. Bake the casserole, uncovered, for about one hour or until a knife inserted in the center comes out clean. Let stand for 10-15 minutes before serving. Garnish with tomato slices and serve. Serves 8.

What's Cookin'

Deviled Eggs Wrapped in Ham Casserole

3 (10-ounce) packages frozen
   chopped spinach, cooked and
   drained
8 hard cooked eggs
1 1/2 teaspoons finely
   chopped onion
1/2 teaspoon dry mustard

1/2 teaspoon salt
3 tablespoons mayonnaise
1 teaspoon Worcestershire
   sauce
8 medium-thin slices ham
1 1/2 cups crushed cornflakes
1/4 cup butter, melted

Arrange spinach in a rectangular baking dish, 11x7 inches. Slice hard-cooked eggs in half lengthwise. Scoop out yolks and mix with next five ingredients. Fill eggs with stuffing and place 2 halves together to make one whole egg. Wrap one ham slice around each egg. Arrange over spinach. Pour Cheese Sauce over deviled eggs and refrigerate. Sprinkle buttered cornflakes on top and bake at 350° for 30 minutes or until hot and bubbly. Serves 8.

CHEESE SAUCE:

3 tablespoons butter
2 teaspoons chopped onion
3 tablespoons flour
2 3/4 cups milk

1 1/2 cups grated Cheddar
   cheese
1/2 teaspoon salt

In a saucepan melt butter; add onion and simmer 5 minutes. Add flour, then milk, stirring until sauce thickens. Stir in cheese. Season with salt. Mix well, making sure the cheese is melted.

What's Cookin'

Muesli

2 1/4 cups granola
2 cups chopped apples
1/4 cup chopped nuts or
   sunflower seeds

1/4 cup chopped dried fruit
3 cups apple juice

Combine all ingredients. Let soak in the refrigerator several hours before serving.

Of These Ye May Freely Eat

Apple Strata

8 slices whole-wheat bread, cubed	8 eggs
1¹/₂ cups sharp Cheddar cheese, grated	2 cups milk
	¹/₂ teaspoon dry mustard
	¹/₂ teaspoon Worcestershire
1 cup chopped ham	sauce
Freshly ground pepper to taste	¹/₄ cup butter, melted
4 apples, sliced and rolled in cinnamon-sugar	

Layer half the bread, half the cheese and spread all of the ham over the cheese. Top with freshly ground pepper, all of the apple slices, the remaining bread cubes and the remaining cheese. In a blender, combine the remaining ingredients except the butter. Pour over the casserole; top with melted butter and refrigerate for 3 hours. Bake, uncovered, at 350° for 45-60 minutes or until firm to the touch. Serves 6-8.

What's Cookin'

Fried Apples

³/₄ stick cold butter	¹/₂ cup brown sugar
6-8 large cooking apples	Cinnamon to taste
¹/₄ cup white sugar	

Put butter in a cold frying pan. Cut unpeeled apples into pie slices, as many as you think you want. Jonathans and Ida Reds are the favorites because they hold their shape better. Sprinkle sugars and cinnamon over the top. Cover pan so apples will steam, and turn the heat on low. Stir occasionally. Let sugars form a caramel topping. Makes 6-8 servings. Serve with ice cream and nut topping.

Just Inn Time for Breakfast

9-Minute Strawberry Jam

2 quarts strawberries	6 cups sugar

Clean the strawberries; pour boiling hot water over them. Set one minute; drain off water. Put on stove; bring to a boil. Boil 3 minutes, then add 3 cups of sugar; bring to a boil, boiling for 3 minutes. Add the remaining 3 cups of sugar; bring to a boil, cooking 3 minutes.

Set aside; let cool—sometimes overnight. This thickens as it cools. Pour into glasses the next day and seal with wax.

Four Seasons Cookbook

Brunch Reubens

10 slices rye bread, cut into
  3/4-inch cubes
11/2 pounds cooked corned beef
10 ounces Swiss cheese,
  shredded

6 eggs, lightly beaten
3 cups milk
1/4 teaspoon pepper

Grease a 9x13-inch glass baking pan. Arrange bread cubes in bottom. Coarsely shred corned beef and layer over bread. Sprinkle with cheese. Beat eggs, milk, and pepper. Pour over corned beef mixture. Cover with foil; refrigerate overnight. Bake, covered, at 350° for 45 minutes. Uncover and bake an additional 10 minutes. Serve immediately. Yield: 6-8 servings.

Something Special

Caesar Salad Sandwiches

8 cups loosely packed romaine
  lettuce, coarsely shredded
2 cups cooked, skinless
  chicken
1/2 cup herb seasoned
  croutons

1/4 cup grated Parmesan cheese
6 anchovy fillets, finely
  chopped, optional
3 (6-inch) pita bread rounds
1/2 cup bottled Caesar
  dressing

In a large mixing bowl, combine romaine, chicken, croutons, cheese, and anchovies. Set aside. Cut pita in two, making 6 halves. Brush insides with Caesar dressing. Pour remaining dressing into lettuce mixture. Toss and fill pockets. Yield: 6 servings.

Something Special

Soups

Michigan contains a treasure of lighthouses that stand solitary vigils along the state's thousand miles of Great Lakes shore. Marquette Lighthouse.

Coho-Clam Chowder

A fresh Lake Michigan catch is the best, but you may also use other fish.

2 (10-ounce) packages frozen
  mixed vegetables
4-5 stalks celery, chopped
3/4 cup chopped onion
1 teaspoon salt
1 cup water
4 medium potatoes, diced
2 cans tomato soup
1 large can tomatoes (26-30
  ounces), chopped

1/2 teaspoon thyme
1/4 teaspoon pepper
1/2 cup margarine
2 can clams with liquid
2 pounds coho salmon,
  cooked, cooled, flaked and
  boned
3 quarts milk

Cook frozen vegetables, celery, onion, and salt in water over low heat until tender. Add potatoes, tomato soup, chopped tomatoes, thyme, pepper, and margarine and cook 20 minutes. Add clams and juice, coho, and milk and cook for 20 minutes. Thicken with cornstarch and water, or dry mashed potatoes to obtain desired thickness. Serves 12.

Some Enchanted Eating

Cold Madras Soup

1 (10 1/2-ounce) can beef
  bouillon
1 (10 1/2-ounce) can green
  pea soup, undiluted
1 (10 1/2-ounce) can tomato
  madrilene soup

2 cups light cream
1 tablespoon lemon juice
1 tablespoon curry powder
Salt and pepper
1 or 2 tart apples, chopped

Combine the 3 soups and heat until well blended in a 2 1/2-quart saucepan. Cool. Add cream, lemon juice, curry powder, salt and pepper. Chill. Serve in very cold cups over finely chopped apples. Serves 6-8.

Renaissance Cuisine

Michigan French Onion Soup

3¹/₂ pounds onions
¹/₄ cup olive oil
2 cups unpasteurized apple
  cider
3 cups beef broth
1 cup water
2 tablespoons brandy

Salt and pepper to taste
6 (¹/₂-inch-thick) slices
  Italian bread, toasted lightly
3 ounces Roquefort or
  Mozzarella cheese, crumbled
  (about ³/₄ cup)

Halve the onions lengthwise and slice thin. In a heavy kettle, cook the onions in the oil over moderately-high heat, stirring occasionally for about one hour, or until the onions are golden brown. Stir in the cider, broth, water, brandy, salt and pepper. Simmer the soup, uncovered, for 20 minutes. Arrange toast slices on a baking sheet; sprinkle with cheese, and broil the croutons under a preheated broiler about 4 inches from the heat until the cheese begins to melt. Ladle the soup into heated bowls and float a cheese crouton in each serving bowl. Makes about 7 cups, serving 4-6 as a main course. Freezes well and can be doubled.

Woman's National Farm and Garden Association - Rochester
Cookbook Volume II

Big Bear's Potato Soup

15 pounds Idaho potatoes, diced to 1/2-inch squares

3 large green bell peppers, diced to 1/4-inch squares, with seeds

2 large red bell peppers, diced to 1/4-inch squares, with seeds

3 large Spanish onions, diced chunky

2 cups carrots, sliced very thin, cut to about 1/2-inch lengths

5 pounds lean ham, remove all fat, diced to about 1/4-inch squares

1 bunch celery, diced to about 1/4-inch pieces, with leaves

6 cans cream of mushroom soup

1 1/2 gallons whole milk

3/4 cup water

1 (16-ounce) package mushrooms, sliced

Place potatoes in a large pot; bring to a boil until they break but are not mushy (do not overcook). In a separate pan, place vegetables and 3/4 cup water; cover, steam until tender but firm. Drain potatoes, add milk and vegetables, cream of mushroom soup (do not dilute) and ham; simmer over low heat for about 45 minutes. Stir frequently to prevent sticking. Cover and let stand until ready to serve.

Dad's Cook Book

Lemony Basil Mushroom Soup

$^1/_4$ cup margarine
$1^1/_4$ cups chopped onions
 sliced
2 celery stalks, sliced
1 pound fresh mushrooms,
2 carrots, sliced
4 garlic cloves, minced
6 cups water
3 ($10^3/_4$-ounce) can condensed
 chicken broth

1 ($10^3/_4$-ounce) cans cream
 of chicken soup
$^1/_2$ cup chopped fresh basil
1 teaspoon fresh ground
 pepper
1 teaspoon lemon juice
$^1/_2$ cup uncooked wild rice
$^1/_4$ cup uncooked regular rice
 1 lemon, sliced
Grated Parmesan cheese

In 6-quart Dutch oven, melt margarine. Sauté onions, mushrooms, celery, carrots, and garlic in margarine about 5 minutes. Stir in water, chicken broth, chicken soup, basil, pepper, lemon juice, and wild and regular rice; cover and simmer over low heat until wild rice is tender, about 40 minutes. Serve garnished with lemon slices and Parmesan cheese. Makes 16 (1-cup) servings.

Home Cookin': Almont Elementary PTA

Potato-Carrot Potage

2 cups diced onions
$^1/_2$ cup butter or margarine
$1^1/_2$ cups chopped celery
4 cups peeled, thinly sliced
 carrots
8 cups peeled, diced potatoes

2 quarts chicken broth,
 seasoned
1 cup heavy cream or sour
 cream, for garnish
4 tablespoons chopped
 chives, for garnish

In a 6-quart soup pot, sauté onions in hot butter or margarine for 3 minutes over medium heat. Add celery and continue to sauté 3 additional minutes. Add carrots, potatoes, and chicken broth. Bring to a boil, reduce temperature, and simmer for one hour or until potatoes and carrots are very soft. Purée about $^1/_3$ of soup in a blender or food processor. Return purée to soup pot to thicken broth. At serving time, pour one tablespoon heavy cream in each bowl, or add a dollop of sour cream and sprinkle with chopped chives. Serves 10-12.

Cranbrook Reflections

Mom's Capusta
(Cabbage Soup)

Serve with loaf of dark pumpernickel and lots of whipped butter. You won't have to fix anything else with the soup—it's really a meal in itself. And this is even better the next day.

1 cup split yellow peas
1 slab spare ribs (or pig's
  knuckles)
Salt and pepper
1 medium onion, chopped
1 bay leaf (whole)
1 large can Silverfloss
  sauerkraut

1/2 medium head sweet
  cabbage, shredded
2 stalks celery, cut up, leaves
  and all
1/2 cup leftover mashed
  potatoes
1 palmful caraway seeds
1 handful dry mushrooms

Soak yellow peas for at least an hour before starting soup. Cut ribs into serving-size portions (2 or 3 ribs). Boil ribs for about 5 minutes to remove fat. Throw out first water and wash ribs off good. Rinse pot clean, too. Put ribs back in pot with just enough water to cover. Add yellow peas. Remember not to add too much water here—the peas have to cook until they get kind of mushy, and if there's too much water, they'll just jump around the pot.

After about an hour, throw in a handful of salt and some pepper. Add chopped onion, bay leaf, sauerkraut, shredded sweet cabbage, and celery. Add mashed potatoes (if they're cold, you might want to push them through a strainer. I put the strainer right in the soup, then put the potatoes in the strainer and mash them through with a wooden spoon. This makes sure that the potatoes disintegrate in the soup.) Add caraway seeds and dry mushrooms (optional). Cook for at least 2 hours.

Note: Make sure you have a big enough pot to start with—there's a lot of stuff going into this soup.

If you don't have any leftover mashed potatoes, instant is just as good; prepare as directed on package. You won't taste them in the soup—they're just used to give the soup some thickness. You can substitute barley or yellow lima beans for the yellow split peas.

Ferndale Friends Cook Book

Italian Cabbage Soup

1 pound Italian sausage (hot)
2 cups dry red wine
1-2 cloves garlic, minced
1/2 cup finely chopped onion
1 or 2 slices bacon
1 (28-ounce) can tomatoes,
    cut up

1 cup water
1 medium head Savoy
    cabbage, chopped
Salt and pepper

Using fork, prick sausage casing several times. Cut into 2-inch pieces. Place sausage in large bowl; add wine and garlic. Set aside to marinate for 30 minutes.

Drain sausage, reserving marinade. In large saucepan, cook sausage, onion, and bacon till meat is done and onions are tender. Add the reserved wine marinade. Cover and simmer 20 minutes. Stir in undrained tomatoes, water, and cabbage. Cover and simmer 20 minutes more, stirring occasionally. Season to taste with salt and pepper. Serve with crusty bread.

Tasteful Art

Fresh Cabbage Soup

5 slices bacon, diced
1 pound cabbage, chopped
2 carrots, diced
2 potatoes, diced
1 stalk celery, sliced

1 1/2 quarts water
2 tablespoons flour
2 tablespoons butter or
    margarine, softened
Salt and pepper to taste

Fry bacon until golden in large saucepan; drain fat. Add vegetables and water; bring to boil, then simmer 20 minutes or until vegetables are tender. Blend flour into butter until smooth; stir into soup. Bring soup to boil, stirring well. Shut off heat, add seasonings, stir and serve.

Historically Delicious

Owosso was the home of Thomas E. Dewey (1902 - 1971), Presidential hopeful in 1944 when he ran against Franklin Roosevelt. In 1948 he ran again, where he was erroneously reported to have defeated Harry Truman.

Sharon's Broccoli and Cheese Soup

In a word: Excellent.

4 cups fat-free broth, low
   sodium
12 ounces frozen shredded
   has brown potatoes (about 2
   cups)
1 cup celery, chopped
1 cup onions, chopped

1 cup carrots, chopped
4 cups broccoli, chopped
3 tablespoons flour
2 cups skim milk
8 ounces fat-free pasteurized
   cheese, cubed
Salt and pepper to taste

Put broth and vegetables in a large stock pot and bring to boil. Simmer until vegetables are tender, about 15 minutes. Blend flour with milk and add to vegetables, stirring constantly until soup thickens. Remove from heat. Add cheese cubes and stir until cheese is melted and smooth. Season to taste. Serves 8.

Options: Use more cheese, if you prefer a cheesier flavor. Sprinkle a bit of paprika on each bowl before serving. If you want your broccoli to remain bright green, put it in the soup about 5 minutes after the other vegetables.

Nutrition: (per serving): Cal 144; Sat Fat 0g; Total Fat 1g; Prot 13g; Carb 22g; Chol 6mg; Fiber 1 g; Vit A 4691 IU; Sod 440mg; Iron 1mg; Vit C 49mg.

"Life Tastes Better Than Steak" Cookbook

Broccoli Soup

1 (10-ounce) package
   chopped broccoli
1 cup chopped onion
4 tablespoons butter
1 (49-ounce) can clear
   chicken broth

2 cups Cremora
$1/2$ cup raw Minute rice
2 carrots, sliced thin
2 potatoes, sliced thin

Cook and drain broccoli. Cook onion in 4 tablespoons butter until transparent. Bring broth to boil; add Cremora and blend well. Add onion, rice, carrots, and potatoes. Cook 15 minutes. Add broccoli. Cook 15 minutes more.

Note: You can also use spinach or asparagus.

Come and Dine

Quick Cream of Broccoli Soup

$1/_2$ pound broccoli, blanched
  3 minutes
2 cans cream of mushroom
  soup

$1^1/_2$ soup cans milk
$1/_2$ pound Cheddar cheese,
  grated

Simmer all ingredients together 20 minutes. Enjoy!

Crystal Clear Cooking

Curried Squash Soup

This soup is rich enough to serve as a main course for a light supper. It is good with a hearty rye bread and a chilled bottle of your favorite white wine.

1 cup chopped onion
2 tablespoons olive oil or
  vegetable oil
$1^1/_2$ teaspoons curry powder
2 small ($1^1/_4$-pound)
  butternut squash, peeled, cut
  into 1-inch cubes
2 medium Winesap apples,
  peeled, chopped
1 (14-ounce) can chicken
  broth

$1^1/_2$ cups water
$1^1/_4$ teaspoons salt
Pepper to taste
$1^1/_2$ cups half-and-half or 1
  (12-ounce) can evaporated
  skim milk
Chopped parsley or chives
  (for garnish)
Sour cream (for garnish)

Sauté the onion in heated olive oil in a 4-quart saucepan over medium heat for 15 minutes or until tender. Stir in the curry powder. Cook for one minute longer. Add the squash, apples, chicken broth, water, salt and pepper. Bring to a boil and reduce the heat to low. Simmer for 10-15 minutes or until the squash is very tender, stirring frequently. Process the mixture in several portions in a food processor until smooth. Combine the portions in a saucepan. Add the half-and-half and mix well. Cook until heated through, stirring occasionally. Garnish the servings with parsley or chives and sour cream. Serves 4.

The Dexter Cider Mill Apple Cookbook

Cheese Tortellini and Spinach Soup

Very easy and makes a great meal when served with crusty bread and a salad.

2 tablespoons olive oil
3 ounces bacon or turkey
  bacon
3 cloves garlic, crushed
1 medium onion, chopped
  finely
2 1/2 cups chicken broth
1 tablespoon dried Italian
  herbs

9 ounces cheese tortellini
1 (28-ounce) can crushed
  tomatoes
8 ounces fresh spinach, rinsed
  and coarsely torn
Salt and pepper, to taste
1 cup freshly grated Parmesan
  cheese

Heat olive oil in a stockpot over medium-high heat. Add bacon, garlic, and onion. Cook, stirring frequently until lightly browned, 10-15 minutes. Add chicken broth and herbs. Bring to boil. Add tortellini. Simmer uncovered until tortellini is cooked, 10-12 minutes. Stir in tomatoes. Simmer 5 more minutes. Add spinach. Cook until wilted, about 3 minutes. Season to taste. Sprinkle liberally with cheese. Serves 6-8.

The Bountiful Arbor

Chicken Barley Soup with a Kick

Choose the strength of the kick with mild, medium or hot salsa.

2 cups chopped, cooked
  chicken breasts
7 cups water
1 (16-ounce) jar salsa
1 onion, chopped
2 chicken bouillon cubes
1 cup chopped carrots
1/2 cup chopped green bell
  pepper

1 cup chopped celery
2/3 cup barley
Chopped parsley to taste
1 teaspoon salt
1 teaspoon pepper
1 teaspoon basil
1/2 teaspoon Worcestershire
  sauce

Combine the chicken, water, salsa, onion, and bouillon cubes in a large stockpot. Bring to a boil; reduce heat. Simmer for 1 1/2 hours, stirring occasionally. Add the carrots, green pepper, celery, and barley; mix well. Stir in the parsley, salt, pepper, basil, and Worcestershire sauce. Simmer soup until the vegetables are tender. Yield: 6 servings.

Dawn to Dusk

Simple Split Pea Soup

8 cups water
2 cups dry split peas
2 tablespoons olive oil
2 cups chopped onions
2 cups chopped celery and/or
 carrots

2 bay leaves
1 1/2 tablespoons onion
 powder
1 teaspoon garlic powder
2 teaspoons salt

Put first 2 ingredients into pot. Bring to boil, reduce heat, cover and simmer for 1/2 hour. Add remaining ingredients and simmer covered for one hour. Remove cover and simmer for 30 more minutes. Stir occasionally. Yield: 9 1/2 cups.

Country Life: Vegetarian Cookbook

So Close to Lelli's Minestrone

Lelli's is a popular local eatery in Detroit and Auburn Hills that is well-known for its 'unbelievable, best-ever' minestrone and Italian food.

1 large onion, chopped
1 clove garlic, chopped
1/2 stick butter
2 (16-ounce) cans Veg-All
2 (14-ounce) cans chicken
 broth
20-ounces Northern white
 kidney beans
1 (14-ounce) can whole
 tomatoes
1/2 package frozen spinach
 (or fresh)

2 tablespoons tomato paste
2 teaspoons garlic powder
2 teaspoons chopped parsley
1 teaspoon salt
1/4 teaspoon pepper
1/2 teaspoon basil
1/3 cup cooked small
 macaroni
1/2 cup heavy whipping cream
1/4 cup Parmesan cheese
A small amount of chickpeas
 (optional)

Sauté onion and garlic in butter. In a large soup pot, put Veg-All, chicken broth, Northern beans, whole tomatoes (chopped), and all liquid from cans. Add spinach, tomato paste, garlic powder, parsley, salt, pepper, basil, and the sautéed onion and garlic. Cook slowly 1 1/2 hours. Take 1/2 of the soup and blend in food processor. Pour it back into soup pot. Add macaroni and heavy cream; sprinkle with Parmesan cheese. Stir. Cook slowly 1/2 hour.

The Fruit of Her Hands

Dill Pickle Soup

8 cups chicken stock

2 medium carrots

2 cups peeled and cubed potatoes

1 cup celery, chopped

5 coarsely grated Polish dill pickles

$^1/_2$ cup milk

2 tablespoons flour

1 egg

5 tablespoons sour cream

Combine stock, carrots, potatoes, and celery. Cook, covered, until potatoes are soft. Do not over cook. Add pickles and cook about 15 minutes more. In bowl, beat milk and flour until smooth. Stir a small amount of hot soup into mixture. Mix until smooth and return to pot, stirring frequently until soup is slightly thickened. Remove from heat. In a bowl, beat egg into sour cream until smooth. Return sour cream mixture to soup pot and stir until smooth. Keep soup warm but do not boil as soup will curdle. Garnish with parsley and dill. 10 servings.

Recipes & Remembrances II

Michigan is this country's #1 state in pickling cucumber production. In the heart of Michigan's cucumber country, the "World's Christmas Pickle Capital" blends its pickling panache with a German Christmas custom. On Christmas Eve, parents hide a glass pickle ornament in their Christmas tree for the children to find the next morning. The discover recieves an extra gift.

Salads

Michigan's state capitol building rises majestically at the center of downtown Lansing.

Great Lakes German Potato Salad

8 medium-sized potatoes
3/4 cup chopped onions
8 slices bacon, cut in 1-inch
   pieces
3 tablespoons bacon drippings
2 tablespoons flour

1 1/2 teaspoons salt
1/4 teaspoon pepper
4 tablespoons sugar
1 cup water
1/2 cup vinegar

Peel potatoes and onions. Dice potatoes and cook in lightly salted water until tender. Drain and keep warm. While potatoes are cooking, fry bacon until crisp. Chop onions. Remove bacon and discard all but 3 tablespoons of drippings. Add onion and cook until tender, about 5 minutes. Mix together dry ingredients. Add to onions and stir to blend. Add water and vinegar. Bring to boil until thickened. Pour over hot cooked potatoes. Add bacon and toss gently. May be kept in oven at 200° or in crockpot on low setting. Serves approximately 8 people.

How to Make A Steamship Float

White Potato Salad

5 pounds new potatoes
3 small onions, minced
1/2 cup water
1/2 cup white vinegar
1/2 cup sugar

2 cups Hellmann's mayonnaise
   (do not substitute)
1/4 cup heavy cream
1 tablespoon salt
Olive oil

The night before, boil potatoes unpeeled for 20 minutes from boiling point. Do not let them get too soft. Boil water, vinegar, and sugar together. Pour over onions. Let stand until potatoes are peeled and sliced very thin. Pour above mixture over potatoes. In separate bowl, mix mayonnaise, cream, and salt. Make sure mixture is smooth and creamy. Pour over potatoes and mix carefully together. Be sure all potatoes get saturated. Dribble olive oil over top. Cover and let stand in refrigerator overnight. Do not cover with foil. Salad will appear watery when you finish, but will absorb moisture overnight. Salad will keep in refrigerator 4 or 5 days. Serves 16.

A Century of Recipes Through the Windows of Time

Big Bear's Mashed Potato Salad

8-10 potatoes, cut into small
  chunks (thirds or fourths)
Miracle Whip to taste (about
  1 cup)

1 cup purple onion, diced fine
1 cup celery, diced fine
1 cup green bell pepper,
  diced fine

Boil potatoes in salted water. Mash potatoes, adding Miracle Whip to desired texture. Add onion, celery, and bell pepper to potatoes; mix well. Level or texture surface, and sprinkle with paprika and parsley flakes. Serve hot or cold.

Variations: Add sweet pickles, to taste and/or pimentos, for color.

Dad's Cook Book

Tuscan Blue and White Bean Salad

3 tablespoons corn oil
1¼ cups corn kernels, fresh
  or frozen (thawed)
1 (16-ounce) can black beans
  (rinsed and drained)
1 (16-ounce) can great
  Northern white beans (rinsed
  and drained)
1 cup chopped red onion

2 tablespoons fresh lime juice
3 large garlic cloves, pressed
1 large jalapeño chile, seeded
  and minced
1 tablespoon minced fresh
  oregano (or 1 teaspoon dried)
1 tablespoon chili powder
1½ teaspoons ground cumin

Sauté corn in oil until brown; transfer to large bowl. Add a little more oil and remaining ingredients. Season with salt and pepper. Serve with tortilla chips.

Recipes and Memories

Picnic Pasta Salad

8 ounces uncooked macaroni,
  any style
8 ounces Italian dressing
1 tablespoon Dijon-style
  mustard
1/4 teaspoon black pepper

2 cups assorted frozen
  vegetables, thawed, drained
1 medium red or green pepper
1/2 cup sliced ripe olives
2 tablespoons chopped fresh
  parsley

Cook macaroni according to package directions; drain and rinse with cold water until completely cool. Blend Italian dressing, mustard, and pepper in large bowl; stir in vegetables, red and green pepper, olives, and parsley. Add macaroni; toss well. Cover; chill at least 2 hours.

Four Seasons Cookbook

Gatehouse Chicken Pasta Salad

DRESSING:

2/3 cup olive oil
5 tablespoons red wine
  vinegar
1/4 cup chopped fresh basil
  leaves (or 2 tablespoons dried
3 tablespoons grated
  Parmesan cheese

1 tablespoon fresh oregano
  (or 1/2 tablespoon dried)
1 teaspoon salt
1/2 teaspoon ground black
  pepper

Prepare dressing first. In a large blender, mix together all ingredients and set aside.

SALAD:

4 cups cooked, cubed chicken
8 ounces rotelle pasta,
  cooked, rinsed, and drained
1 red pepper, sliced thin
1 green pepper, sliced thin
1 1/2 cups broccoli florets,
  cooked 2 minutes, rinsed,
  chilled

1/2 cup sliced, pitted black
  olives
1 cup cherry tomatoes, sliced
  in half
1/2 cup mayonnaise (or
  mayonnaise-base salad
  dressing)

In a large bowl, combine chicken, pasta, and vegetables; toss salad with oil and vinegar dressing. Refrigerate 8 hours or overnight. At serving time toss salad with 1/2 cup mayonnaise. Serves 6-8.

Cranbrook Reflections

Rice Salad

3 cups cold, cooked brown
  rice
1¹/₂ cups diced raw zucchini
2 teaspoons minced red onion
2 cups chopped tomatoes
1¹/₂ cups finely chopped
  green pepper
1 cup finely chopped fresh
  parsley

2 teaspoons salt
¹/₄ cup olive oil
¹/₄ - ¹/₂ teaspoon garlic
  powder
2 tablespoons lemon juice
¹/₂ cup chopped chives or
  scallions (with tops)

Put all ingredients into a bowl and mix together well. Cover and chill. May serve on lettuce leaves garnished with tomato wedges. Yield: 5¹/₂ cups.

Country Life: Vegetarian Cookbook

Anniversary Chicken and Wild Rice Salad

Simply irresistible! The perfect main event for a summer buffet.

SALAD:

1 cup wild rice
1 teaspoon salt
4 cups shredded, cooked
   chicken
7 ounces marinated artichoke
   hearts, drained
4 ribs celery, julienned
7 scallions, cross-cut, finely
   sliced
2 carrots, diced
8-10 radishes, thinly sliced

1 onion, diced
1 head cauliflower, cut in
   small florets
1/4 cup finely chopped parsley
1 cup pine nuts or pecans
Dressing
1 sweet red pepper, sliced
   (for garnish)
6 ounces pitted black olives,
   drained (for garnish)

Rinse wild rice twice in a fine mesh strainer. In a saucepan, add rice and salt to 3 cups water and cook, covered, for 40 minutes or until tender. In a large bowl, combine chicken, rice, vegetables, and nuts. Toss. Stir in Dressing, cover bowl, and refrigerate overnight. At serving time, mound rice salad in a shallow bowl and garnish with sliced red pepper and black olives.

DRESSING:

1 cup mayonnaise
2 tablespoons curry powder
1 cup olive oil
1/3 cup vinegar

1 tablespoon Dijon mustard
1 garlic clove, finely minced
1 teaspoon salt
Ground black pepper

Mix together above salad dressing ingredients in a quart jar. Shake to blend. Serves 12-16.

Cranbrook Reflections

Basil Chicken Salad

2 celery stalks, diced
2 scallions, chopped fine
1/3 cup crushed almonds

10 leaves fresh basil
1 can chicken meat
2 tablespoons Miracle Whip

Chop celery, scallions, nuts, and basil. Mix with chicken and Miracle Whip. Serve on lettuce bed and garnish with basil.

Herbal Favorites

Chilled Chicken Salad with Fruit and Rice

2¹/₂ cups cooked, cubed
  chicken
1¹/₂ cups cooked brown or
  white rice
1 cup green grapes, sliced in
  half
³/₄ cup thinly sliced celery
1 small can pineapple tidbits,
  drained

1 small can mandarin
  oranges, drained
¹/₂ cup slivered almonds,
  toasted in a teaspoon of butter
¹/₂ cup mayonnaise
1 cup ranch dressing
Salt and freshly ground
  pepper to taste
Lettuce leaves

In a large bowl combine all ingredients except the lettuce. Toss gently.
Serve on lettuce-lined plates. Serves 4.

What's Cookin'

Dried Cherry Chicken Salad

1 cup dried tart red cherries
4 chicken breast halves,
  cooked, torn into large pieces
3 stalks celery, coarsely
  chopped
2 Granny Smith apples,
  coarsely chopped

1 cup coarsely chopped
  pecans
1¹/₄ cups mayonnaise
¹/₂ cup chopped parsley
1 tablespoon raspberry
  vinegar
Salt and pepper to taste

Mix the one cup cherries, chicken, celery, apples, and pecans in a large
bow. Combine the mayonnaise, parsley, and raspberry vinegar in a
bowl; mix well. Add to the chicken mixture and toss lightly to coat
well. Season with salt and pepper. Chill 2 hours or longer. Serve on
a bed of red leaf lettuce. Garnish with additional cherries. Serves 6.

The Dexter Cider Mill Apple Cookbook

Spinach Salad & Sour Cream Dressing

1 (1-pound) bag fresh spinach
1/2 cup sour cream
1/2 cup sugar
3 tablespoons vinegar
4 teaspoons horseradish

1/2 teaspoon mustard
1/4 teaspoon salt
1 (15-ounce) carton small
   curd cottage cheese
1 cup pecans, halved

Rinse, remove stems and break up spinach. Blend next 6 ingredients and pour over spinach. Add cottage cheese and pecans. Toss and serve. Servings: 10.

Bringing Grand Tastes to Grand Traverse

Spinach Salad with Sliced Apples

Looks and tastes as good as it sounds.

1 bunch spinach
1 apple, unpeeled
4 strips bacon, slivered and
   fried crisp

1 bunch green onions,
   chopped
2 ounces Amish or jack
   cheese, cubed

Wash and dry spinach. Remove stems, then tear leaves into bite-size pieces. Cut apple in half lengthwise, then crosswise. Removing core, thinly slice. Place spinach and apple slices in salad bowl, along with bacon, chopped onions, and cheese.

DRESSING:
1/4 cup olive oil
3 tablespoons white wine
   vinegar with tarragon
1 teaspoon sugar

1/2 teaspoon dry mustard
Garlic salt to taste
Freshly ground pepper

Whisk together above ingredients and pour over salad. Lightly toss. Serves 4-6

Hollyhocks & Radishes

Spinach and Strawberries with Poppy Seed Dressing

1/3 cup raspberry vinegar
1 teaspoon salt
1/2 cup sugar
1 teaspoon dry mustard
1 1/2 tablespoons minced
   onion
1 cup vegetable oil

1 1/2 tablespoons poppy
   seeds
1-2 pounds spinach, washed
   and torn
1 pint strawberries, sliced
1/2 cup pecan halves

Put vinegar, salt, sugar, mustard, and onion in blender. Blend slowly. Add oil. When thick, add poppy seeds. Just before serving, toss spinach, strawberries, and pecans with dressing.

**Woman's National Farm and Garden Association - Rochester
Cookbook Volume II**

Spinach Orange Salad

DRESSING:
1/4 cup vegetable oil
2 tablespoons white sugar
2 tablespoons white vinegar
1 tablespoon snipped parsley

1/2 teaspoon salt
1/4 teaspoon black pepper
Dash of Tabasco sauce

Combine all ingredients; cover. Shake well and refrigerate.

SALAD:
1/4 cup sliced almonds
4 teaspoons white sugar
Fresh spinach, washed, dried
   and chilled (enough for 6-8
   people)

1 cup thin bias-cut celery
2 tablespoons chopped green
   onion tops
1 (11-ounce) can mandarin
   oranges, drained

Place almonds and sugar in small skillet. Stir over medium heat, watching closely, until almonds are golden brown. Remove to small bowl; cool.

Place spinach in large salad bowl. Add celery, green onion, and oranges. At serving time, add dressing and almonds; toss lightly. Serves 6-8.

Heavenly Helpings

Mandarin Salad

DRESSING:

1/2 teaspoon salt
Dash of pepper
2 tablespoons sugar
2 tablespoons vinegar

1/4 cup vegetable oil
Dash of red pepper sauce
1 tablespoon snipped parsley

SALAD:

1/4 cup sliced almonds
1 tablespoon plus 1 teaspoon
  sugar
1/4 head lettuce
1/4 head romaine

1 cup chopped celery
2 green onions (with tops),
  thinly sliced
1 (11-ounce) can mandarin
  oranges

Shake dressing ingredients in tightly covered jar; refrigerate. Cook almonds and sugar over low heat, stirring constantly, until sugar is melted and almonds are coated. Cool; break apart. Store at room temperature. Tear lettuce and romaine into bite-size pieces (about 4 cups). Place greens in plastic bag; add celery and onion. Fasten bag securely and refrigerate.

Five minutes before serving, pour dressing into bag. Add mandarin orange segments, drained. Fasten bag securely and shake until greens and oranges are well coated. Add almonds and shake. Makes 4-6 servings.

Note: If serving immediately, do not refrigerate dressing or salad. Do not store longer than 24 hours.

Woman's National Farm and Garden Association - Rochester
Cookbook Volume II

Broccoli Salad

2 large bunches fresh broccoli
5 small chopped green onions
$^1/_2$ - $^3/_4$ cup raisins
9 slices fried bacon

1 cup mayonnaise
2 tablespoons white vinegar
2 tablespoons sugar

Remove broccoli top and break into pieces. Rinse well; drain and put in medium-sized salad bowl. Add chopped onions, raisins, and crumbled bacon. Mix mayonnaise, vinegar, and sugar; pour over salad mixture and toss. Serves 6.

Country Cookbook

Broccoli Salad

1 bunch broccoli, stalks
  removed
$^1/_2$ pound bacon, fried and
  crumbled

1 cup Mozzarella cheese,
  shredded or cubed

Wash and separate broccoli flowerettes, drain. Cook bacon and crumble.

DRESSING:
$^1/_4$ cup sugar
1 tablespoon red wine vinegar
  (do not substitute)

$^1/_2$ cup Hellmann's lite
  mayonnaise

Combine sugar and wine vinegar and heat until sugar is dissolved. Do not overheat. Combine with mayonnaise. Toss with broccoli mixture.

Home Cookin': First Congregational United Church of Christ

 Except for California, Michigan has the largest variety of agricultural products in the nation. Michigan ranks in the top five in production of 23 different crops.

Korean Salad

2 bags spinach, cleaned and
  dried
2 cups water chestnuts, sliced
4 hard boiled eggs, sliced
1 can bean sprouts, drained

$^1/_2$ pound bacon, sliced, diced
  and cooked
1 medium Bermuda onion,
  sliced into rings

DRESSING:
1 cup oil
$^1/_4$ cup cider vinegar
$^1/_3$ cup tomato catsup
$^1/_2$ cup sugar

2 teaspoons salt
1 tablespoon Worcestershire
  sauce

Place all salad ingredients in a large salad bowl. Mix dressing ingredients together and set aside. (Dressing can be made ahead of time.)
Just before serving, pour over remaining ingredients and toss. To serve
as a luncheon salad, add shrimp. Serves 10.

Renaissance Cuisine

Cucumbers in Sour Cream

4 large cucumbers
1 teaspoon salt
Water
$^1/_2$ cup sugar

3 tablespoons cider vinegar
1 small container sour cream
1 medium Spanish onion

Peel and slice cucumbers into $^1/_4$-inch slices. Put them in a good-size
bowl, sprinkle with salt, and cover with water. Refrigerate several
hours, then drain, rinse and put in a strong dish towel and wring out
very well. (Can use a potato ricer to squeeze out.) They will look
limp.

Mix together the sugar, vinegar, sour cream. This should seem
sweet, so taste and add more vinegar or sugar. Pour over cucumbers
and add thinly sliced Spanish onion. Mix well and refrigerate until
very cold. Will keep several days in refrigerator.

Halvorson-Johnson Family Reunion Cookbook

Bleu Cheese Coleslaw

The bacon and bleu cheese give a face-lift to those tired old coleslaw recipes.

2 tablespoons Mucky Duck*
  mustard
1 tablespoon chopped garlic
1/4 cup white wine vinegar
3/4 cup vegetable oil
4 slices bacon, coarsely
  chopped

1 head cabbage, shredded
4 ounces bleu cheese,
  crumbled
Freshly ground pepper to
  taste

Combine mustard, garlic, and vinegar in blender container. Add oil gradually, processing constantly. Process until thickened. Cook bacon in skillet until crisp; remove from heat. Stir dressing into bacon and drippings in skillet. Combine cabbage and bleu cheese in large bowl. Pour dressing over top; toss to mix. Season with pepper.

*Sweet-tangy mustard.

Mucky Duck Mustard Cookbook

Beet Salad

This recipe has no specific amounts for ingredients, it depends upon how much you want to make—just for yourself or for a crowd.

Beets, cooked, peeled, diced
  small
Raw onions, diced small

Salt and pepper, to taste
Mayonnaise

Mix together beets, onions, salt and pepper. Add just enough mayonnaise to make it moist. Will keep in refrigerator approximately 3-4 days.

Crystal Clear Cooking

Well over 100,000 acres of sugar beets are planted in Michigan each year. The beets are stored outside before being processed and are kept cool naturally by cooler fall temperatures. The storage piles are 20 feet high, 120 feet wide and can be up to one-quarter mile in length. One beet is processed into about 5 ounces of pure beet sugar, along with some by-products such as molasses and beet pulp.

Oriental Cabbage Salad

1 (3-ounce) package oriental
  noodles with chicken flavor
4 cups shredded cabbage
4 green onions, sliced
2 tablespoons sesame seeds
3 tablespoons vinegar

2 tablespoons sugar
2 tablespoons salad oil
1/2 teaspoon salt
1/2 cup slivered almonds,
  toasted

Crush noodles slightly; place in colander. Pour boiling water over noodles to soften slightly. Drain well. In large mixing bowl, combine noodles, cabbage, onions, and sesame seeds.

For dressing, in a screw-top jar, combine seasoning packet from noodles, vinegar, sugar, oil, salt, and pepper; shake to mix well. Pour over cabbage mixture and toss. Cover and chill several hours or overnight. Before serving, stir in almonds. Serves 6-8.

The Fruit of Her Hands

Smashed Salad

1 large head romaine lettuce
1 large head iceberg lettuce
2 avocados, cut into chunks
1/4 cup onion, grated
1 cup Cheddar cheese, grated
1/2 cup black olives, pitted
  and sliced
1/2 cup walnuts, chopped
1/2 cup grated Parmesan
  cheese

2 cups Doritos, coarsely
  smashed
1 cup Catalina dressing,
  sweet French
2 tablespoons chili powder
Green peppers and tomatoes,
  if desired

Wash and tear lettuce into bite-sized pieces. Toss in large bowl with avocados, onion, cheese, olives, walnuts, and Parmesan cheese. Just before serving add smashed Doritos. In a small bowl, add Catalina dressing and chili powder. Pour over salad. Add peppers and tomatoes, if desired. Serves 12-14.

Renaissance Cuisine

Midwest Apple Salad

DRESSING:

1/2 - 3/4 cup olive oil
3 tablespoons lemon juice
2 tablespoons cider vinegar
3 tablespoons honey
1 large shallot, finely chopped

1/2 teaspoon dried thyme
 leaves
1/2 teaspoon salt or to taste
1/4 teaspoon coarsely ground
 pepper or to taste

In screw top jar, combine 1/2 cup olive oil and remaining dressing ingredients. Cover and shake well. If too tart, add remaining olive oil to taste.

SALAD:

Lettuce, washed and broken,
 use several varieties
 including leaf, bib and 1 bunch
 watercress (1 cup per person)
2-3 golden Delicious apples,
 thinly sliced (do not peel)

1 - 1 1/2 cups toasted nuts
 (honey roasted almonds are
 especially good)
1/4 cup finely chopped parsley

Arrange greens in salad bowl. Distribute apple slices over top and sprinkle with toasted nuts and parsley. Just before serving, drizzle some of dressing over top. Toss gently to coat lightly with dressing. (Don't use too much dressing). Add freshly ground pepper to taste.

Note: If you have leftover dressing, it can be refrigerated and used later.

The Bell Tower Cookbook

Chinese Tossed Salad

DRESSING:

1/2 cup Mazola oil
2 teaspoons salt
4 tablespoons Japanese rice
  vinegar (unseasoned)

2 tablespoons toasted sesame
  seeds (toast in Teflon frying
  pan)
4 teaspoons sugar

Mix ingredients and refrigerate at least one day.

SALAD:

1 head lettuce
1/2 cup shredded cooked
  chicken
1-2 scallions, finely chopped
1 cup alfalfa sprouts
1/3 cup green pepper, thinly
  sliced

2 tablespoons grated carrots
1/3 cup celery, thinly sliced
1/4 cup radishes, thinly sliced
1/3 cup roasted peanuts
1/3 cup deep-fried wonton
  skins or 1 can LaChoy chow
  mein noodles

Wash and tear lettuce into bite-size pieces. Drain and refrigerate till ready to assemble. Just before serving, add chicken and vegetables. Pour on dressing and add roasted peanuts and wonton skins, broken into small pieces. Serves 8-10.

Note: Can be prepared in advance.

The Bell Tower Cookbook

Horseradish Salad

1 (3-ounce) package lemon
  Jello
1 1/3 cups hot water
2 tablespoon lemon juice,
  divided
3 ounces cream cheese, softened

1 (4-ounce) jar fresh horseradish,
  drained
1/2 pint whipping cream,
  whipped
Sliced stuffed olives

Dissolve Jello in hot water. Add 1 tablespoon lemon juice. Cool for 30 minutes then whip. Mix cream cheese, horseradish, and 1 table-spoon lemon juice. Fold into Jello. Fold in whipped cream. Turn into Jello mold. Garnish with olives. Refrigerate for 4 hours. Excellent accompaniment for ham, corned beef, etc. Servings: 10.

Bringing Grand Tastes to Grand Traverse

Cucumber Cottage Cheese Mold

1 unwaxed cucumber,
(garden, or 1/3 seedless
cucumber)
1 small onion
1 pound fine curd cottage
cheese

1/2 cup salad dressing
2 tablespoons vinegar
1/2 teaspoon salt, if desired
1 small box lime Jello (may
use sugar-free)
1/2 cup boiling water

Grind cucumber and onion with medium blade of food grinder, or in processor. Add cottage cheese, salad dressing, vinegar, and salt. Dissolve Jello in boiling water and add to mixture. Chill until set in 8x8-inch flat pan or mold and cut to serve.

Seasoned Cooks II

Strawberry Jello

2 (6-ounce) boxes strawberry
Jello
40 ounces frozen strawberries
1 (16-ounce) can crushed
pineapple, save juice

4 bananas, mashed
1 cup sour cream, at room
temperature

Dissolve Jello in 3 cups boiling water. Add remaining ingredients, including pineapple juice, and mix well. Pour 3/4 of mixture into a glass 13x10x2-inch pan and let set. When mixture is firm, spread sour cream on top, then spoon the remaining Jello mixture on top. Refrigerate.

From Our Home to Yours

Strawberry and Pretzels Mold

2 cups coarsely crushed
   pretzels
1 cup plus 2 tablespoons
   sugar, divided
3/4 cup margarine, melted
1 (6-ounce) package
   strawberry gelatin
2 cups boiling water

2 (10-ounce) packages frozen
   strawberry halves, slightly
   thawed
1 (8-ounce) packages cream
   cheese, softened
1 teaspoon vanilla extract
2 cups whipped topping

Preheat oven to 400°. In a large mixing bowl, combine crushed pretzels, 2 tablespoons sugar, and melted margarine. Mix well. Pat mixture into the bottom of a 9x13-inch baking dish. Bake for 12 minutes. Remove from oven and cool.

Meanwhile, in a large bowl, combine strawberry gelatin and boiling water, stirring until gelatin dissolves. Add strawberry halves, stirring until thawed. Chill in refrigerator 15-20 minutes or until partially set.

Meanwhile, in a medium mixing bowl, beat together cream cheese, remaining one cup of sugar, and vanilla until smooth. Gently fold in whipped topping. Spread mixture evenly over pretzel crust. When gelatin is partially set, remove from refrigerator and pour over cream cheese layer. Chill overnight. If desired, garnish with additional whipped topping sprinkled with crushed pretzels. Serves 24 (1-inch each). Contains 225 calories and 10 grams total fat.

The Fruit of Her Hands

Apricot Cream Cheese Salad

1 (6-ounce) package apricot
  Jello
1 large can undrained crushed
  pineapple
3/4 cup sugar
2 small jars strained apricot
  baby food

1 (8-ounce) package cream
  cheese
1 large can evaporated milk,
  chilled
2/3 cup nuts, finely chopped

Combine Jello and pineapple. Heat until mixture simmers. Add sugar, apricots, and softened cream cheese. Continue heating, stirring occasionally, until cheese melts. Remove from heat; chill until mixture mounds when dropped from spoon. Whip chilled evaporated milk until stiff peaks form; fold into apricot mixture. Pour into a 9x13-inch pan. Chill until firm. Top with chopped nuts. Serves 15.

Centennial Cookbook

Hot Fruit Ambrosia

1 (8-ounce) package pitted
  bing cherries
1 can peach slices, cut up
  (save juice)
1 can pears, cut up (save
  juice)

1/4 cup lemon juice
2 tablespoons cornstarch
1/2 teaspoon cinnamon
1/4 teaspoon nutmeg
2 or 3 bananas

Heat juices with cornstarch and sugar until thickened. Mix in fruit, adding cinnamon and nutmeg. Add bananas last. May be served in a chafing dish for a brunch or buffet.

A Century of Recipes Through the Windows of Time

In the late 1800's the residents of Mackinac (Mack-in-aw) Island passed an unusual and very charming law: no motorcars allowed. Stroll the streets, use a horse-drawn carriage, or ride a bike. Mackinac Island's Grand Hotel boasts a 700-foot verandah that is visible from the mainland seven miles away. After opening in 1898 it suffered the ups and downs of the nation's economy and the whims of the resort trade. It was purchased in 1933 by W. Stewart Woodfill, who started as a desk clerk in 1919.

Black Fruit Salad

1¹/₂ cups black cherries,
  pitted
1¹/₂ cups black grapes
³/₄ cup blueberries

¹/₂ cup brown sugar
Juice of 1 lemon
1¹/₂ cups sour cream
Fresh mint sprigs, optional

In large mixing bowl, combine fruits; sprinkle with brown sugar and lemon juice. Let stand 2 hours, tossing several times. Lift fruit out with slotted spoon. Divide evenly among 6 goblets or other individual serving dishes. Stir sour cream into juices remaining in mixing bowl. Spoon juice over fruit. Serve with a dollop of sour cream and fresh mint sprigs. Yield: 6 servings.

Something Special

City Club Salad Dressing

The favorite dressing at the Grand Rapids Women's City Club.

¹/₃ cup sugar
3 tablespoons honey
1 teaspoon salt
1 teaspoon dry mustard

1 teaspoon celery seed
1 teaspoon paprika
1 cup salad oil
¹/₄ cup vinegar

Mix sugar, honey, and seasonings. Gradually add oil and vinegar alternately, beating with rotary beater or blender. Perfect topping for grapefruit sections and avocado. Yield: 1²/₃ cups.

The Junior League of Grand Rapids Cookbook I

 The first regularly-scheduled passenger flight in the United States took off for Detroit from Cassard Field in Grand Rapids, July 31, 1926.

Pasta, Rice, Etc.

The Renaissance Center in Detroit is the tallest building in all of Michigan.

Pasta Primavera

Sin*sational!* *This dish is best prepared and served immediately, although if you need time with your guests, it can be prepared an hour ahead of time and reheated in the oven.*

1/2 cup butter
1 medium onion, minced
1 pound thin asparagus, diagonally cut into 1/4-inch pieces, tips left intact
1/2 pound mushrooms, thinly sliced
6 ounces cauliflower, broken into small flowerets
1 medium zucchini, sliced 1/4-inch thick
1 small carrot halved lengthwise, cut diagonally in 1/8-inch slices
1 cup whipping cream
1/2 cup chicken stock

2 tablespoons fresh basil or 2 teaspoons dried basil
1 large garlic clove, minced
1 cup frozen peas, thawed or 1 cup fresh young peas
5 green onions, thinly sliced
1 pound linguine, fettucine or thinly sliced noodles, cooked to al dente, thoroughly drained
1 cup freshly grated Parmesan or Romano cheese
2 ounces chopped prosciutto or cooked ham*
1 pound shrimp or scallops, optional

Heat wok over medium-high heat. Add butter, onion, and garlic and sauté about 2 minutes. Mix in asparagus, mushrooms, cauliflower, zucchini, and carrots and stir-fry 2 minutes.

(At this point, remove several asparagus tips for garnish later on.) Increase heat to high, add cream, stock, and basil and bring to boil to slightly reduce, about 3 minutes. Stir in peas, ham, and onion and cook one minute longer. Season to taste with fresh ground pepper. Add pasta and cheese, tossing until thoroughly combined and pasta is heated through. Turn out on large serving platter or individual side dishes and garnish with asparagus tips. Serve immediately! Serves 4-6 main course/6-8 first course or side dish.

*Prosciutto is a thinly sliced dry Italian ham, found in Italian shops and better butcher shops; well worth searching for! Vegetables can be chopped in advance and refrigerated; vegetable variations can be made, too, according to personal taste.

For a *sin*sational variation, try adding one pound of shelled shrimp or scallops to this dish. Guaranteed to bring many raves!

Some Enchanted Eating

Pasta with Cauliflower in Spicy Pink Sauce

3 cups tomato purée
1 1/2 cups whipping cream
1/2 cup freshly grated
  Romano cheese
1/2 cup coarsely shredded
  Fontina cheese
2 tablespoons ricotta cheese
1 teaspoon crushed red
  pepper

1 teaspoon kosher salt
Salt to taste
5 quarts water
1 head cauliflower, coarsely
  chopped
1 pound penne
3 tablespoons unsalted butter

Mix the tomato purée, whipping cream, Romano cheese, Fontina cheese, ricotta cheese, pepper, and kosher salt in a bowl; set aside. Bring salted water to a boil in a large saucepan. Add the cauliflower and pasta. Cook for 5 minutes; drain.

Add the pasta mixture to the cheese mixture, tossing to combine. Spoon into a baking dish or 6-8 individual shallow ceramic baking dishes. Top with the butter. Bake at 500° for 7-10 minutes or until bubbly and browned. Yield: 6-8 servings.

Dawn to Dusk

Ceccolini's Linguine

Simple and fresh tasting.

1/3 cup olive oil
1 large onion, chopped
1/4 cup chopped parsley
1 tablespoon minced garlic
1/2 teaspoon red pepper
  flakes
1 (28-ounce) can Italian
  tomatoes, chopped, undrained

1 teaspoon sugar
1 teaspoon salt
1/4 teaspoon pepper
1 pound medium shrimp,
  shelled, deveined and cut in
  half horizontally
1 pound linguine or spaghetti,
  cooked

In saucepan, heat olive oil over medium heat. Sauté onion until trans-lucent, 5 minutes. Stir in parsley, garlic, red pepper flakes, tomatoes, sugar, salt, and pepper. Reduce heat to low; cook 20 minutes or until sauce is thickened, stirring occasionally. Stir in shrimp. Cook until shrimp turns pink, about 3 minutes. Add pasta to sauce, toss well. Serves 6.

The Bountiful Arbor

Sweet and Sour Shrimp with Noodles

6 ounces (3 cups) uncooked
  noodles (your choice)
2 tablespoons butter, melted
1 cup sliced celery
1 cup thinly sliced carrots
1 medium green pepper, cut
  into thin strips
1 tablespoon light oil

1 (20-ounce) can pineapple
  chunks, drained (reserve
  juice)
1/4 cup cider vinegar
2 tablespoons brown sugar
2 tablespoons cornstarch
2 tablespoons soy sauce
1 pound cooked shrimp

Cook noodles as directed on the package. Drain; rinse with hot water. Toss noodles with butter and keep warm. Meanwhile, in a large skillet sauté celery, carrots, and pepper in oil until crisp-tender, about 5 minutes. Remove from heat. In a bowl combine reserved pineapple juice, vinegar, sugar, cornstarch, and soy sauce. Add to vegetables. Cook over low heat for 4 minutes or until clear and thickened. Stir in pineapple chunks and shrimp. Continue to cook until everything is hot and bubbly. Serve over the cooked noodles. Serves 5-6 persons.

What's Cookin'

Bow Tie Pasta & Chicken

1 (8-ounce) package bow-tie
  pasta
3/4 cup sun-dried tomatoes
Small amount of water
2 cloves garlic, finely chopped
2 tablespoons olive oil
1/2 pound chicken breast,
  julienned into 1/2-inch strips
1 1/2 cups broccoli florets,
  very small

1 teaspoon basil
Pinch of red pepper flakes,
  crushed
Salt and ground pepper to
  taste
1/4 cup white wine
3/4 cup chicken broth
1 tablespoon Parmesan
  cheese

Cook and drain pasta. Simmer tomatoes in water until softened. Drain and slice tomatoes. Sauté garlic in olive oil in large skillet, stirring constantly. Add chicken and broccoli, sauté until tender. Add sun-dried tomatoes, basil, seasonings, wine, and broth. Cook 3-5 minutes, stirring occasionally. Toss in bow-tie pasta. Add Parmesan cheese. Servings. 4.

Bringing Grand Tastes to Grand Traverse

Chicken Spaghetti

3 pounds chicken breasts,
  cooked
2 cups chopped celery
2 cups chopped green
  peppers
2 cups chopped onions
1 (12-ounce) can mushroom
  stems and pieces
1 pound grated Cheddar
  cheese

1 can cream of chicken soup
4 cans cream of mushroom
  soup
2 cans chicken broth
1 (12-ounce) jar chopped
  pimento
1 (8-ounce) can sliced ripe
  olives
1 (20-ounce) box spaghetti

Cut chicken into bite sizes. Sauté celery, peppers, and onions in olive oil. Add mushrooms, cheese, soups, broth, pimentos, olives, and chicken. Cook spaghetti noodles and mix with other ingredients. Heat as a casserole at 350° for 20 minutes. Serves 16. Can be frozen and reheated.

Our Best Home Cooking

One Step Lasagne

2 (15½-ounce) jars
  spaghetti sauce
2 pounds ground beef, cooked
1 (24-ounce) box lasagne
  noodles
1 (12-ounce) package
  Mozzarella cheese

1 (15-ounce) carton ricotta
  cheese or 16 ounces cottage
  cheese (either may be mixed
  with 2 eggs and/or sour cream
  for easier spreading
1 cup Parmesan or Cheddar
  cheese

Combine spaghetti sauce and ground beef in bowl. Cover bottom of lasagne dish with 2 cups sauce. Arrange layer of uncooked noodles. Spread ½ of cheese mixture and ½ of cheese. Repeat layers. Pour remaining sauce evenly to cover. Sprinkle with more Parmesan cheese. Cover with plastic wrap and let set several hours or overnight to soak noodles. (If overnight, refrigerate.) Remove plastic wrap and cover with foil for part of the baking time. Bake at 350° for one hour or longer or until knife goes easily through the pasta. Let stand covered for at least 10 minutes to thicken and set before serving. Serves 12 generously. If your baking pan is deep enough it could be done in three layers. Water may be added to sauce if it needs to go further.

Centennial Cookbook

Lasagne Swirls

8 uncooked lasagne noodles
1 (10-ounce) package frozen
  chopped spinach, thawed and
  squeezed
1 cup grated Parmesan
  cheese

1⅓ cups ricotta cheese or
  cottage cheese
½ teaspoon salt
¼ teaspoon pepper
¼ teaspoon nutmeg

Cook noodles as directed on package, rinse with cold water and drain. Mix together spinach, ¾ cup Parmesan cheese, ricotta, salt, pepper, and nutmeg. Spread about ⅓ cup cheese mixture along entire length of noodle. Roll noodles up and stand on end in a greased 7- or 8-inch round casserole dish at least 2½ inches deep.

CONTINUED

SAUCE:

2 cloves garlic, minced
1 large onion, chopped
2 tablespoons salad oil
1¹/₂ pounds ground beef
1 (12-ounce) can tomato sauce
1 teaspoon sugar

¹/₂ teaspoon salt
¹/₂ teaspoon crumbled basil
¹/₂ teaspoon crumbled
    oregano leaves
¹/₄ teaspoon pepper

Sauté garlic and onion over medium heat until limp. Add ground beef and brown. Add tomato sauce, sugar, salt, basil, oregano, and pepper. Simmer, uncovered, for 5 minutes. Pour sauce over noodles. If making ahead, cover and refrigerate. Bake, covered, in a 350° oven until rolls are heated through, about 30 minutes (50-60 minutes if rolls are cold). Remove from oven and sprinkle with remaining ¹/₄ cup Parmesan cheese. Makes 6 servings.

The Junior League of Grand Rapids Cookbook I

Jennifer's Spinach Lasagna

No need to precook the noodles; this is a delicious time-saver!

1 (25¹/₂-ounce) jar of fat-free
    spaghetti sauce
1 (4-ounce) carton fat-free egg
    substitute
2 cups fat-free ricotta or
    cottage cheese
1 (10-ounce) package frozen
    chopped spinach, thawed and
    drained

1 (16-ounce) package
    shredded fat-free Mozzarella
    cheese
¹/₄ cup fat-free Parmesan
    cheese
1 (8-ounce) box of lasagna
    noodles

Combine egg substitute, cottage cheese, and spinach. Spread ³/₄ cup spaghetti sauce in lightly sprayed 13x9x2-inch baking dish. Layer ¹/₂ each: uncooked lasagna noodles, spinach mixture, Mozzarella cheese, and Parmesan cheese. Spread spaghetti sauce over top. Repeat for second layer. Cover with remaining spaghetti sauce. Cover dish securely with aluminum foil and bake at 350° for one hour. Let stand 10 minutes before serving. To reduce sodium, look for low sodium spaghetti sauce. Serves 8.

Nutrition: (per serving): Cal 265; Sat Fat 0g; Total Fat 1g; Prot 32g; Carb 32g; Chol 15mg; Fiber 0g; Vit A 3009 IU; Sod 691mg; Iron 2mg; Vit C 9mg.

"Life Tastes Better Than Steak" Cookbook

Cheese and Pasta in a Pot

2 pounds lean ground beef
Vegetable oil
2 medium onions, chopped
1 garlic clove, crushed
1 (14-ounce) jar spaghetti
  sauce
1 (1-pound) can stewed
  tomatoes
1 (3-ounce) can mushrooms,
  sliced and broiled

1 (8-ounce) package large
  shell macaroni
1¹/₂ pints dairy sour cream
¹/₂ pound provolone, thinly
  sliced
¹/₂ pound Mozzarella cheese,
  thinly sliced

Cook ground beef in a little vegetable oil in a large deep frying pan until brown, stirring often with a fork. Drain off any excess fat. Add onions, garlic, spaghetti sauce, tomatoes, and undrained mushrooms; salt and pepper to taste. Mix well. Simmer for 20 minutes, or until onions are soft. I also add one tablespoon brown sugar. Cook macaroni shells according to package directions. Cook only ¹/₃ of time, since casserole will be baked. Drain macaroni and rinse with cold water. Pour ¹/₂ the shells into a deep casserole. Cover with ¹/₂ the tomato-meat sauce. Spread ¹/₂ the sour cream over sauce. Top with slices of provolone. Repeat, ending with Mozzarella cheese. Bake, covered, for 35-40 minutes at 350°. Remove cover; continue baking until Mozzarella melts and browns slightly. Serves 8.

Pleasures from the Good Earth

Herbed Orzo

Great as a side dish to accompany grilled seafood or chicken.

1 pound rice shaped pasta (orzo)

1/2 teaspoon leaf marjoram (2 teaspoons if available fresh)

3 tablespoons fresh parsley, finely chopped

1 tablespoon fresh rosemary (or other fresh herb)

1 cup diced red or yellow bell pepper

1/4 cup green onion tops, finely chopped

1/2 teaspoon green peppercorns, ground

1 teaspoon finely chopped lemon zest

1/2 teaspoon salt

1/8 teaspoon freshly grated nutmeg

1 tablespoon *olive oil

Cook pasta until al dente; drain and toss with remaining ingredients. Serve warm or at room temperature. Makes 8 cups.

Variations: Add one tablespoon finely chopped sun-dried tomatoes, use the *olive oil from the oil cured sun-dried tomatoes in place of the one tablespoon called for in the ingredient list. Add one tablespoon fresh garlic tops, finely chopped (these are similar to chives with a hint of garlic flavor).

Per one cup serving: Cal 230; Prot 7g; Fat 3g; (1% Sat); Carb 44g; Dietary fiber trace; Chol 0mg; Sod 136mg; Cal 25mg; Iron 2mg. Exchanges: Bread 2¹/₂; Vegetable ¹/₂; Fat ¹/₂.

High Fit - Low Fat

Rice

2 cups Uncle Ben's Converted Rice

1 can beef consommé soup

1 can French onion soup

1 stick oleo

3 soup cans water

Mix all ingredients together and bake at 350° for one hour.

Heavenly Helpings

Absolutely Wonderful Rice

1¹/₂ cups cooked white rice
1 cup sour cream
1 tablespoon Mucky Duck*
  mustard
1 teaspoon salt
1 (4-ounce) can chopped
  green chilies, drained

8 ounces Monterey Jack
  cheese, shredded
1 tablespoon butter or
  margarine

Combine rice, sour cream, mustard, and salt in bowl; mix well. Spoon
¹/₂ the mixture into 8-inch square baking dish. Sprinkle with chilies
and ³/₄ of the cheese. Add remaining rice mixture; dot with butter.
Top with remaining cheese. Bake at 350° for 25 minutes.

Note: *Sweet-tangy mustard. Do not use a minute rice for this popular buffet dish. To double recipe, use 2 cups rice, 1¹/₂ cups sour cream,
2 tablespoons mustard, 6 ounces chilies, 2 tablespoons butter, and 12
ounces cheese.

Mucky Duck Mustard Cookbook

Vegetable Rice Pizza

3 cups cooked rice
¹/₄ cup egg substitute
3 cups Mozzarella cheese,
  divided (shredded)
1 cup tomato pizza sauce
8 ounces fresh mushrooms,
  cleaned and sliced

1 green pepper, chopped
1 red pepper, chopped
1 small package sliced
  Canadian bacon

Preheat oven to 400°. Spray a 12-inch pizza pan or 10-inch pie pan
with vegetable oil or cooking spray. In a large bowl combine rice, egg
substitute and one cup Mozzarella cheese. Stir well. Press mixture
into prepared pan. Bake for 5 minutes. In a small bowl pour pizza
sauce. Spread over baked rice crust. Layer ¹/₂ cup Mozzarella cheese,
mushrooms, red and green peppers and Canadian bacon over sauce.
Top with remaining Mozzarella cheese. Bake 400° for 10-14 minutes
or until cheese is lightly browned.

The Bell Tower Cookbook

Spartichokes

Nice party or buffet dish.

2 cups cooked brown rice
4 eggs, beaten
²/₃ cup milk
2 tablespoons margarine,
 melted
2 tablespoons chopped onion
2 tablespoons chopped
 parsley

1 teaspoon seasoned salt
¹/₂ teaspoon salt
1 cup cooked, drained,
 chopped spinach
1 cup chopped artichoke
 hearts
2 cups shredded Cheddar
 cheese

Mix together rice, eggs, milk, margarine, onion, parsley, and salts. Add spinach, artichokes and Cheddar cheese; stir until blended. Pour into casserole and bake at 325° for 45 minutes. Serves 6-8.

Some Enchanted Eating

Creole Jambalaya

³/₄ cup chopped onion
¹/₂ cup chopped celery
¹/₄ cup chopped green pepper
2 garlic cloves, minced
2 tablespoons butter or
 margarine
2 cups cubed, fully cooked
 ham
1 (28-ounce) can tomatoes
 with liquid, cut-up
1 (10¹/₂-ounce) can
 condensed beef broth

1 cup uncooked long grain
 white rice
1 cup water
1 teaspoon sugar
1 teaspoon dried thyme
¹/₂ teaspoon chili powder
¹/₄ teaspoon pepper
1¹/₂ pounds fresh/frozen
 uncooked shrimp
1 tablespoon chopped fresh
 parsley

In a Dutch oven, sauté onion, celery, green pepper, and garlic in butter until tender. Add next 9 ingredients; bring to a boil. Reduce heat; cover and simmer until rice is tender, about 25 minutes. Add shrimp and parsley; simmer, uncovered, until shrimp are cooked, 7-10 minutes. Makes about 8 servings.

Home Cookin': Almont Elementary PTA

Rice with Raisins and Pine Nuts

Very nice side dish with chicken and veal.

2 tablespoons butter	1 cup rice
3 tablespoons chopped green onion	1/2 cup golden raisins
	1 1/2 cups chicken broth
1/2 teaspoon finely minced garlic	1/4 cup pine nuts

Melt one tablespoon butter in saucepan and add onion and garlic. Cook, stirring until soft. Add the rice and stir. Add raisins and chicken broth and bring to boil. Cover and let simmer exactly 17 minutes. Stir to fluff rice while blending in the pine nuts and remaining butter. Serves 4.

Some Enchanted Eating

Varenyky
(Filled Dumplings)

This is a favorite dish of the Ukrainian people.

2 cups flour	1/2 cup cold water
1 egg	Potato-Cheese Filling

Place the flour in a deep bowl. Add water and egg to make a medium-soft dough. Knead until smooth. Cover and let rest for 10 minutes. Prepare the filling. It should be thick enough to hold its shape. Roll the dough quite thin. Cut rounds with a 3-inch cutter. Put the round on the palm of the hand. Place a spoonful of the filling on it, fold over to form a half circle and press the edges together with the fingers. Place the Varenyky on a floured tea towel and cover. At this time, they can be frozen. To cook, drop a few Varenyky at a time into a large quantity of rapidly boiling water. Stir very gently to separate. Cooking time will depend on size and thickness. They are ready when well puffed (approximately 5 minutes). Remove and drain.

POTATO-CHEESE FILLING:

1 tablespoon grated onion	1 cup cottage cheese or
1 tablespoon butter	grated Cheddar cheese
2 cups cold mashed potatoes	Salt and pepper to taste

Combine all ingredients. Should be thick.

Historically Delicious

Cheese Sauce

1 cup water
1/2 cup cashews
1/2 cup sunflower seeds
1/4 cup yeast flakes
1/4 cup lemon juice

1/3 cup pimento, optional
1 teaspoon salt
1 teaspoon onion powder
1/4 teaspoon garlic powder

Blend smooth all ingredients. Chilling will make sauce thicken. Use over salads, cooked vegetables, pasta, rice, potatoes or on pizza or lasagna.

Variations: (1) Substitute other nuts or seeds for cashews and sunflower seeds. (2) To give an orange color add one of the following suggestions to the blender while blending cheese sauce: 1/3 cup pimento or 2 tablespoons tomato paste and an additional 2 tablespoons water. (3) Replace cashews or sunflower seeds with 2 tablespoons Emes Plain Kosher-Jel. Place Emes and lemon juice in blender. Soften 2 minutes. Heat the water from the original recipe to a boil. Add half of the water and remaining ingredients to the blender. Blend smooth. Add remaining water while blending. Chill several hours then slice or cut in cubes. Melts when exposed to heat. Freezes well.

Of These Ye May Freely Eat

Salsa Di Calamari
(Squid Sauce)

1 tablespoon olive oil	1 can tomato sauce
3 cloves garlic, chopped	1 can crushed tomatoes
Salt and pepper to taste	1/2 cup white wine
1 pound squid (fresh, frozen or canned)	1 tablespoon parsely, chopped

Sauté garlic in olive oil and when golden, add the squid (fresh squid has to be cleaned and washed thoroughly before using). Add remaining ingredients and simmer until sauce has thickened. Serve with pasta of choice or polenta. Add garlic bread and a salad and a glass of white wine. Enjoy. Amore e'gioia!

Variation: Can be used with other seafood if squid is not available.

Sharing Our Best Volume II

Vegetables

Editor Gwen McKee and husband Barney in Greenfield Village. The characters in the tower play chimes every 15 minutes. Dearborn.

Artichoke & Mushroom Casserole

1 (10-ounce) frozen
  artichokes, prepared as
  directed
3 cups sliced, fresh
  mushrooms
1/2 cup sliced green onions
  with tops
4 tablespoons margarine
2 tablespoons flour

1/4 cup milk
3/4 cup water
1 teaspoon chicken bouillon
  granules
1 teaspoon lemon juice
1/8 teaspoon nutmeg
3/4 cup soft bread crumbs
1 tablespoon melted
  margarine

Sauté onion and mushrooms in margarine. Remove from pan. Blend flour and 1/8 teaspoon salt in pan. Add milk, water, bouillon, lemon juice, and nutmeg. Cook and stir until bubbly. Add mushrooms and artichokes and put into casserole dish. Top with a mixture of melted margarine and bread crumbs. Bake at 350° for 20 minutes.

Note: One can of artichokes can be used in place of frozen artichokes.

Recipes & Remembrances II

Zucchini Casserole

3 tablespoons butter
3 tablespoons flour
1 (14-ounce) can stewed
  Italian tomatoes
1 small onion, chopped
1 small green pepper,
  chopped

1 tablespoon brown sugar
1 teaspoon salt
3 zucchini, peeled and sliced
Grated cheese
Bread crumbs

Melt butter, add flour and blend. Add tomatoes, onion, and green pepper. Add brown sugar and salt. Pour over zucchini in 2-quart casserole dish or larger depending on size of zucchini. Cover with grated cheese and bread crumbs. Bake at 350° for one hour.

Blissfield Preschool Cookbook

Cranberry Acorn Squash

2 acorn squash (about 2 cups)
1 tablespoon diet margarine,
   softened
3 tablespoons packed brown
   sugar

1/2 teaspoon cinnamon
1 cup fresh or frozen
   cranberries

Cut squash lengthwise. Remove seeds. Combine margarine, sugar, and cinnamon. Stir in cranberries. Fill squash halves with mixture. Place in microwave shallow dish. Microwave for 5 minutes on HIGH. Turn and cook additional 5 minutes or until done. Makes 4 servings.

Woman's National Farm and Garden Association - Rochester
Cookbook Volume II

Acorn Squash à la Cherries

5 acorn squash
5 tablespoons butter
5 teaspoon brown sugar

1 1/4 cups tart cherries (out of
   a 21-ounce can)

Cut squash in half and remove seeds. Add to each, one tablespoon butter, one teaspoon brown sugar, and 1/4 cup cherries. Bake at 350°, covered with foil, for 60 minutes, or until tender. Servings: 10.

Bringing Grand Tastes to Grand Traverse

Stuffed Acorn Squash

3 small acorn squash, washed,
  halved, seedy centers
  removed
1/2 cup chopped green
  pepper, membrane and seeds
  removed
3 tablespoons margarine
2 cups canned whole-kernel
  corn, drained, or fresh corn

1 teaspoon basil, crushed
1 cup soft fine bread crumbs
3 tablespoons margarine,
  melted
3 tablespoons toasted sesame
  seeds
3 tablespoons shredded
  Parmesan cheese

Place squash halves, cut-side-down, in a shallow baking pan; pour in 1/4-inch boiling water. Bake at 400° about 35 minutes. In a skillet, cook green pepper in hot margarine 5 minutes, stirring occasionally. Remove from heat. Add corn and basil; mix; set aside. Mix bread crumbs with margarine, seeds, Parmesan cheese; set aside.

Remove squash from oven, turn right-side-up. Spread margarine in each cavity; spoon corn mixture into cavities. Sprinkle sesame seeds and crumbs evenly over top. Return to oven and continue baking about 20 minutes. Makes 6 servings.

Cook Book: The Best of Michigan

Broccoli Soufflé
with Mushroom Cheese Sauce

SOUFFLE:

3 tablespoons margarine
3 tablespoons flour
1 cup milk
1 teaspoon salt
1 tablespoon lemon juice

1¹/₂ teaspoons grated onion
1 cup finely chopped, cooked
   broccoli, well drained
4 eggs, separated

Melt margarine; blend in flour. Gradually add milk. Cook over medium heat, stirring constantly, until mixture thickens. Stir in salt, lemon juice, onion, and broccoli. Beat egg whites until stiff but not dry. Beat egg yolks until thick; add broccoli mixture. Mix thoroughly. Fold in egg whites. Pour into 1¹/₂-quart casserole; place in pan of hot water. Bake in moderate oven (350°) 40 minutes, or until knife inserted halfway between edge and center comes out clean. Serve at once with Mushroom Sauce.

MUSHROOM SAUCE:

2 tablespoons margarine
2 tablespoons flour
¹/₄ teaspoon salt
Dash of pepper

1 cup milk
1 (3 - 4-ounce) can sliced
   mushrooms, drained
¹/₂ cup grated sharp cheese

Melt margarine; blend in flour, salt, and pepper. Gradually add milk. Cook, stirring constantly, until mixture thickens. Add mushrooms and cheese; heat until cheese melts. Makes 6 servings (256 calories per serving).

From Our Kitchens with Love

Each year thousands of visitors from around the world come to Cranbrook House and Gardens to delight in the formal gardens and terraces enhanced by sculpture and fountains. The estate in Bloomfield Hills is a reflection of a gracious style of living from the early part of this century.

Asparagus Bundles

A JLAA Special Event favorite.

45-50 asparagus spears,
   trimmed to about 4 inches
10 small red tomatoes
$3/4$ cup olive oil
2 teaspoons grated Parmesan
   cheese

$1/2$ cup lemon juice
1 teaspoon sugar
$1/2$ teaspoon oregano
1 teaspoon chopped garlic
$1/8$ teaspoon black pepper

Clean and cut tips off asparagus spears. Blanch spears. Slice tomatoes and hollow out to make rings. Place 4-5 spears in each ring and cut ends to equal length. Beat remaining ingredients together and pour over bundles just before serving. Serves 10.

The Bountiful Arbor

Carrot Casserole

$1/2$ pound margarine
3 cups herb Pepperidge
   Stuffing Mix
4 cups sliced cooked carrots
1 small onion, chopped

1 cup sharp Cheddar cheese,
   grated
1 can cream of celery soup
1 cup milk

Pour melted margarine over stuffing mix. Reserve one cup for topping. In buttered casserole layer carrots, stuffing mix and onion and cheese. Repeat layers, cover with reserved stuffing. Pour soup and milk (well mixed) over all. Bake at 350° for 25 minutes. Serves 8.

Allen Park Garden Club Recipe Book

Zucchini, Corn and Tomatoes

2 medium-size zucchini, about
   2 pounds or 4 cups sliced
$1/2$ cup onion, thinly sliced
$1 3/4$ teaspoons salt
$1/2$ teaspoon oregano

$3/4$ teaspoon basil
$2 1/2$ cups tomatoes, fresh or
   canned, chopped
$1 1/2$ cups corn
$1/4$ cup water

Slice zucchini on diagonal. Combine all ingredients. Simmer until tender. Serve as is or over brown rice or noodles. Vary the vegetables. Try summer squash, broccoli, carrots, okra or green beans instead of zucchini.

Of These Ye May Freely Eat

Two Corn Casserole

¹/₂ cup margarine
¹/₄ cup chopped onion
³/₄ cup chopped green pepper
1 (17-ounce) can whole kernel
　corn (undrained)
1 (17-ounce) can cream-style
　corn

3 eggs, well beaten
1 box corn muffin mix
4 ounces grated Cheddar
　cheese (optional)

Heat oven to 350°. Grease 2-quart casserole. In small skillet, melt margarine. Add onion and pepper. Sauté until crisp. In large bowl, combine 2 corns, eggs, and muffin mix. Blend well. Add onion and pepper. Mix. Pour into casserole and sprinkle with cheese (optional). Bake at 350° for 55-65 minutes or until firm and set. Let stand 5 minutes before serving.

The Fruit of Her Hands

Onions Onions Onions

3 tablespoons butter
2 large sweet (Vidalia) onions,
　thinly sliced
2 red onions, thinly sliced
2 Bermuda or Spanish onions,
　thinly sliced
2 leeks, washed and thinly
　sliced

1¹/₂ cups grated Havarti
　cheese
1 (6-ounce) package herbed
　Boursin or Allouette cheese,
　crumbled
1¹/₂ cups grated gruyére
　cheese
³/₄ cup white wine

Preheat oven to 350°. Butter a large baking dish. Layer onions in dish—¹/₃ of each type. Sprinkle with salt and pepper. Top with Havarti. Make another layer and top with the herbed cheese. Make another layer and top with gruyére. Dot top with butter. Pour wine over all. Bake one hour. Cover with foil, if getting too dark.

Tasteful Art

Peppers are a fruit—not a vegetable. Naturally rich in Vitamin C, peppers also supply Vitamin A to our diets. Michigan grows more than 13 million pounds of peppers a year and usually ranks 7th among states producing peppers.

Eggplant Pancakes

1 eggplant (about 1 pound)
2 large eggs
Salt and freshly ground
  pepper to taste
2 tablespoons finely chopped
  onion

5 tablespoons bread crumbs
  or matzo meal
1 tablespoon chopped parsley
Vegetable shortening for
  frying

Peel the eggplant and dice into 1/2-inch pieces. Place in boiling salt water to cover and simmer, uncovered, about 10 minutes or until tender. Drain well.

In a mixing bowl, combine the eggs, salt, pepper, onion, bread crumbs or matzo meal, and chopped parsley. Fold in the eggplant, adding more bread crumbs or matzo meal if needed to hold together.

Heat a griddle or nonstick pan, then smear with vegetable shortening. Drop heaping tablespoons of the eggplant batter into the pan and pat down. Fry on each side and serve.

The Fruit of Her Hands

Baked Eggplant Moussaka

The most famous eggplant recipe in all the Near East is called moussaka. Though the origin is not known for certain, the recipe was probably carried to Greece by the Arabs when they introduced the eggplant in the Middle Ages.

3 eggplants	1/4 teaspoon nutmeg
Vegetable oil	2 tablespoons chopped
2 pounds ground beef	parsley
1 (6-ounce) can tomato paste,	1 cup dry bread crumbs
diluted in 1 cup water	1 cup grated kefalotyri or
1 cup dry white wine	Parmesan cheese
Salt and pepper	

Peel and slice eggplant into 1/4-inch thick slices. Salt well on both sides of slices. Let stand for one hour; rinse in cold water and drain. Heat oil in frying pan and add eggplant. Cook for 3-4 minutes. Remove from pan and drain on absorbent paper.

In separate pan, sauté onion in butter. Add meat and cook until well browned. Add diluted tomato paste, wine, nutmeg, parsley, and season to taste with salt and pepper. Simmer until ingredients are well blended.

WHITE SAUCE:

1/2 stick (1/8 pound) butter	3 eggs, beaten
1 cup flour	1/2 cup grated cheese
1 quart milk, heated	

Melt butter in saucepan. Add flour gradually, stirring until well blended. Add heated milk and stir until thickened. Stir in well beaten eggs, nutmeg, and salt and pepper to taste. Cook for one minute, stirring constantly. Add cheese and stir until melted into sauce.

Sprinkle bread crumbs on the bottom of 13x9-inch baking dish. In layers, add 1/2 of eggplant, 1/2 of meat mixture, 1/3 of cheese, and then 1/3 of bread crumbs. Repeat layers. Pour on white sauce and top with remaining cheese and bread crumbs. Bake at 350° for 1/2 hour or until golden brown. Cool slightly before cutting. Makes 10 servings.

Opaa! Greek Cooking Detroit Style

Spinach Soufflé

This soufflé is so easy to prepare. For spinach lovers who prefer a low cholesterol spinach soufflé, use egg beaters and low cholesterol cheese. I have prepared this recipe both ways. Believe me, you can't tell the difference.

20 ounces frozen chopped
  spinach
2 pounds small curd creamed
  cottage cheese
1/4 pound sharp Cheddar
  cheese, grated
1/4 pound Swiss cheese,
  grated

6 eggs, beaten
6-7 tablespoons flour
1/4 pound butter, melted
4 scallions, chopped and
  sautéed

Allow spinach to stand at room temperature to defrost completely (do not soak in water). Squeeze very dry and combine with remaining ingredients, mixing well. Pour into greased 9x13-inch baking dish. Bake in preheated 350° oven for one hour, or until brown. Serve with a crisp tossed salad and crusty bread. Makes 6 servings.

Opaa! Greek Cooking Detroit Style

Baked Herbed Spinach

1 cup finely chopped onion (1
  large)
2 cloves garlic, minced
1/4 cup butter or margarine
5 (10-ounce) packages frozen
  chopped spinach, thawed
1 cup heavy cream
1 cup milk
1/2 cup grated Parmesan
  cheese

1/2 cup packages bread
  crumbs
1 teaspoon leaf marjoram,
  crumbled
1/4 teaspoon pepper
1/4 cup grated Parmesan
  cheese

Heat oven to 350°. Sauté onion and garlic in butter or margarine just until tender. Combine all ingredients, except for 1/4 cup grated cheese. Turn into greased 2-quart baking dish. Sprinkle top with reserved cheese. Bake 30 minutes or until cheese on top is browned. Makes 12 servings.

From Our Kitchens with Love

Baked Garlic with Sun-Dried Tomatoes

An unusual twist to traditional baked garlic.

4 large heads garlic	1 tablespoon dried basil
2¹/₂ tablespoons butter, thinly sliced	1 tablespoon dried oregano
	Pepper to taste
¹/₄ cup olive oil	6 ounces goat cheese, sliced
2 cups chicken broth	Fresh basil leaves
2 cup sun-dried tomatoes	1 loaf Italian bread, sliced

Cut ¹/₄-inch slice from top of garlic heads; discard. Remove any loose papery peeling. Place the garlic cut-side-up in a medium baking dish. Arrange butter slices over garlic; pour olive oil over garlic. Pour chicken broth around garlic; arrange sun-dried tomatoes in broth. Sprinkle with basil, oregano, and pepper. Bake at 375° for one hour and 15 minutes or until garlic and tomatoes are tender, basting with broth every 15 minutes. Arrange goat cheese around garlic.

Bake for 10 minutes longer or until goat cheese is almost melted. Garnish with fresh basil. Serve with Italian bread slices. Yield: 16 servings.

Dawn to Dusk

Fried Green Tomatoes in Cream

We try never to let a tomato get away from us. When the days shorten, so that our bounty of tomatoes can no longer catch enough sun to turn them a rich red, we bring them in to store in our fruit cellar or paper bags. The window sill is not the answer. They'll look awful pretty there but they'll taste awful poorly. In the total dark, they will ripen nicely after about 2-3 weeks. If we can't wait that long, we make good things like India Relish or Green Tomato Apple Pie or for dinner, Fried Tomatoes in Cream....a favorite taste treat.

4 green tomatoes, unpeeled	2-3 tablespoons butter
Flour	2 teaspoons brown sugar
Salt and freshly ground pepper	1/2 cup heavy cream

Slice tomatoes 1/2-inch thick. Dredge in flour mixed with salt and freshly ground pepper to taste. In a large, heavy skillet, melt butter over medium heat. When it begins to sizzle, add tomato slices, sprinkling each with a pinch or so of brown sugar. When lightly browned, turn. Sprinkle each again with brown sugar. When slices have browned and are just beginning to soften, turn off heat and immediately pour in cream. Gently turn tomatoes in the thickening cream, then serve immediately. Serves 4.

Hollyhocks & Radishes

Bean Casserole

1 pound spicy ground sausage	1 cup brown sugar
1 medium onion, chopped	1 can stewed tomatoes
1 medium green pepper, chopped	1 can pork & beans
1/2 stick butter	1 can kidney beans, drained
1 cup catsup	1 can butter beans, drained
	1 can lima beans, drained

Brown sausage, set aside. Brown onion and green pepper with butter or oleo. Combine drained sausage, onion mixture and all remaining ingredients. Place in ovenproof dish and bake at 350° for one hour or more. Great for picnics or pot lucks.

Seasoned Cooks II

Baked Beans

1 (3-pound) jar white
    Northern beans, precooked
1 onion, sliced
2 teaspoons dry mustard

1 cup brown sugar
3/4 cup ketchup
4 slices bacon, cut up

Combine beans, onion, mustard, ketchup, brown sugar, and bacon. Bake at 325° for 2 hours, uncovered.

Trendfully Cookin'

Ludington Cassoulet

Cassoulet is one of southwestern France's most famous stews. It's really a white bean casserole with strong, earthy flavors that develop from the meats with slow cooking.

1 pound sliced onions
1/2 cup Michigan red wine
2 teaspoons minced garlic
3 teaspoons tomato paste
1 1/2 pounds chopped tomato
    concasse
2 1/4 teaspoons chopped
    rosemary
1 1/4 tablespoons chopped
    thyme

4 ounces beef stock
3/4 pound cooked Great
    Northern beans
4 ounces duck breast
6 ounces pork tenderloin
6 ounces Pleva cherry
    sausage (may substitute)
1 1/2 cups chicken base
1 1/2 ounces bread crumbs

Preheat oven to 350°. Sauté the onions in a dry pan until browned. Add about 1/4 of the wine. Mix in garlic, sauté until the aroma is strong, then add the tomato paste. Sauté, stirring constantly, until there is a nice aroma. Add the rest of the wine to deglaze the pan. Reduce to a heavy consistency. Add half of the chopped tomatoes, and the herbs. Sauté over high heat until the juices from the tomatoes have reduced and some of the sugars caramelize. Add a pinch of salt, beef stock, and cooked beans. Simmer gently until the flavors combine and the stew is fairly dry.

In a separate pan sauté the sausage, pork, and duck, stirring gently. Add chicken base, simmer for a few minutes. Fold this mixture into the beans. Add the rest of the tomatoes. Top with bread crumbs and bake until the stew is moist and has cooked to a nice consistency.

Per serving: Cal 354; Cal from Fat 16%; Sod 662mg; Chol 45mg.

Michigan Gourmet Cookbook

Black Beans and Rice

1¹/₂ pounds cubed pork loin
1 tablespoon oil
1 can cream of chicken soup
1 can black beans, rinsed and
   drained
1 (16-ounce) can diced
   tomatoes (do not drain, may
   use 2 cans)

2 cans chopped green chilies
2-3 tablespoons salsa
1 cup uncooked Minute rice
¹/₄ cup water
1 teaspoon cumin
Shredded Cheddar cheese

Brown cubed pork in oil; drain excess oil. Add remaining ingredients, except cheese, in large pot and bring to boil. Add pork. Place ingredients in 9x13-inch baking dish. Bake in 350° oven for 30 minutes. After removing from oven, sprinkle top with cheese and let melt. May substitute chicken for pork.

Home Cookin': Almont Elementary PTA

They're full of beans and proud of it at the tip of the Lower Peninsula's "thumb." Known as one of the bean capitals of the world, the Huron, Tuscola, and Sanilas county area ranks as one of the world's top producers. Michigan produces more dry beans than any other state. There are about 440,000 farm acres planted with them.

Old Settler's Beans

1/2 pound ground beef	1/2 cup brown sugar
1/4 pound bacon, cut up	1/2 cup sugar
1 small onion	1/4 cup catsup
1 can red kidney beans	1/2 teaspoon mustard (not dry)
1 can B&M Pork & Beans	2 tablespoons molasses
1 can butter beans	

Brown beef, bacon, and onion. Mix all ingredients and put in casserole dish. Heat uncovered one hour or more, as desired at 350°. Can be made ahead of time.

Renaissance Cuisine

Pan-Roasted Vegetables

1/3 cup butter	2 cups broccoli flowerets
1/2 teaspoon thyme leaves	2 cups carrots, cut into small
1/4 teaspoon salt	strips
1/4 teaspoon pepper	2 small onions, quartered
3 cups cauliflower flowerets	

Heat oven to 400°. In 9x13-inch baking pan melt butter in oven (5-6 minutes). Stir in thyme, salt and pepper. Add remaining ingredients; toss to coat. Cover with foil; bake for 22-27 minutes or until vegetables are crisply tender.

Blissfield Preschool Cookbook

Sweet Potato St. Cecilia

4 sweet potatoes	1/2 cup orange juice
1/2 cup butter	4 oranges
1/2 cup sugar	Miniature marshmallows
2 teaspoons cinnamon	

Boil sweet potatoes until soft (30 minutes). Cool and peel. Mash potatoes and add butter, sugar, cinnamon, and orange juice. Mix well. Halve the oranges; remove the meat and juice. Stuff each half with sweet potato mixture. Top with marshmallow. Bake at 350° for 15-20 minutes. Makes 8 servings.

The Junior League of Grand Rapids Cookbook I

Devonshire Potato and Mushroom Pie

Delicious.

3 cups cooked mashed
  potatoes
1¹/₂ cups sliced fresh
  mushrooms
¹/₄ cup chopped onion

2 tablespoons butter
1 teaspoon lemon juice
¹/₄ teaspoon salt
Dash black pepper
¹/₂ cup dairy sour cream

Place a layer of 1¹/₂ cups mashed potatoes in a buttered 9-inch pie pan. Sauté mushrooms and onion in butter. Add lemon juice, salt and pepper. Mix well. Spoon over potato layer. Spread sour cream over mushrooms and onion layer. Top with another 1¹/₂ cups mashed potatoes. Bake at 350° for 45 minutes or until browned. If desired, paprika may be sprinkled on top for additional color. Serves 6.

Ferndale Friends Cook Book

Potato Pancakes

2 cups grated, raw potatoes
2 tablespoons flour
2 eggs, well beaten

1 small onion, grated
1 teaspoon salt

Add last 4 ingredients to grated potatoes and beat well. With spoon, drop mixture on hot greased griddle and spread thin. Fry on both sides. Serve with sour cream and sprinkle with sugar.

From Our Home to Yours

Potato Zucchini Pie

1 pound potatoes, cooked and
  mashed
2 tablespoons butter, divided
2 eggs
8 ounces grated Mozzarella
  cheese

¹/₂ cup grated Parmesan
  cheese
1 large zucchini, grated
¹/₄ cup minced onion
Salt and pepper to taste
2 tablespoons bread crumbs

Mash potatoes with one tablespoon butter, eggs, and cheese. Add zucchini, onion, salt and pepper. Stir well. Put in 9-inch pie plate. Top with one tablespoon butter and bread crumbs. Bake for 30 minutes in a 400° oven.

The Bell Tower Cookbook

Michigan Spuds Bake

Excellent for family or guests.

12 medium potatoes (or
  enough to fill a 9x13-inch pan)
1/2 cup margarine, cut up
1/2 cup chopped onions
2 cups shredded Cheddar
  cheese

2 cups sour cream
1 teaspoon salt
1/4 teaspoon pepper

Boil potatoes until done but still firm. Drain well and refrigerate. Peel and grate potatoes coarsely. Gently mix with all of remaining ingredients. Bake in greased 9x13-inch casserole at 350° for 30-40 minutes or until bubbly. Cool for 5 minutes and cut into squares for serving. Serves 12.

Some Enchanted Eating

Potato Wedges

Use your own favorite seasoning in this recipe. Instead of Italian seasoning, you may want to try substituting grated Parmesan cheese, garlic salt, basil, paprika or something to compliment the main course for the meal.

4 medium Michigan potatoes
1/4 cup butter or margarine
1 teaspoon Italian seasoning

Salt
Pepper

Preheat oven to 450°. Cut each potato into 4 lengthwise wedges. Place on ungreased cookie sheet with skin-side-down. Melt butter or margarine. Stir in Italian seasoning. Brush potatoes with seasoned butter. Season with salt and pepper, as desired.

    Bake at 450° for 30-35 minutes, or until potatoes are tender. Arrange on serving platter. If desired, garnish with parsley.

Good Food From Michigan

Michigan produces lots of soybeans--an ideal food helpful in lowering cholesterol and in the prevention of many cancers. Soybean oil is used in more than 80% of all cooking oils and salad dressings, and in 90% of all margarines produced. Ford, in 1940, was the first to use soybean plastics in automobiles.

Tater Tot Casserole

1 large package frozen tater
  tots
Onions, chopped
1 can cream of mushroom
  soup

1 can cream of celery soup
Cheese, grated, such as
  Cheddar

Place frozen tater tots in 8x8-inch square pan and sprinkle chopped onions over top. In saucepan heat undiluted soups together; pour over tater tots and onions. Sprinkle with grated (Cheddar) cheese. Bake at 350° for one hour.

Crystal Clear Cooking

Gingered Carrots and Apples

2 cups bias-sliced carrots
1/3 cup orange juice
2 teaspoon grated fresh
  ginger root
2 tablespoons butter or oleo

2 medium apples, cored and
  cut into 1/4-inch slices
1 teaspoon sugar
2 tablespoons snipped fresh
  chives

Cook carrots, orange juice, and ginger root in butter or oleo for 5 minutes in covered skillet. Add apples and simmer 2-4 minutes in covered pan. Stir in sugar and top with chives. Serves 4.

Come and Dine

Harvest Nut Roast

1 1/2 cups chopped onions
3 tablespoons water
2 tablespoons oil (olive is best)
2 1/2 cups finely chopped celery
3/4 cup chopped walnuts
3/4 cup ground pecans or sunflower seeds

1 1/2 teaspoons salt
2 cups soy milk
1 1/4 teaspoons basil
1/2 teaspoon sage or 1 1/4 teaspoons thyme
3 cups whole grain bread crumbs

Sauté onions in water and oil until clear. Put into bowl and add remaining ingredients, omitting bread crumbs. Stir together well. Fold in bread crumbs. Pour into lecithin-oiled 8x8-inch baking dish. Bake at 350° for 60 minutes. To prevent overbrowning on top, may need to cover with foil near end of baking. Delicious served with Country Style Gravy. Yield: 6 cups or 8x8-inch baking dish or medium loaf pan.

COUNTRY STYLE GRAVY:

2 cups water
1/2 cup cashew pieces or 3 tablespoons whole wheat flour
1 tablespoons onion powder
1/4 teaspoon garlic powder
1/4 teaspoon salt

2 tablespoons oil (omitting if using nuts)
3 tablespoons soy sauce or gomasio
1 tablespoon yeast flakes
1 tablespoon cornstarch

Blend all ingredients on high 2-3 minutes until creamy. Pour into saucepan and cook on medium-high until thick, stirring constantly. Serve over entrée roasts or loaves, potatoes, or biscuits. Yield: 2 1/2 cups.

Country Life: Vegetarian Cookbook

Michigan is the Apple Variety State. There are 15 types of apples grown commercially in its hilly terrain. The state has ideal fall weather—sunny days and cool nights—to bring out the natural color and flavor of apples. There are more than 100 cider mills in Michigan.

Michigan Farm Apple Relish

This is a recipe Chef Robert Nelson learned from his mother more than 50 years ago. His Farm Relish will liven up grilled meats, or provide a tangy topping for an omelette.

2 quarts chopped tomato
2 cups sliced Michigan
  Empire apples
1 cup diced celery
1 cup chopped onions
2 chopped green peppers
2 chopped red peppers

1¹/₂ cups Michigan apple
  cider vinegar
1 whole cinnamon stick
2 tablespoons yellow mustard
  seed
¹/₂ tablespoon whole cloves
2³/₄ cups Michigan beet sugar

Combine all ingredients in large kettle. Simmer slowly for one hour or until mixture is thick and clear. Fish out cinnamon stick. Cool and store. Serves 64.

Per serving: Cal 44; Cal from Fat 4%; Sod 13mg; Chol 0mg.

Michigan Gourmet Cookbook

Swiss-born Louis Chevrolet came to America to sell a wine pump he invented. He went on to design the first cars for the company that bore his name, now a division of General Motors. The Dodge brothers started out as bicycle manufacturers. After working briefly for Henry Ford, they founded Dodge Brothers, then later sold it to Chrysler.

Poultry

The high banks of the Michigan International Speedway, the world's fastest race track, hosts the U.S. 500 IndyCar race. Brooklyn

Chicken Florentine

6 chicken breasts (boneless)
1/4 cup butter
2 tablespoons oil
2 (10-ounce) packages
chopped spinach
1/2 cup mayonnaise
1/4 cup sour cream

1 can condensed cream of
chicken soup
1 tablespoon lemon juice
1 teaspoon curry powder
Salt and pepper
1/2 cup grated sharp cheese
1/2 cup cornflake crumbs

Sauté chicken in butter and oil for 10 minutes. Cook spinach; drain and squeeze dry. Spread spinach in bottom of greased 2-quart casserole. Top with chicken breasts. Mix remaining ingredients except for cheese and corn flake crumbs. Pour over chicken. Sprinkle with cheese; top with crumbs. Bake at 350° for 25 minutes.

Home Cookin': Almont Elementary PTA

Cherry-Orange Chicken

2 (3-pound) fryers or chicken
breasts
4 tablespoons oleo, melted
1 cup brown sugar
1/2 teaspoon orange peel

1/4 teaspoon ground ginger
1/2 cup orange juice
1 (16-ounce) can dark sweet
cherries, drained

Cut up and place chicken in 9x13-inch baking pan. Melt and pour oleo over chicken. Mix and pour next 4 ingredients over chicken. Bake at 350° for 45 minutes. Remove from oven. Top with cherries. Bake for 30 minutes longer until tender and golden. Servings: 6.

Bringing Grand Tastes to Grand Traverse

Curried Chicken Bake

Casseroles that can be made ahead and baked at the last minute after work or play are especially welcome.

3 Empire apples, peeled,
  thickly sliced
1 tablespoon butter or
  margarine
1 tablespoon sugar
4 chicken breast halves

$^1/_2$ cup mayonnaise
$^1/_2$ teaspoon soy sauce
$^1/_2$ teaspoon Dijon mustard
$^1/_2$ teaspoon prepared
  horseradish
2 teaspoons curry powder

Preheat the oven to 350°. Sauté the apples in the butter in a skillet over low heat for 5-7 minutes. Add the sugar and increase the heat to medium. Sauté until the apples are brown. Spread in a greased 9x13-inch baking dish. Rinse the chicken in cold water and pat dry. Combine the mayonnaise, soy sauce, mustard, horseradish, and curry powder in a bowl; mix well. Spread over both sides of the chicken. Arrange chicken skin-side-up over the apples. Bake at 350° for one hour or until chicken is cooked through. You may chill the dish for up to 24 hours before baking, or double the recipe if desired. Serves 4.

The Dexter Cider Mill Apple Cookbook

Wingfield's Chicken Francaise

4 boneless chicken breasts,
  remove skin (8 ounces each)
Salt and pepper to taste
$^1/_2$ pound flour
3 eggs

$^1/_2$ cup butter, for sautéing
  (must use butter)
$^1/_2$ cup cooking oil, for sautéing
$^1/_2$ cup more butter
Juice from 1 fresh lemon

Pound the chicken breasts slightly; sprinkle with salt and pepper. Roll the breasts in flour, shaking off excess. Beat the eggs in a bowl and dip each breast in the eggs. In a large skillet, melt $^1/_2$ cup butter and oil until foaming. Place the breasts in the pan and cook until golden brown on both sides. When the breasts are golden, remove skillet from heat, drain off and discard butter and oil. Add $^1/_2$ cup more butter and the lemon juice; reheat the skillet, turning each breast to coat with lemon butter and serve immediately.

Chelsea Cooks

Chicken Breasts En Papillote

2 whole chicken breasts,
  boned, skinned and pounded
  to 1/4-inch thickness
Salt and freshly ground
  pepper to taste
1 1/2 teaspoons olive oil for
  brushing chicken
1 tablespoon olive oil
1 shallot, minced

2 large garlic cloves, minced
1/2 pound mushrooms, sliced
1/2 teaspoon chopped fresh
  rosemary
1/4 teaspoon dried thyme
3 tomatoes, peeled, seeded
  and chopped
1/2 cup dry white wine
Zest of 1 lemon

Preheat oven to 375°. Sprinkle chicken lightly with salt and pepper. Cut 4 large double thicknesses of aluminum foil, large enough to fold loosely over each chicken breast. Brush foil with olive oil and set a chicken breast half on each piece. Heat one tablespoon of olive oil in a large skillet and sauté the shallot and garlic until shallot is tender, but not brown. Add the mushrooms and sauté until the mushrooms begin to release some of their liquid, about 10 minutes. Add the rosemary, thyme, and tomatoes and sauté over medium heat, stirring occasionally, for another 10 minutes. Remove from the heat and stir in the wine and lemon zest. Taste and season accordingly. Spoon some of this sauce over each of the chicken breasts. Fold the foil over and crimp the edges tightly together. Bake in a preheated oven for 20 minutes. Serve in the foil with whipped potatoes that are piped on a greased baking sheet and browned in the oven. Serves 4.

What's Cookin'

Chicken Supreme

4 whole chicken breasts,
  skinned, boned, and split
4 slices Swiss cheese
1 can cream of chicken soup

2 cups Pepperidge Farm
  Stuffing Crumbs
1/4 pound melted butter

Place chicken in shallow baking pan. Top each piece of chicken with 1/2 slice of cheese. Thin soup with 1/4 - 1/2 can of water. Pour over chicken. Mix stuffing with butter. Toss. Sprinkle over top of chicken. Bake 325° for 1 1/2 hours. Serves 8.

Woman's National Farm and Garden Association - Rochester
Cookbook Volume II

Cheesy Tomato Basil Chicken Breasts

SAUCE:

3 tablespoons butter
2 cups cubed tomatoes
1/3 cup chopped onion
1 (6-ounce) can tomato paste
1 tablespoon basil leaves
1/2 teaspoon salt

1/4 teaspoon pepper
2 teaspoons minced fresh
    garlic
3 whole chicken breasts,
    skinned and cut in half

TOPPING:

1 cup fresh bread crumbs
1/4 cup chopped fresh parsley
2 tablespoons melted butter

6 ounces Mozzarella cheese,
    cut into strips

Heat oven to 350°. In 9x13-inch baking pan, melt 3 tablespoons butter in oven. Meanwhile, stir together remaining sauce ingredients; set aside. Place chicken in baking pan, turning to coat with butter. Spoon sauce mixture over chicken. Bake for 30-40 minutes or until chicken is no longer pink. Stir together all topping ingredients except cheese. Place cheese strips over chicken; sprinkle with topping mixture. Continue baking 5-10 minutes or until chicken is fork tender and bread crumbs are browned.

Blissfield Preschool Cookbook

Broccoli Cheese Chicken

1 tablespoon margarine or
    butter
4 chicken breast halves,
    boneless, skinless
1 can condensed broccoli
    cheese soup

¹/₃ cup water or milk
2 cups broccoli, cut into
    ¹/₂-inch pieces
¹/₈ teaspoon pepper

In skillet over medium-high heat, in hot margarine, cook chicken for 10 minutes or until browned on both sides. Spoon off fat. Stir in soup and water. Add broccoli and pepper. Heat to boiling. Reduce heat to low. Cover, cook 10 minutes or until broccoli is tender and chicken is no longer pink, stirring occasionally.

Trendfully Cookin'

Chicken and Asparagus Quiche

There is nothing finer than the very first spring crop of Michigan asparagus.

1 unbaked 8- or 9-inch pie
    shell
³/₄ cup finely diced cooked
    chicken
¹/₄ cup finely diced ham
2 cups cut cooked asparagus,
    ¹/₂-inch pieces

1 cup shredded Swiss cheese
3 eggs
Milk or light cream
Pinch of nutmeg
Pinch of pepper
6 whole cooked asparagus
    spears, for garnish

Preheat oven to 425°. Into unbaked pie shell, place chicken, ham, asparagus, and Swiss cheese. Break 3 eggs into a large measuring cup; add enough milk or cream to make 1¹/₄ cups. Add pinch each of nutmeg and pepper. Beat well with fork. Pour over mixture in pie shell. Decorate with cooked asparagus spears. Bake for 15 minutes. Reduce heat to 300° and bake 30-40 minutes, or until cold knife inserted into center comes out clean. Serves 6-8.

Cranbrook Reflections

An excellent source of Vitamin C, B6, dietary fiber and glutathione, asparagus takes three to five years to mature before it can be harvested. The 23,000 acres in Michigan planted with asparagus produce about 25 million pounds per year. The short harvesting season requires that most be fresh-frozen or canned.

Golden Chicken Nuggets

Our testers loved these dipped in honey or low-fat ranch dressing.

2¹/₂ pounds boneless
   chicken breasts cut into
   1-inch pieces
1¹/₂ cups flour
1 cup whole wheat flour
2 teaspoons dried parsley
1¹/₂ teaspoons poultry
   seasoning

¹/₂ teaspoon salt
¹/₂ teaspoon pepper
1 cup plain yogurt
3 cups crushed wheat thin
   crackers

Preheat oven to 400°. Spray 2 cookie sheets with nonstick cooking spray. In a large plastic bag with a zip closure, combine the flours with the dried parsley, poultry seasoning, salt and pepper. Add the chicken pieces, a handful at a time, to the flour mixture. Close the bag and shake to coat. Place ¹/₂ of the yogurt in a small bowl. In a separate small bowl, place the crushed wheat thin crackers. Dip the flour coated chicken pieces into the yogurt and roll in the cracker crumbs. Place the coated pieces on the prepared cookie sheets. Bake 10-12 minutes.

Nutrition per serving: Cal 112; Fat 2g; Prot 14g; Carb 10g; Chol 33mg; Fiber 0g; Vit A 30IU; Sod 82mg; Iron 1mg; Vit C 0mg.

Smart Snacks

Marinated Fried Chicken
(Kotopoulo Tiganito Marinato)

Hellenes like marinades, especially the Greeks of Detroit. They have the best concept of why Greek chicken dishes are so exciting.

MARINADE FOR CHICKEN:

1/4 cup olive oil	1/2 onion sliced thin
1/4 cup lemon juice	1 teaspoon oregano
1/2 cup white wine vinegar	1 bay leaf, crushed
1/4 cup white wine	2 peppercorns, crushed
2 cloves garlic, sliced	4 coriander seeds, cracked

In a large bowl, combine all the ingredients and beat with a fork.

1 (2¹/2-pound) frying chicken, cut into serving pieces	Corn or peanut oil for frying
	Parsley for garnish, chopped and sprinkle
Salt and pepper	Flour for coating

Dip chicken in the marinade, coating the pieces on all sides. Cover and refrigerate for at least 2 hours. Drain, then season with salt and pepper to taste. In a paper bag add flour and chicken pieces. Shake lightly until chicken is coated with flour. Pour oil into a heavy skillet and heat until almost to the smoking point. Place the chicken in oil and fry to a light color on all sides. Remove chicken to a baking pan, and bake in a 350° oven for 50 minutes or until tender, pouring off oil as it collects in the pan. The chicken will be crisp and chestnut brown. Serve with a tomato, cucumber salad and crusty bread. Makes 4 servings.

Opaa! Greek Cooking Detroit Style

Oven-Fried Sesame Chicken

Really tasty!

3 tablespoons sesame seeds
2 tablespoons flour
1/4 teaspoon pepper
4 chicken breast halves,
   skinned

2 tablespoons soy sauce
2 tablespoons margarine,
   melted

Preheat oven to 400°. Combine sesame seeds, flour, and pepper. Dip chicken pieces into soy sauce, dredge in sesame seed mixture. Arrange chicken, bone-side-down, in a large shallow baking dish. Drizzle margarine over chicken. Bake for 40-45 minutes or until tender. Serves 4.

The Bountiful Arbor

Picnic Drumsticks

1 1/2 cups plain yogurt
1/3 cup lemon juice
6 cloves garlic, minced
1/2 teaspoon salt
1/2 teaspoon cayenne pepper
1/3 cup Mucky Duck*
   mustard
30 drumsticks (about 6
   pounds), skinned

3 cups finely crushed saltine
   crackers
2 tablespoons oregano
1 tablespoon paprika
1/2 teaspoon salt
1/2 teaspoon cayenne pepper
6 tablespoons unsalted butter
   or margarine, melted

Combine yogurt, lemon juice, garlic, 1/2 teaspoon salt, 1/2 teaspoon cayenne pepper and mustard in medium bowl; mix well. Spoon into 2 shallow dishes. Rinse drumsticks; pat dry. Arrange in prepared dishes, turning to coat well. Marinate, covered, in refrigerator for 3 hours to overnight.

Combine cracker crumbs, oregano, paprika, 1/2 teaspoon salt, and 1/2 teaspoon cayenne pepper in paper or plastic bag. Add drumsticks several at a time, shaking to coat with crumb mixture. Arrange in foil-lined baking pans; drizzle with butter. Bake at 375° for about 45 minutes or until golden brown. Serve hot or at room temperature.

*Sweet-tangy mustard. Chicken can be wrapped in foil and refrigerated after cooking for next-day picnic or tailgate party.

Mucky Duck Mustard Cookbook

Asparagus and Chicken Stir-fry

1 teaspoon sesame seeds
1 boneless chicken breast,
  sliced into thin strips
1/2 pound asparagus spears
  (about 12 spears), cleaned
  and diagonally sliced

3 green onions, sliced
1 tablespoon soy sauce
2 teaspoons sugar
Salt
Pepper
Hot, cooked rice

Preheat a skillet or wok; add sesame seeds. Stir frequently and continue cooking until sesame seeds are lightly toasted. Add the chicken; stir-fry until chicken is cooked and no longer pink, stirring often. Push chicken to side of pan. Add asparagus and green onion to skillet. Stir-fry until vegetables are crisp-tender. Stir together vegetables and chicken. Stir soy sauce and sugar into mixture in skillet. Season with salt and pepper, as desired. Serve immediately with hot, cooked rice. Yield: 2 servings.

Good Food From Michigan

Chicken Kapama

Excellent with pork chops, too.

1 (3-pound) chicken, cut up
2 tablespoons butter
1 (16-ounce) can whole
  tomatoes
1 onion, chopped

1 stick cinnamon
2 cups water
Salt and pepper
1 cup rice

Brown chicken in butter. Break tomatoes into small pieces. Pour tomatoes, onion, cinnamon, water, and salt and pepper over chicken. Cover and bring to a boil. Simmer for 30 minutes, turning chicken once. Sprinkle rice into the liquid and bring to a boil. Cover and simmer 20-30 minutes longer or until rice and chicken are tender.

Canned tomatoes containing green pepper and onions give a different flavor to this dish and make an interesting variation. Can be made day ahead and freezes very well. Makes 4 servings.

The Junior League of Grand Rapids Cookbook I

Hot Chicken Salad

2 cups cooked chicken, cubed
2 cups celery, diced
$1/2$ teaspoon salt
2 teaspoons grated onion
2 tablespoons lemon juice

$1/2$ cup toasted almonds
1 cup mayonnaise
1 cup potato chips, crushed
$1/2$ cup grated American cheese

Mix well first 6 ingredients; add mayonnaise and mix again. Pile lightly in a buttered casserole and sprinkle with potato chips and cheese mixture. Bake at 450° for 15 minutes.

Come and Dine

Chicken Casserole

1 (6-ounce) package brown
   rice, cooked
2 cups chicken, cooked and
   cubed (3-4 breasts)
$1/4$ pound mushrooms, sliced
   or 1 (4-ounce) can
1 can of mushroom soup

$1/2$ cup milk
1 ($4^1/4$-ounce) can black
   olives, chopped
2 cups Cheddar cheese,
   grated
$1/2$ cup almonds, sliced

Butter a 3-quart baking dish. Spread rice evenly in bottom. Top with chicken or turkey. Sprinkle on the mushrooms. Pour the soup combined with the milk over top. Add a layer of olives and top with cheese. Sprinkle with almonds. Bake at 350° for 45 minutes, until heated through. Can be frozen, thawed, and reheated in low oven.

Pleasures from the Good Earth

Honey and Mustard Glazed Chicken

1/4 cup butter or margarine
1/2 cup honey
1/4 cup prepared mustard
1 tablespoon soy sauce

1 teaspoon lemon juice
1/2 teaspoon salt
1 (3 - 4-pound) frying chicken,
  cut-up

Preheat oven to 375°. Melt butter or margarine. Add honey, mustard, soy sauce, lemon juice, and salt. Whisk together until smooth. Pour honey mixture into a greased shallow baking pan. Roll each piece of chicken in honey mixture and place in baking pan meat-side-up. Bake at 375° for 50-60 minutes, or until chicken is thoroughly cooked and tender. Yield: 4-6 servings.

Good Food From Michigan

Chicken and Rice Hawaiian

1 (20-ounce) can chunk
  pineapple
1 medium onion
1/2 cup celery
2 tablespoons oil
2 cups cooked chicken, cut in
  chunks
1 cup catsup

1/2 teaspoon salt
1/4 teaspoon pepper
2 tablespoons cornstarch
3 tablespoons soy sauce
1 medium green pepper, cut
  in 1/4-inch strips
Cooked rice (4 servings)

Drain pineapple, reserving juice. Cook onion and celery in oil until tender. Add chicken. Blend catsup and juice with enough water to make 2 1/2 cups liquid. Stir salt and pepper into liquid mixture. Mix cornstarch with soy sauce and add to mixture, stir to thicken. Add green pepper and pineapple. Cover and cook 5 minutes. Serve over hot rice. Makes 4 servings.

Heavenly Helpings

Chicken and Rice Casserole

2 cups diced, cooked chicken
2 cups chopped celery
2 cups cooked rice
2 tablespoons chopped onion
1 can water chestnuts,
  drained and sliced

1/2 cup slivered almonds
2 cans cream of chicken soup
  (undiluted)
1 cup mayonnaise
Salt and pepper

TOPPING:
1 cup crushed cornflakes

1/4 cup melted butter

Mix together first 8 ingredients with salt and pepper. Place in buttered casserole. Top with mixture of cornflakes and butter. Bake at 350° for 45 minutes, uncovered. Serves 8.

Home Cookin': First Congregational United Church of Christ

The Great Lakes State is not only surrounded by four of the five Great Lakes, but has more than 11,000 inland lakes, and 36,000 miles of rivers and streams. No doubt it offers the best freshwater beaches, boating and fishing to be found anywhere.

French Garlic Chicken

The French love garlic! Although the number of cloves may appear overwhelming at first, the results are magnifique!

2 large heads garlic (20-25 cloves)
1¹/₂ cups chicken stock
2 tablespoons butter
1 tablespoon oil
3¹/₂ - 4 pounds chicken parts

1 lemon, peeled and thinly sliced
2 tablespoons flour
¹/₂ cup dry white wine
Salt and pepper

Preheat oven to 350°. Separate cloves of garlic, set in a saucepan, cover with water, simmer 5 minutes. Drain and cover with cold water. Discard water and peel cloves. Simmer poached, peeled garlic cloves, partially covered, in stock for 30 minutes. In a heavy skillet, melt butter and oil. When hot, brown chicken until golden. Transfer to a 9x13-inch pan and cover with garlic cloves (save stock) and lemon slices. Prepare sauce in skillet with flour, garlic stock, and wine. Skim fat, if necessary, and pour sauce over chicken. Cover with foil and bake for 45-55 minutes. Serve with French bread to spread with poached garlic. May be made ahead and reheated. Serves 4-6.

Cranbrook Reflections

Chicken Pot Pie

1 chicken, cooked and deboned
1 medium bag frozen vegetables, cooked and drained (use fresh if available, microwave to soften)

1 medium onion, chopped
Salt and pepper to taste
2 cans cream of chicken soup or 1 can soup and 1 can broth from chicken

Mix together and put in a 13x9-inch pan. Cover with Topping.

TOPPING:
1 cup self-rising flour
1 stick butter or oleo

1 cup milk

Pour over chicken mixture. Bake at 400-425° until brown, 30-40 minutes.

Centennial Cookbook

White Chili

A health-conscience recipe.

1 1/2 pounds boned chicken
  breast
2 (14-ounce) cans chicken
  broth
3 (16-ounce) cans white navy
  beans (do not drain)
2 cups chopped onion

2 tablespoons garlic
1 tablespoon oil
1 (4-ounce) can green chilies
  (do not drain)
2 teaspoons cumin
2 teaspoon oregano
1/4 teaspoon cayenne pepper

Bake chicken. Cut into pieces. Combine broth and beans in soup pot, set aside on low heat. Sauté onion and garlic in oil. Add chilies. Add onion mixture and chicken to soup pot. Add remaining ingredients. Simmer 30 minutes. Serves 5.

Recipes & Remembrances II

Grilled Turkey Tenderloins

1/4 cup soy sauce
1/4 cup oil
1/4 cup sherry
2 tablespoons lemon juice
2 tablespoons onion,
  dehydrated

1/4 teaspoon ginger
Dash of pepper
Dash of garlic salt
1 pound turkey tenderloins,
  1-inch thick

Mix first 8 ingredients. Add turkey and coat. Marinade overnight. Grill 6-8 minutes per side. Servings: 4.

Bringing Grand Taste to Grand Traverse

Sautéed Duck Breasts

Carve the breasts from 4 mallards at the time they are shot. This eliminates plucking the birds and also conserves freezer space. Defrost the breasts in a plastic bag, saving any juice that accumulates.

1/4 pound butter	4 tablespoons currant jelly
2 cloves garlic, minced	1 tablespoon Worcestershire
8 duck breasts	sauce
Rind of 1 orange, cut in	Salt and pepper to taste
julienne strips and poached 2	7 ounces Marsala
minutes	
4 tablespoons chopped	
parsley	

In a large skillet, melt butter. Add minced garlic. When the butter is bubbling, add the duck breasts, and sauté them for one minute on each side. Remove the breasts to a warm platter. Add to the butter in the skillet the juices from the defrosted breasts, the poached orange rind, the chopped parsley, the currant jelly, the Worcestershire sauce, salt and pepper to taste, and the Marsala. Blend this mixture well, then return the breasts to the sauce and simmer gently 2 more minutes. The breasts should be pink inside. Serve the breasts with wild rice and any remaining sauce.

Mrs. Boone's Wild Game Cookbook

Wild Partridge

Partridge breast	1 onion, sliced
Vinegar	1 can cream of chicken soup
Water	1 can cream of mushroom
Flour	soup
Oil	1 cup milk

Soak partridge breast in vinegar and water overnight. Rinse and roll in flour. Brown in oil on both sides. Remove from pan and place in casserole dish. Add remaining ingredients and bake at 350° for 2 hours.

Crystal Clear Cooking

Seafood

When the water freezes on Michigan's more than 11,000 lakes, ice fishing can produce a tasty evening meal.

Lake Michigan Fish Boil

Share your catch with a crowd.

1-2 new potatoes per person
2 small onions per person
1 cup uniodized salt, divided

1/2 pound lake fish per
  person, skinned, filleted and
  cut in 2-inch chunks

Use a fish boil cooker or a large pot with basket that allows room beneath the basket for potatoes and onions. Put potatoes and onions in water in bottom of cooker. Water should cover the bottom of the basket. Bring to a boil; add 1/2 cup salt. Bring again to a boil; boil 12 minutes. Add fish to basket. Water should cover fish. Bring to boil; add 1/2 cup more salt. Cook 15-18 minutes or until fish flakes. Drain. Serve with drawn butter. Serves 10-12.

Variations: Steelhead, trout, Chinook or coho may be used.

Some Enchanted Eating

Open Fire Walleye Fish Fry

Here's one for walleye that's a bit different. It works best over an open fire.

1/2 cup Jiffy, Bisquick or
  pancake mix
1 teaspoon Italian seasoning
1 teaspoon poultry seasoning

1 egg
1 1/2 cups club soda or beer
2 walleye fish fillets
Some flour

Combine all ingredients, except the walleye and flour, for the batter. This batter must be thin. Add milk or more club soda (or beer) until it is the consistency of a thin pancake batter. Roll fillets in flour. Dip in batter, and fry in deep fat or oil until brown at the edges. Flip and cook until done. Serves 4.

Mrs. Boone's Wild Game Cookbook

At 200 feet wide and 50 feet tall, the Upper Tahquamenon Falls is the second-largest falls east of the Mississippi River (only Niagara is bigger).

Broiled Walleye

1 medium-size walleye fillet per person	Dash garlic powder
1 stick butter, divided	Juice of 1 fresh lemon
1 package slivered almonds	Dash Worcestershire sauce
	1/2 teaspoon mixed herbs

Place fillets in broiling pan. In a frypan melt 1/2 stick butter, add almonds and a dash of garlic powder. Sauté until almonds are toasted. Set aside.

Place 1/2 stick butter, lemon juice, Worcestershire sauce, and mixed herbs in blender and mix well. Chill until firm.

Place walleye fillets in oven and broil 20 minutes. Remove and pour slivered almonds over top. Return to broiler for a few minutes. Place a fillet on each plate and serve with a tablespoon of herbed butter over each fillet.

Fish & Game Menu Cookbook

Marinated Grilled Tuna with Tomato-Basil Sauce

The tomato-basil sauce can double as a lovely fresh summer pasta sauce.

6 fresh tuna steaks (about 6
  ounces each)
Pepper, to taste
6 tablespoons olive oil

2 tablespoons lemon juice
2 tablespoons chopped fresh
  oregano, or 2 teaspoons dried

Sprinkle tuna steaks on both sides with pepper. Combine oil, lemon juice, and oregano in a shallow glass dish just large enough to hold tuna in a single layer, and stir to blend. Add tuna, turning to coat both sides. Set aside at room temperature and let marinate for one hour, turning once or twice.

Build a charcoal fire in a grill, or preheat broiler. When grill or oven is ready, cook fish for about 4-5 minutes on each side for medium rare.

TOMATO-BASIL SAUCE:

1¹/₂ tablespoons butter
1¹/₂ tablespoons olive oil
3 tablespoons finely chopped
  shallot
2 tablespoons red wine
1 tablespoon sherry vinegar
1 pound plum tomatoes,
  peeled, seeded, and diced

1¹/₂ tablespoons chopped
  fresh basil leaves
Salt and pepper, to taste
6 small sprigs fresh oregano,
  for garnish
6 small fresh basil leaves, for
  garnish

Melt butter with olive oil over medium heat. Add shallot and cook until softened, about 3 minutes. Add wine and vinegar and cook over high heat, stirring, for about one minute. Reduce heat to medium-low; add tomatoes and simmer for 5-6 minutes, or until most of the liquid is evaporated. Stir in basil, season with salt and pepper, and simmer for 30 seconds. Keep warm. Serve fish immediately with warm sauce and garnish. Serves 6.

Note: If swordfish is substituted, increase cooking time by 5-6 minutes per side. Sauce can be made a few hours in advance and reheated just before serving.

The Bountiful Arbor

Tuna or Shrimp Stack-Up

15 slices bread
Butter
1 cup tuna or chopped shrimp
1 small can of mushrooms,
    drained
4 hard cooked eggs, chopped

1/2 cup chopped ripe olives
1/4 cup chopped green onions
1/4 cup mayonnaise
1 can cream of chicken soup
1 cup sour cream

Trim bread; butter both sides. Combine all ingredients (except chicken soup and sour cream); spread on 10 bread slices. Assemble 5 triple-decker sandwiches; fasten corner with toothpicks. Toast on baking sheets in 350° oven 20 minutes or until crisp and lightly browned. Mix soup and sour cream; heat and stir until hot. Serve over hot sandwiches.

Allen Park Garden Club Recipe Book

Red Snapper à la Greektown

Both ancient and modern Greeks have been devoted to the sea. Some of the favorite fish of the Greeks are, unfortunately, not available in this country. However, we do have in America an abundance of fish to keep alive the recipes and tradition of Greek fish cookery.

4 (1-pound) whole red
    snapper
Olive oil
3 teaspoons salt

2 teaspoons oregano
1/2 teaspoon black pepper
4 cloves fine chopped garlic

Wash fish, drain, and pat dry. Brush olive oil on all parts of fish. Set aside. In a bowl mix all the spices including garlic. Sprinkle spices all over fish and cavity. Let it stand for 30 minutes before broiling. Broil (or charco-broil) for 20 minutes or until brown and flaky.

LEMON OIL SAUCE:

1 cup olive oil
1/2 cup lemon juice

1/4 cup parsley, chopped
1/2 teaspoon salt

Mix all ingredients thoroughly in a saucepan and heat slowly. Spoon sauce over broiled fish. Serve with rice pilaf and a glass of dry white wine. Makes 4 servings.

Opaa! Greek Cooking Detroit Style

Red Snapper with Sour Cream Topping

1 large onion, chopped	4 red snapper fillets
2 tablespoons butter	1 cup sour cream
2 cloves garlic, crushed	1/4 cup grated Swiss cheese
Salt and pepper	

In frying pan, sauté onion in butter until tender and begins to brown. Add the garlic, salt, and pepper; sauté for another minute or two. Remove from heat and let cool a little. Butter a casserole that is large enough to hold the 4 fish fillets, without having them overlap. Wash and pat-dry fillets, and place skin-side-down. Skin can be removed, if you prefer.

Salt and pepper fish. Divide the onion mixture and spread it evenly over the 4 fillets. Add sour cream over each fillet and sprinkle grated cheese over sour cream. (The fish can be cooked now or placed in the refrigerator until baking time.) Bake 25-30 minutes in a 375° oven till top is lightly browned. Serve immediately. Serves 3-4 persons.

Note: Other fish can be used in this recipe. Any firm-fleshed white-fish fillet of about 1/2-inch thickness will work. If your fillets are much thinner, you will have to shorten baking time.

From Our Kitchens with Love

Baked Fish Fillets in Parchment

Inspired by a memorable dinner in Nashville! We like to use salmon for this recipe, although Cape bluefish, swordfish or black cod would also be delicious. The parchment seals in the flavors and keeps the fish moist.

1¹/₂ pounds fish fillets
1 tablespoon prepared mustard
2-3 teaspoons green peppercorns, crushed, to taste
1 medium sweet, mild onion,
  thinly sliced (optional)
¹/₂ cup scallions, finely chopped
2 tablespoons lemon thyme or
  fresh herb of choice, finely chopped

18 slices sun-dried tomatoes
  (about 1¹/₂ ounces) or 6
  pieces oil-cured, cut julienne
¹/₄ cup dry vermouth
Parchment paper, cut into 6
  approximately 12-inch
  squares, enough to wrap the
  fish in securely

Preheat oven to 450°. Cut the fish into 6 serving-size pieces and place them on the parchment. Spread each piece lightly with the mustard. Sprinkle with the crushed green peppercorns then arrange the onion, scallions and herb on top. Arrange 3 sun-dried tomato slices on the very top; drizzle each fillet with 2 teaspoons of vermouth and wrap up the package. Take care to fold the edges over several times for a tight seal. Place in the middle of the preheated oven for 15-20 minutes, depending on the thickness of the fish. Allow 10 minutes per inch of thickness plus 10 minutes more for this dish. Serve immediately in their wrapping. Delicious accompanied with steamed fresh vegetable in season and a baked potato with non-fat yogurt sour cream. Makes 6 servings.

Per serving: Cal 170; Prot 24g; Fat 5g; (1% Sat); Carb 4g; Dietary fiber 1g; Chol 67mg; Sod 104mg; Cal 30mg; Iron 1mg. Exchanges: lean meat 3; Vegetable 1; Fat (-1).

High Fit - Low Fat

Planked Fish: Indians used to plank their whitefish by lashing them to a piece of wet driftwood which they set upright in the sand. They then cooked them vertically next to the hot fire. Though practically a lost art, it can be done by oiling a warmed plank and placing the fish, skin-side down in the middle. Brush with lemon butter, season liberally, and bake about 15-20 minutes till it flakes easily with a fork. (This also works just fine in a greased skillet, and extra good to lay some bacon strips over the top of the fish before cooking.)

Stuffed Fish Fillets

3 tablespoons nonfat plain
  yogurt
1 tablespoon nonfat milk
3 slices fresh French bread
  cubes
2 tablespoons lemon juice
2 tablespoons finely chopped
  onion
2 tablespoons finely chopped
  green pepper

2 tablespoons sliced pimiento
  stuffed olives
4 fillets of orange roughy, cod,
  or sole
Salt and pepper
Paprika
Dill weed

Preheat oven to 350°. Spray baking dish with Pam. In a small bowl, combine all ingredients, except last 4. Mix well. Sprinkle both sides of the fillets lightly with salt, pepper, and paprika. Place 2 fillets in baking dish. Spread stuffing evenly over fillets; place second fillet on top of stuffing like a sandwich. Cut both in half; sprinkle tops with paprika and dill weed. Bake 20-25 minutes or till fish flakes.

Note: If fillets are large, use same amount of stuffing and cut fillets to serve 6-8. Not for freezing. Low cholesterol.

Woman's National Farm and Garden Association - Rochester
Cookbook Volume II

Baked Salmon

3 pounds filleted and skinned
  salmon
Salt and pepper to taste

Butter
1 thinly sliced small onion
1 thinly sliced fresh lemon

Place salmon in baking dish; season to taste, dot with butter, and place onion and lemon over fish. Cover with Saran Wrap and place in microwave at HIGH power for 3 minutes. Remove from microwave and check with a fork for doneness (thickest part of fish should flake when fork is inserted).

Fish & Game Menu Cookbook

Spicy Lime-Ginger Grilled Shrimp

Wonderful!!

MARINADE:

3/4 cup lime juice (fresh)
1 tablespoon minced fresh
  ginger
2 medium garlic cloves, minced
2 small shallots, finely chopped
2 tablespoons finely chopped
  fresh cilantro

1/2 teaspoon salt
1/8 teaspoon black pepper
1/8 teaspoon crushed red
  pepper flakes or to taste
2 1/2 tablespoons orange
  marmalade
1/3 cup olive oil

Combine all ingredients in small mixing bowl, whisking in oil last.

SHRIMP:

1 1/2 pounds shrimp (medium
  large or jumbo) shells left on
  until after cooking
4 large carrots, peeled
1 large European cucumber,
  halved and seeded, peel left on

1 head red leaf lettuce
2 tablespoons finely chopped
  cilantro for garnish

Thread shrimp on skewers (4-6 per skewer) and lay them flat in a
19x13-inch non-aluminum dish. Pour 1/2 the marinade over shrimp
and marinate for 1/2 hour. Meanwhile, shred carrots and cucumber;
put in medium mixing bowl. Add about 2 tablespoons of remaining
marinade; reserve rest for dipping.

When ready to serve, prepare the barbecue for medium-high heat
and place skewered shrimp flat on grill. Baste and grill until just pink.
Arrange lettuce leaves on platter and mound cucumber-carrot mixture
on top. Place skewered shrimp on top of vegetables and let guests help
themselves. Garnish with chopped cilantro and pass remaining marinade for dipping.

Note: If using bamboo skewers, soak in water overnight before
skewering shrimp. This will prevent them from catching fire on the
grill.

Recipes and Memories

Shrimp Stroganoff

2 tablespoons butter or
  margarine
2 tablespoons finely chopped
  onion
8 ounces fresh shrimp,
  peeled, deveined
1 (10-ounce) can cream of
  shrimp soup

1/2 cup skim milk
1/2 cup low-fat sour cream
1/4 teaspoon paprika, or to
  taste
Salt and pepper to taste
8 ounces egg fettuccini,
  cooked

Melt the butter in a skillet. Add the onion. Sauté until the onion is
tender. Add the shrimp. Cook until the shrimp turn pink. Blend in
the soup and skim milk. Cook until heated through; do not boil. Stir
in the sour cream and paprika. Season with salt and pepper. Serve
over the hot fettuccini. Yield: 4-6 servings.

Dawn to Dusk

Barbecue Shrimp

24 large shrimp, peeled and deveined

12 slices bacon

Peel and devein the shrimp, leaving the tails on. Cook the bacon halfway in a skillet, chill, and cut in half lengthwise. Wrap the shrimp in bacon, holding together with a toothpick.

BARBECUE SAUCE:

1¹/₂ cups orange juice concentrate

6 tablespoons soy sauce

1 cup ketchup

³/₄ cup molasses

4 teaspoons Worcestershire sauce

2 teaspoons Tabasco

1¹/₂ cups chili sauce

2 tablespoons Dijon mustard

2 cloves garlic, chopped fine

2 tablespoons fresh lemon juice

¹/₂ cup chicken broth

2 teaspoons salt

In a large bowl mix together all the ingredients for the BBQ sauce. Place the bacon-wrapped shrimp on a sheet tray. Ladle the BBQ sauce generously over each shrimp, leaving the tails unsauced. Place the shrimp under a low-heat broiler; cook for 6 minutes. Turn shrimp and cook for another 6 minutes. To serve, place the shrimp on a large decorative platter, with napkins on the side. Yields: 8 servings.

Recipe by Chef Chuck "Rocky" Rachwitz.

The Simply Great II Cookbook

In 1917 Dr. Oscar Kraft was boating on Lake Michigan when his boat caught fire and he was forced to come ashore off Lake Michigan. Coming over the dunes to look for assistance, he discovered an abandoned lumber town. Two rows of dilapidated homes and businesses stood empty on another smaller lake now known as Lower Herring Lake. Oscar recognized the charm and beauty of the surrounding area and purchased the entire town. Today his niece and her children run this breathtaking hideaway known as Watervale.

Shrimp Casserole à la Roditys

The Kolpos, hundreds of bays which encompass the coastline of Greece, are the home of garithes, the best shrimp you'll ever eat. If you can't get to the Kolpos, I suggest you try this tasty dish instead.

1 pound medium-sized raw
  shrimp
2 tablespoons butter
3 tomatoes, peeled and
  chopped
1 onion, chopped

1 clove garlic, minced
1 tablespoon brandy
1 tablespoon red wine
$1/4$ pound feta cheese
Salt and pepper

Use a small sharp knife to pick off shell of shrimp. Slit shrimp down the back; clean off the back vein down the back of the shrimp. Rinse in cold water.

Bring one cup of water to a boil. Add shrimp, cover, and cook one minute. In a skillet, melt butter and add shrimp; cook over medium heat for 3 minutes or until shrimp are pink. Remove shrimp to a casserole dish. In skillet, add tomatoes, onion, and garlic and cook for 5 minutes. Add brandy, wine, and salt and pepper to taste; cook for 3 minutes longer. Pour sauce over shrimp and top with thin slices of feta cheese. Serve hot. Rice pilaf is a must! Makes 4 servings.

Opaa! Greek Cooking Detroit Style

Ship-to-Shore Shrimp

2 tablespoons oil
Garlic
Onions
Shrimp

1 package Japanese frozen
  (or fresh) vegetables
Soy sauce

Sauté garlic in oil until brown. Add onions and shrimp. Mix, cover and cook over medium heat until shrimp is done. Add vegetables and season with soy sauce to taste.

Note: Use as much or as little shrimp and onion as you like. Serves approximately 6-8 people.

How to Make A Steamship Float

Shrimp Stuffed Peppers

4 medium to large firm green
  peppers
1/4 pound lean bacon, sliced
1 1/2 cups onions, chopped
1/2 cup green pepper, chopped
3 tablespoons celery, chopped
1 tablespoon garlic, finely minced
1 cup ripe tomatoes, coarsely
  chopped (1 large or 2 small)
1 pound fresh shrimp in the
  shell, deveined and cut into
  1/2 - 3/4-inch pieces

1 1/2 teaspoons salt
1/2 teaspoon pepper, freshly
  ground
3/4 teaspoon thyme
2 bay leaves, crushed
3 tablespoons parsley, finely
  minced
1/8 teaspoon cayenne
1/2 cup green onions, chopped
1/2 cup white bread, crumbled
  and slightly dampened
  (crusts removed)

Cut off and discard the top 1/4 of the green peppers (or use for the stuffing). Remove seeds and membrane. Place peppers upright in about 1/2-inch of salted water in a heavy saucepan that will hold them snugly but not tightly. Bring water to boil, cover the pan, reduce heat and cook for 5 minutes. Remove the peppers from pan, drain thoroughly, then set aside to cool while you prepare the stuffing. Fry bacon in large heavy sauté pan until almost crisp. Add onions, green pepper, celery, garlic, tomatoes, and green onions. Sauté just until vegetables begin to turn soft, about 8 minutes. Add salt, pepper, thyme, bay leaves, parsley, and cayenne. Mix well with wooden spoon. Add shrimp and cook over low heat just until shrimp turn pink. Add bread and blend well. Stuff peppers and bake, uncovered, in preheated 350° oven for 30 minutes, or until slightly browned on top.

Pleasures from the Good Earth

Baked Crabcakes with Fruit Salsa

3 tablespoons butter
1/4 cup chopped onions
1/2 cup chopped celery
1 garlic clove, minced
1/2 cup finely chopped green
 onion
3 tablespoons chopped fresh
 parsley
1 pound crabmeat

1/3 cup low-fat mayonnaise
1 teaspoon dry mustard
Dash of cayenne pepper
1 teaspoon Mrs. Dash
 (original)
1 1/2 cups fresh saltine
 cracker crumbs (low salt)
1 egg white, beaten

Preheat oven to 450°. Melt butter in a medium skillet over medium heat. Sauté onions, celery, garlic, and green onions until wilted. Do not brown. Remove from heat and stir in parsley, then the crabmeat. Mix in mayonnaise, mustard, pepper, and Mrs. Dash. Mix in 1/3 cup of cracker crumbs. Fold in beaten egg white. Form into 12 patties. Roll in the remaining crumbs. Place on a baking sheet that has been sprayed with Pam. Bake for 10 minutes; turn the patties over and bake for 15 minutes more.

FRUIT SALSA:
3 firm peaches, finely chopped
1/2 cup finely chopped fresh
 pineapple
2 ripe tomatoes, chopped
 (with seeds removed)
3 green onions, sliced
 (include tops)
3 tablespoons chives

1 jalapeño pepper, finely
 chopped (seeds removed)
3 tablespoons fresh cilantro,
 chopped
4 tablespoons canola oil
4 tablespoons white wine
 vinegar
2 tablespoons honey

Combine all but last 3 ingredients; whisk oil, vinegar, and honey. Pour over the other ingredients. Let salsa marinate for one hour. Serves 6.

What's Cookin'

Thousands of islands rise in the waters that surround the Great Lakes State. Early settlers depended on these patches of wilderness as way stations. Later, fishermen used their shores as bases for plying remote waters. Today, Michigan's island hold a special allure for vacationers.

Sharon's Seafood Salad

2 cups crabmeat, chopped
2 cups lobster, chopped
1 pound small shrimp,
 cooked, peeled and deveined
4 stalks celery, finely chopped

1 (16-ounce) jar prepared
 sour cream dill salad dressing
2 tablespoons fresh dill,
 chopped
Sliced almonds

In large mixing bowl, combine crabmeat, lobster, shrimp, and celery. In small bowl, combine dressing and dill. Add to seafood mixture and toss gently. Refrigerate several hours or overnight. Stir before serving on lettuce leaves; sprinkle top with sliced almonds. Yield: 6 servings.

Something Special

Crabmeat Cobbler

1/2 cup Crisco
1/2 cup green pepper,
  chopped
1/2 cup onion, chopped
1/2 cup flour, sifted
1 teaspoon dry mustard
1/2 teaspoon Accent
1 cup milk

1 cup shredded American
  cheese
1 (6¹/2-ounce) can crabmeat
2 tablespoons Worcestershire
  sauce
1¹/2 cups drained tomatoes
1/2 teaspoon salt

Melt Crisco in pan. Add green pepper and onion and cook until tender, about 10 minutes. Blend in sifted flour, dry mustard, Accent, milk, and American cheese; cook, stirring constantly, until cheese is melted and mixture is very thick. Add crabmeat, Worcestershire sauce, tomatoes, and salt.

CHEESE BISCUIT TOPPING:
1 cup flour, sifted
2 teaspoons baking powder
1/2 teaspoon salt

1/4 cup shredded American cheese
2 tablespoons Crisco
1/2 cup milk

Sift together flour, baking powder, and salt. Add American cheese and Crisco. Cut in until mixture resembles coarse meal. Add milk. Mix only until all flour is dampened. Drop by rounded teaspoonsful on top of crabmeat mixture. Bake in 450° oven for 15-20 minutes.

Allen Park Garden Club Recipe Book

The northern reaches of Michigan's Lower Peninsula is a skiers' paradise. Here the slopes have somjething for everyone. Many hills are of modest proportions, but several are steep moraines which sprang up along the shoulders of the glaciers that carved Lake Mighigan.

Sparty statue on the campus of Michigan State University. Lansing.

Michigan Meat Balls

2 pounds hamburger
1 cup sour cream
1 package Lipton Dry Onion
  Soup Mix
1 egg
1¹/₂ cups bread crumbs

¹/₂ cup flour
1 teaspoon paprika
¹/₄ cup butter
1 can cream of chicken soup
¹/₄ cup water

Mix hamburger, sour cream, soup mix, egg, and crumbs. Mix well.
Form into walnut-size balls. Roll in flour and paprika and brown in
butter. Blend soup with water; pour over meat balls and simmer.
Crockpot works good.

Country Cookbook

Royal Swedish Meat Balls

2 pounds ground round
1 pound ground lean pork
2 eggs, beaten
1 cup mashed potatoes
1 cup dry bread crumbs
1 tablespoon brown sugar
1 cup milk
2¹/₂ teaspoons salt

¹/₂ teaspoon pepper
¹/₂ teaspoon ginger
¹/₂ teaspoon nutmeg
¹/₂ teaspoon cloves
¹/₂ teaspoon allspice
Flour
1 pint cream

Combine all ingredients except flour and cream; mix well. Form into
small balls. Dip in flour. Brown. Put in baking dish. Pour cream
over them. Bake in slow oven, 325°. They may be fried in pan
instead of baked.

Halvorson-Johnson Family Reunion Cookbook

Crazy Meat Balls

2 pounds ground beef
1 cup bread crumbs

1 package dry French onion
soup

Mix ground beef, crumbs, and French onion soup. Shape into balls.

SAUCE:

1 bottle chili sauce
1 cup cranberry sauce
1 can drained sauerkraut

¹/₂ cup brown sugar
1 cup water

Simmer chili sauce, cranberry sauce, sauerkraut, brown sugar, and water till mixed. Pour over meatballs in 9x13-inch pan. Bake at 325° for 2 hours.

Home Cookin': First Congregational United Church of Christ

Hungarian Meatballs

1 cup condensed tomato soup
1 cup sour cream
1 pound ground beef
¹/₃ cup fine, dry bread crumbs
1 teaspoon salt
Dash of pepper
1 egg

1 tablespoon shortening
¹/₂ cup minced onion
1 clove garlic, minced
1 teaspoon paprika
1 teaspoon lemon juice
1 bay leaf
Noodles, cooked and drained

Blend soup and sour cream. Add ¹/₄ cup of this mixture to beef, bread crumbs, salt, pepper, and egg. Shape into 1-inch balls (12 or more); brown in shortening.

Add onion and garlic and brown lightly; stir in remaining soup mixture and seasonings. Cover and simmer 30 minutes, stirring occasionally. Uncover and simmer about 5 minutes or until sauce has thickened slightly. Remove bay leaf. Serve meatballs on hot buttered noodles. Makes 6 servings.

Ferndale Friends Cook Book

Greek Style Meatloaf

2¹/₂ pounds ground chuck
¹/₂ pound finely diced feta
  cheese
10 pitted black olives,
  chopped
1 small onion, peeled and
  diced
1 tablespoon oregano

1 tablespoon ground cumin
1 tablespoon paprika
1 teaspoon black pepper
1¹/₂ teaspoons salt
1 tablespoon garlic powder
1 egg
¹/₂ cup bread crumbs

In a large bowl, mix all the ingredients thoroughly. In a jelly-roll pan, shape meat into a loaf, making sure there are no bubbles. For easier and firmer shaping, wet hands before shaping.

Bake in a preheated 350° oven for one hour, or until the temperature registers 165° on a meat thermometer. If meat seems to be browning too quickly, cover with foil. Remove from oven; let meatloaf stand for 15 minutes to firm up. Slice and serve with mashed potatoes and gravy. Makes 8 servings.

Opaa! Greek Cooking Detroit Style

Hamburg Cups

Children love them. Can be made with smaller cups for party trays.

1 pound ground beef
4 tablespoons ketchup
1 tube Hungry Jack biscuits

Sliced or grated Cheddar
  cheese

Cook beef till it's light brown; drain. Add ketchup; stir well. Line muffin tins with biscuits. Place ground beef mixture in biscuit lined cups. Top with cheese. Bake according to biscuit directions. Remove with fork and serve!

Come and Dine

 Detroit comes from the French d'etroit, meaning "of the straits." Almost 300 years old, it was only of modest size until Henry Ford set up an auto assembly line; within 30 years, Motor City had five times as many people, growing to become the nation's sixth-largest metropolitan area. It also holds the distinction of being the only major U.S. city north of Canada.

Hamburger Gravy

2 pounds ground beef
1 cup beef soup base
1 can mushroom soup
1/2 package Lipton Onion
   Soup Mix

Cornstarch
Water

Brown and drain ground beef. Add soup base, soup, and onion mix. Cook slowly to boiling point. Thicken with cornstarch and water. Serve over mashed potatoes.

Crystal Clear Cooking

Not-So-Sloppy Joes

These Joes can be served open-faced and are super for Super Bowl Sunday supper.

1 onion, chopped
2 cloves garlic, crushed
3/4 cup grated carrots
3/4 cup chopped mushrooms
2 tablespoons vegetable oil
1 pound ground beef
1 cup tomato sauce
3 tablespoons Mucky Duck*
   mustard
2 tablespoons red wine
   vinegar

2 tablespoons catsup
1 tablespoon molasses
1 teaspoon Worcestershire
   sauce
1 teaspoon paprika
1 teaspoon chili powder
Salt and freshly ground
   pepper to taste
6 hamburger buns, warmed
4 ounces Cheddar cheese,
   shredded

Sauté onion, garlic, carrots, and mushrooms in oil in large skillet for 5 minutes. Add ground beef. Cook until brown and crumbly, stirring frequently. Stir in tomato sauce, mustard, vinegar, catsup, molasses, Worcestershire sauce, paprika, and chili powder. Simmer, covered, for 15 minutes. Season with salt and pepper. Spoon over bun bottoms; top with cheese and place on baking sheet. Broil until cheese melts. Add bun tops. Serve hot. Yield: 6 servings.

*Sweet-tangy mustard.

Mucky Duck Mustard Cookbook

Stuffed Cabbage Rolls

1 large head cabbage	1 teaspoon salt
1 pound hamburger	1/4 teaspoon pepper
2 eggs	1 small onion, cut fine
1/2 cup rice (uncooked)	

Simmer cabbage leaves to soften. Combine remaining ingredients and mix well. Place mixture into cabbage leaves and roll up. Place layer of cabbage leaves in bottom of pan. Place rolls on top. Make sauce.

SAUCE:

1 large onion	1/4 teaspoon pepper
2 (8-ounce) cans tomato sauce	1 teaspoon salt
2 (1-pound, 13-ounce) cans tomatoes	1 teaspoon Worcestershire sauce
2 tablespoons lemon juice	1/2 - 1 cup brown sugar

Bring sauce to a boil and pour over rolls. Place in 375° oven covered for one hour. Bake uncovered at 250° for 2 hours.

Country Cookbook

Stuffed Cabbage in Egg Lemon Sauce

1 medium onion, chopped	1 head cabbage
2 tablespoons margarine	1 egg, separated
1 1/2 pounds ground chuck	2 tablespoons lemon juice
1/2 cup rice, uncooked	

Sauté onion in margarine, add meat and brown. Add rice and set aside. Boil cored cabbage (whole) until leaves are soft and peel off (between 10-14 leaves). Holding leaf in hand, fill with browned meat mixture (about 2 tablespoons). Wrap tightly and place in 4-quart pot. When frying pan is empty, add water and pour over stuffed cabbage in pot. Cover stuffed cabbages with a plate to prevent floating. Bring to boil, lower heat and simmer one hour. Allow to sit for 1/2 hour.

In a separate bowl, beat egg white until stiff. Add yellow, continue to beat. Add lemon juice, continue to beat; add juice from pot, mix in. Pour this mixture over stuffed cabbages and warm for 10 minutes. Serves 4-6. Serve with warm bread.

Ferndale Friends Cook Book

Cabbage Rolls

1/2 cup cooked rice
1 cup milk
1 1/4 pounds ground beef
2 teaspoons salt
1/4 teaspoon pepper

1 small onion (chopped)
Cabbage
2 tablespoons brown sugar
1/2 cup hot water

Mix together rice, milk, ground beef, salt, pepper, and onion. Roll in steamed cabbage leaves and place in baking dish. Mix brown sugar and water and sprinkle over rolls. Cover and bake at 350° for about one hour.

Northcountry Kitchens Cookbook

Beef - Potato Nacho Casserole

2 pounds ground beef
3/4 cup chopped onion, divided
1 (1 1/4-ounce) package taco seasoning mix
3/4 cup water
1 (8-ounce) can tomato sauce
1 (4-ounce) can chopped green chilies, drained
1 (16-ounce) can red kidney beans, rinsed and drained
1 (24-ounce) package frozen potatoes, thawed
1 (11-ounce) can nacho cheese soup (undiluted)
1/2 cup milk
1/4 cup chopped green pepper
1/4 teaspoon sugar
1 teaspoon Worcestershire sauce
Paprika

Brown beef. Add 1/2 cup onion in skillet; drain. Stir in taco mix, water, and tomato sauce. Bring to boil and simmer one minute. Spread meat mixture into greased 9x13-inch pan. Top with green chilies, beans, and potatoes.

In bowl combine soup, milk, 1/4 cup onion, green pepper, sugar, and Worcestershire sauce. Pour over potatoes. Sprinkle with paprika. Cover with foil and bake at 350° for one hour. Remove foil and bake 15 minutes more until light golden brown. Let stand 10 minutes before cutting. Makes 8 servings.

Heavenly Helpings

Wet Burritos

1 pound hamburger
1 can refried beans
1 package taco or burrito seasoning
2 jars chicken gravy
1 small can mild enchilada sauce
1 (10-count) package 6-inch flour tortillas
Cheddar cheese
Mozzarella
Lettuce
Chopped onion
Chopped tomatoes
Sour cream

Brown hamburger; drain, then add beans and taco seasoning. In saucepan, heat chicken gravy and enchilada sauce. Fill shells with meat, then put in long (8x13-inch) pan. Cover with sauce and cheese. Bake at 350° for 15-20 minutes. Can be baked a little longer to brown cheese (15 minutes). Top with lettuce, onion, tomatoes, and sour cream.

Chelsea Cooks

Big Bear's Spaghetti Sauce

3 pounds 85% lean ground
  beef
2 pounds all ham sausage
4 large green bell peppers,
  diced, with seeds
2 large red bell peppers,
  diced, with seeds
3 large Spanish (sweet)
  onions, diced
1 bunch celery, diced with
  leaves
6-8 large tomatoes, diced

12 Roma tomatoes, diced
4 jalapeño peppers, diced
6-8 cloves garlic, diced
16 ounces mushrooms, sliced
2 cans tomato paste
1/2 cup catsup
1/2 cup barbecue sauce
1/8 cup soy sauce
5 bay leaves
2 tablespoons oregano
1/2 tablespoon sweet basil
1/4 cup parsley

Place ground beef and sausage in a frying pan over medium heat;
break up and blend as it cooks. Drain off excess fat and water. Place
vegetables, tomato paste, catsup, barbecue sauce, soy sauce, and spices
in a large stockpot over low heat until tender but not mushy—they
will create their own liquid. Cover vegetables (about 2 1/2 - 3 inches)
with water, mix, add beef and pork. Simmer until ready to serve.

Dad's Cook Book

Enchilada Casserole

1 cup chopped onion
1 clove garlic, minced
2 tablespoons butter
2 pounds ground beef, lightly
  browned
1 (10³/₄-ounce) can
  mushroom soup
1 (8-ounce) can tomato sauce
1 (6-ounce) can tomato paste

2 to 4-ounce can peeled,
  chopped green chilies
1 teaspoon salt
1 (8-ounce) package tortilla
  chips or cheese flavored chips
³/₄ pound shredded American
  or Longhorn cheese
Sour cream, optional
Parmesan cheese, optional

Sauté onion and garlic in butter. Add meat; brown. Stir in soup,
tomato sauce, tomato paste, chilies, and salt. Cook just to boiling.
Place half of the tortilla chips in bottom of a 13x9-inch baking dish.
Pour meat mixture over chips. Top with remaining chips and cheese.
Bake at 375° for 20-25 minutes. Serve with sour cream or sprinkle
with Parmesan cheese. Add hot pepper sauce or hot chilies if you
prefer a hotter dish. Serves 8.

Renaissance Cuisine

Deep Dish Taco Squares

¹/₂ pound ground beef
¹/₂ cup sour cream
¹/₃ cup salad dressing
¹/₂ cup shredded sharp
  Cheddar cheese (2 ounces)
1 tablespoon chopped onion

1 cup Bisquick
¹/₃ cup milk
1-2 medium tomatoes, sliced
  thin
¹/₂ cup chopped green pepper

Heat oven to 375°. Cook and stir ground beef till brown; drain off
fat. Mix sour cream, salad dressing, cheese, and onion; set aside.
Mix baking mix and milk till dough forms a ball. Pat into a 8x8-inch
pan, half way up sides. Layer beef, tomato, and green pepper; spoon
sour cream over top. Sprinkle with paprika. Bake for 25-30 minutes.

Seasoned Cooks II

Chili Burger

1 teaspoon vegetable oil
1 small onion, finely chopped
1 clove garlic, minced
1 jalapeño pepper, seeded
  and finely chopped
2 teaspoons ground cumin
1 cup cooked black beans
3/4 pound lean ground beef
2 tablespoons tomato paste
2 tablespoons chopped fresh
  cilantro

1 teaspoon dried thyme
1/2 teaspoon salt
1/2 teaspoon freshly ground
  black pepper
4 kaiser rolls, split and
  toasted
Tomato salsa for garnish
Shredded lettuce for garnish

In a small nonstick skillet, heat oil over medium heat. Add onion and sauté until golden brown, about 3 minutes. Add garlic, jalapeño, and cumin; sauté until fragrant, about 2 minutes longer (if mixture becomes too dry, add one tablespoon water). Transfer the mixture into a medium-size bowl.

Prepare grill or preheat broiler. Add beans to the onion mixture and mash coarsely with a potato masher. Add beef, tomato paste, cilantro, thyme, salt, and pepper; mix thoroughly but lightly. Shape the mixture into 4 (3/4-inch) thick patties. Grill or broil the patties on a lightly oiled rack until browned and cooked through, about 5 minutes per side. Place on rolls and garnish.

From Our Kitchens with Love

Big Bear's Deep Woods Chili

3 pounds lean ground beef
2 pounds pork sausage
3 large Spanish sweet onions,
  chopped chunky
3 large green bell peppers,
  diced, with seeds
1 bunch celery, diced with
  leaves
6-8 large tomatoes, diced

3 (28-ounce) cans of sliced
  tomatoes
1 cup ketchup
1 cup barbecue sauce
1/4 cup soy sauce
6-8 cloves garlic, sliced or
  smashed
2 ounces chili powder
3 cans chili kidney beans

Fry beef and sausage together and drain off excess water and fat. Place fresh vegetables in a pan with one cup water (hold garlic); place over low heat; cover, steam until tender (maintain a little snap). Place canned tomatoes, ketchup, barbecue sauce, soy sauce, garlic and chili powder in a large pot over low heat. Drain excess fat and water from ground beef; add to vegetables, and simmer for about 45 minutes, uncovered.

At the table, for those who would like a little fire, serve hot sauce of your choice or make a Jalapeño Sauce: one cup jalapeño peppers, chopped; place in a blender and purée; add red wine vinegar until it is a thick liquid; add to chili.

Dad's Cook Book

Chili

2 pounds ground burger
1 large onion, chopped
1 large green pepper,
  chopped
1 can pork and beans
1 can chili beans

2 cans stewed tomatoes
1 can tomato soup
1 package dry chili mix
Salt and pepper to taste
Garlic powder to taste

Brown burger with onion and green pepper in large electric frypan. Add all the rest of the ingredients; let simmer for 2 hours.

Fish & Game Menu Cookbook

Beef Stew
(For a crockpot)

2 pounds stew meat
8 carrots, cubed
2 onions, quartered
6-8 potatoes, cubed
2 stalks celery, cut up
1 (15-ounce) can tomato sauce
1/4 cup water

1/8 teaspoon garlic powder
1 teaspoon Worcestershire
  sauce
2 teaspoons salt
1/2 teaspoon pepper
1/4 cup flour

Put meat and vegetables in crockpot. Combine remaining ingredients except for flour and mix with meat and vegetables. Cook on low for 9-11 hours or on high for 5-6 hours in crockpot. Mix flour with 2 teaspoons water and make into a paste. Turn crockpot on high and add paste to stew. Cook another 15 minutes to thicken. Serves 4-6.

From Our Home to Yours

All Day Beef Stew

3 pounds beef stew meat
1/2 cup flour
4 teaspoons salt
1 (10 1/2-ounce) can beef
  broth
2 cups dry red wine
4 medium carrots, cut in
  1-inch pieces

4 medium potatoes, quartered
1 (20-ounce) bag frozen green
  beans
1 1/2 pounds small white
  onions
1 tablespoon brown sugar
1 bay leaf

Trim and cut meat into 1-inch cubes. In Dutch oven, toss meat, flour, and salt until meat is well coated. Stir in undiluted beef broth and remaining ingredients. Cover and bake at 250° for 5-6 hours or until meat and vegetables are tender, stirring occasionally. Makes 8-10 servings.

Woman's National Farm and Garden Association - Rochester
Cookbook Volume II

The Stew of Distinction

1¹/₂ pounds beef, veal or
 lamb for stew
3 tablespoons lard or
 drippings
1¹/₂ teaspoons salt
Pepper
3 cups water

4-6 medium carrots
4-6 medium white onions
1 small bunch celery, cut into
 4-inch pieces
Tomato Dumplings
Paprika

Brown meat slowly in lard or drippings. Season. Add water. Cover and simmer about 2¹/₂ hours for beef, 2 hours for veal, 1¹/₂ hours for lamb. About 30 minutes before meat is tender, add carrots, onions, and celery. Fifteen minutes before serving, drop Tomato Dumplings on top of meat and vegetables. Cover and cook 12 minutes without removing cover. Remove stew to hot platter, arranging vegetables and dumplings in separate mounds around meat. Sprinkle dumplings with paprika. Thicken liquid with flour for gravy, if desired. Makes 4-6 servings.

TOMATO DUMPLINGS:

1¹/₂ cups sifted enriched
 flour
1 teaspoon salt
1 tablespoon baking powder

1 egg, beaten
1 tablespoon lard, melted
¹/₂ cup tomato juice

Sift together flour, salt, and baking powder. Combine egg, melted fat and tomato juice. Combine mixture with dry ingredients, stirring only until flour disappears.

Recipes & Remembrances II

 There are more than 1,200 Christmas tree growers in Michigan, with an annual harvest of 5,000,000 plus trees supplying nearly 20% of the national market. Michigan produces eight or more varieties of Christmas trees.

Marcy's Beef Brisket

1 (12-ounce) jar chili sauce
1/2 cup brown sugar
2 tablespoons lemon juice
2 tablespoons yellow mustard
Water

Several garlic cloves
1 (10-ounce) package frozen
 baby lima beans, thawed
Beef brisket (about 6 pounds
 trimmed of all fat)

Combine chili sauce, brown sugar, lemon juice, and mustard. Add 2½ jars of water from chili sauce jar. Chop garlic coarsely and scatter in roasting pan. Add lima beans and brisket. Pour chili sauce mixture over brisket. Cover tightly with heavy foil and roast in preheated 350° oven about 4 hours. After 2 hours, remove foil and continue roasting for the other 2 hours. Baste brisket occasionally with pan juices.

Chelsea Cooks

Marv's Pot Roast

What makes this special is the puréeing of the vegetables to make a thick, rich gravy.

1 (3-pound) bottom round pot roast
2-3 tablespoons butter
1 onion, chopped
3 stalks celery (leaves and all), coarsely chopped
3-4 carrots, coarsely chopped
1 clove garlic, crushed
1/4 pound mushrooms, coarsely chopped

1 (10 1/2-ounce) can beef consommé
1/2 cup dry red wine
1 teaspoon salt
Freshly ground pepper to taste
1/2 teaspoon paprika
1 tablespoon capers
1 cup sour cream

Preheat oven to 350°. In a Dutch oven, over medium-high heat, brown meat in butter. Remove meat and reduce heat to medium. Add onion, celery, carrots, and garlic, and sauté until onion is soft. Add mushrooms, consommé, wine, salt, pepper, paprika, and capers.

Return meat to pan. Cover and bake 2-3 hours, or until meat is tender. (Note: You can do this on top of stove instead. Simmer very gently, tightly covered.) Remove meat to a platter and cover with foil to keep warm. Skim any fat, then purée the vegetables in their broth in a food processor or blender. Return to pan and reheat on stove. (If you wish a thicker gravy, mix 3 tablespoons flour with 3 tablespoons water and stir in with a whisk. Cook until thickened.) Stir in sour cream but do not boil. Slice meat, then cover with gravy. Serves 6.

Hollyhocks & Radishes

Smothered Swiss Steak

1 medium onion
2 tablespoons flour
¹/₄ teaspoon paprika
Salt and pepper to taste
1 pound round, Swiss or cubed
  steak, cut into 3-4 pieces

1 teaspoon Kitchen Bouquet
  (optional)
¹/₂ cup water or beef broth

Place layer of onion slices in bottom of crock-pot or baking dish. Mix flour, paprika, salt, and pepper together and dredge steak pieces until lightly coated with flour mixture. Place ¹/₂ meat pieces on onion; add another layer of onions and add remaining meat. Mix water (broth) and Kitchen Bouquet; pour over entire meat mixture. In crock-pot, cook 6-8 hours. In oven, cook 2 - 2¹/₂ hours. If gravy is desired, add more water and thicken with white sauce for the last half hour of cooking.

Centennial Cookbook Welcome Corners

Swiss Steak

Sirloin tips work best for this recipe, but a round steak will work also.

Sirloin tips or round steak
Seasonings
Flour

1 medium can tomato sauce
¹/₂ can water
Onion, to taste

Season meat as you like and then shake in flour; brown. Pour tomato sauce and water over meat. Add onion, to taste. Simmer until done. Thicken juice if desired.

Crystal Clear Cooking

 Strange laws in Michigan: A state law stipulates that a woman's hair legally belongs to her husband. In Detroit, it is illegal to "ogle" a woman from a moving car. In Port Huron, the speed limit for ambulances is 20 mph. Under state law, dentists are officially classified as "mechanics."

Stir-Fry Beef and Beans

1¹/₂ pounds flank steak,
  cut in strips
3 tablespoons peanut oil
2 tablespoons soy sauce
2 tablespoons cornstarch
1 teaspoon ground ginger

2 pounds green beans (frozen)
3 stalks celery, chopped
¹/₂ pound fresh or frozen snow
  peas, strings removed
1 can water chestnuts, drained
1 large onion, chopped

Marinate meat in one tablespoon peanut oil, soy sauce, cornstarch, and ginger for several hours. Stir-fry green beans in one tablespoon peanut oil. Set green beans aside. Stir-fry celery, snow peas, water chestnuts, and onion in one tablespoon peanut oil until crisp-tender. Set aside vegetable mixture. Stir-fry meat until brown. Add beans and vegetable mixture.. Stir-fry until heated through. Serve with white rice.

Come and Dine

Vegetable and Beef Stir-Fry

1 (20-ounce) can pineapple
  chunks in natural juice
¹/₄ cup soy sauce
2 tablespoons red wine
  vinegar
1¹/₂ tablespoons cornstarch
1 pound sirloin tip steak
4 tablespoons vegetable oil

2 cups broccoli flowerets
1 cup carrots, thinly sliced
1 medium onion, cut in
  wedges
¹/₂ medium red pepper cut in
  strips
Instant or long-grain rice

Drain pineapple, reserve juice. Combine juice, soy sauce, vinegar, and cornstarch; set aside. Thinly slice beef across grain; cut into 1¹/₂-inch strips. Heat 2 tablespoons oil in uncovered wok over high heat 2 minutes; add meat. Stir-fry 3-5 minutes or until browned. Remove beef and juices. Heat remaining oil; add vegetables. Stir-fry 2-3 minutes. Add juice mixture; stir until thickened. Stir in pineapple chunks and meat. Cover, cook 2 minutes. Serve with hot rice. Serves 4-6.

Four Seasons Cookbook

Marinated Flank Steak

RUM SOY SAUCE:

3 tablespoons dark rum

3 tablespoons low-sodium soy
   sauce

2 cloves garlic, crushed

1 1/2 pounds lean flank steak
   all visible fat removed

Combine rum, soy sauce, and garlic in a saucepan; bring to a boil. Cool. Add flank steak and marinate overnight. Grill on a very hot grill, brushing with marinade from time to time, to desired doneness. Makes 6 servings.

Note: Good for lamb, pork or turkey. For shish-ka-bob, try cutting up the meat and skewering alternately with pearl onions, button mushrooms, red pepper squares, and cherry tomatoes.

Per serving: Cal 213; Prot 23g; Fat 11g; (5g Sat); Carb 1g; Dietary fiber 0g; Chol 57mg; Sod 325mg; Cal 9mg; Iron 2.4mg. Exchanges: Meat 3; Fat 1.

High Fit - Low Fat

Italian Spiedini

This is a delicious one-dish meal certain to become a family favorite. It is also great for parties and company dinners. It freezes well, also.

1 or 2 thin round steaks

Oil

Italian bread crumbs or add
   oregano and grated cheese to
   regular bread crumbs

Salt and pepper

8-10 thinly sliced potatoes

1 large green pepper, cut in
   strips

1 large onion, thinly sliced

Butter or margarine

Pound steaks until tender. Brush with oil and cover both sides with bread crumbs, which have been mixed with salt and pepper. Cut into 4-inch squares; roll and insert toothpicks. In large baking pan, apply oil to bottom, then in layers, insert potatoes, green pepper, and onion, and dots of butter or margarine. Continue doing this, layer upon layer, until at last you top it off with round steak rolls. Cover with tin foil and bake at 350° for 1 1/2 hours. Uncover and brown for 10 minutes.

Simply Sensational

Pasties

All ingredients for pasty are raw to begin. You may also use ground beef instead of the beef and pork cut small, and you may wish to use less meat and more potatoes and vegetables

Pastry
1/2 pound pork and beef (cut
  in small pieces)
1/4 cup onions (diced fine)
1/2 cup potatoes (sliced fine
  or cubed)

1/4 cup carrots or rutabaga
  (sliced or cubed)
Salt and pepper (to taste)
Butter

Roll out pastry into circles (using 8-inch pan for guide). Place filling (remaining ingredients except butter, mixed) on crust and dot with butter (if meat is lean) and bring up edges of crust to meet over the mixture on top, crimp edges of crust together to seal. Bake one hour at 400°.

One secret to a delicious pasty is not to eat it immediately after baking, but leave in oven (slightly cooled oven) for at least half an hour after baking, or remove pasties from oven to racks immediately after baking and cover with towel, and let rest for about half an hour or until cool enough to eat. Serve plain or pass catsup.

Northcountry Kitchens Cookbook

Pasties: Pronounced PASS-tees, these little individual pies were used for miner's meals, and were often reheated on a shovel over the candle the miner wore on his hat. They were filled with hand-chopped meat (suet), onions, potatoes, carrots, or rutabagas, and sometimes an all-in-one-meal had a fruit filler (cherries, peaches, apples) in one end. Not necessarily flaky (it had to be portable), today's cooks add broth, cream, gravy or butter to combat the dryness.

Veal Piccata à la Milanese

1 pound veal, thinly sliced	2 tablespoons olive oil
Flour	Rosemary
1 egg, beaten	Pepper
Bread crumbs	Lemon wedges
3 tablespoons butter	

Cut veal into smaller pieces by trimming fat and gristle. Pound with flour until very thin. Dip in egg and then bread crumbs. Put butter and olive oil in heavy frying pan. Add a pinch of rosemary and dash of pepper. Sauté veal slowly until golden brown. Serve with lemon wedges and drippings. Can be made ahead and then warmed in pan. Makes 4 servings.

The Junior League of Grand Rapids Cookbook I

Lemon Grilled Ribs

Make this sauce ahead of time to have it handy.

1/2 cup water	1/4 cup catsup
1 chicken bouillon cube	1/4 cup lemon juice
3 tablespoons brown sugar	2 tablespoons cornstarch
1 cup pineapple juice	Salt and pepper
2 cloves garlic, minced	3 pounds spare ribs or
1/4 cup onion, minced	country-style ribs

Combine first 9 ingredients in a saucepan, and season to taste with salt and pepper. Bring to a boil, stirring well. Lower heat and simmer 5 minutes; set aside.

Cut ribs into serving-size pieces (3 or 4 ribs per person). Place ribs bone-side down on grill over slow coals. Grill about 20 minutes; turn meaty-side-up again and grill about 20 minutes longer, brush meaty side with sauce mixture. Continue to grill without turning 20-30 minutes; baste occasionally. Brush sauce on both sides of ribs; let cook 2-3 minutes on each side. Makes 4-6 servings.

Great Lakes Cookery

Plum Sauced Barbecued Ribs

8 pounds pork spareribs

Cut ribs into 2-3 rib portions. In large Dutch oven bring salted water to boiling; reduce heat. Simmer ribs, covered, for 45 minutes or until tender; drain.

SAUCE:

1/2 cup chopped onion	1/4 cup chili sauce
2 tablespoons butter or margarine	1/4 cup soy sauce
	2 teaspoons prepared mustard
1 (17-ounce) can purple plums	1 teaspoon ground ginger
1 (6-ounce) can frozen lemonade, thawed	1 teaspoon Worcestershire sauce

In large saucepan cook onion in butter until tender. Drain plums, reserving syrup; remove pits and discard. Place plums and syrup in blender or food processor; cover and process until smooth. Add plum purée and remaining ingredients to onions. Simmer, uncovered, for 10 minutes, stirring occasionally. Grill ribs over low coals about 25 minutes, turning 3-4 times and brushing often with sauce until well coated. Pass remaining sauce. Makes 8 servings.

What's Cookin'

Marinated Pork Loin

This versatile pork dish received rave reviews at the auxiliary recipe tasting parties.

2 pounds pork loin, trimmed

MARINADE:

2 large cloves garlic, minced	Parsley
1 teaspoon coarse (kosher) salt	Cayenne pepper
	1 tablespoon Dijon mustard
1 tablespoon thyme	1 tablespoon oil
1 tablespoon basil	1 teaspoon vinegar
2 teaspoons sugar	

Mix all the marinade ingredients until well blended. Spread over

CONTINUED

pork loin in a non-aluminum pan. Cover with plastic wrap. Refrigerate 12 hours to 2 days. Return to room temperature before baking. Preheat oven to 325°. Roast until internal temperature measures 150°, approximately 1¹/₄ hours, or 160° for no pinkness. Transfer to cutting board, cover with foil, and let rest 15 minutes before slicing. Deglaze roasting pan with ¹/₂ cup water. Bring to boil, thicken with flour and water mixture. Serves 4.

Cranbrook Reflections

Medallions of Pork with Cherry Sauce

1 (2-pound) pork tenderloin
1 cup dried cherries
1 cup port wine
1 teaspoon unsalted butter

1 teaspoon olive oil
Salt and pepper to taste
¹/₄ cup balsamic vinegar

Cut pork into ¹/₄-inch slices; pound thin. In a small saucepan over medium heat, combine cherries with ¹/₃ cup of the port. Bring to a simmer, then turn off heat. Let cherries soak.

In a medium sauté pan (not nonstick) over medium-high heat, cook butter with oil until light brown. Cook pork in 2 batches; brown well around edges (1-2 minutes each side). Put on warm plate and sprinkle with salt and pepper. Remove pan from heat. Add vinegar, scraping pan with a wooden spoon. Return to heat and add remaining ²/₃ cup wine. Boil over high heat until thick, about one minute. Combine with cherries and spoon over meat. Serve immediately.

Come and Dine

Pete's Pork Tenderloin

Very flavorful. Wonderful for a summer barbecue.

1/4 cup soy sauce	1/2 teaspoon crushed red
1 cup minced fresh onion	pepper flakes
2 cloves garlic, crushed	1/4 cup oil
1/4 cup lemon juice	2 pounds pork tenderloin, cut
2 tablespoons brown sugar	in large chunks
2 tablespoons coriander	

Combine all ingredients for marinade in large bowl. Add pork. Marinate for at least 2 hours, overnight is best. Put meat on skewers and barbecue or bake at 350° for 45 minutes to one hour, basting often with marinade. Makes 6-8 servings.

Recipes and Memories

Pork Chops Hawaiian

1 cup soy sauce	2 tablespoons vinegar
1/2 cup water	1/2 cup pineapple syrup
1/4 cup brown sugar	1/2 cup sugar
8 (1-inch) boneless pork chops	1/4 cup ketchup
(trimmed) or boneless loin	1 small onion, sliced
2 tablespoons flour	1 small green pepper
1 teaspoon each salt and	5 slices pineapple, cut in
pepper	wedges

About 6 hours before serving, bring soy sauce, water, and brown sugar to a boil. Cool slightly and pour over meat. Turn every hour for 4 hours. Remove and pat meat dry. Mix flour, salt and pepper. Coat meat and brown in skillet. Remove to baking dish. Combine vinegar, pineapple syrup (pour the syrup off canned pineapple and add sugar to make syrup), ketchup, onion, green pepper chunks, and pineapple chunks. Pour over meat. Cover and bake for 1 1/2 hours at 350°. Serve over rice.

Seasoned Cooks II

Pork Chops Plus

1 loin chop per person with
   most of the fat trimmed off
Flour
Rice, cooked
Carrots, sliced (about one per
   person)
Celery, chopped

Salt
Butter
Herb seasoning
1 green pepper, sliced
1 onion, sliced
Catsup

Sprinkle chops with flour, brown on one side and turn. Lower heat while adding one tablespoon cooked rice on top of each pork chop. Add sliced carrots and chopped celery to each. Add salt, butter, and herb seasoning. Top with a green pepper ring, sliced onion, and about one teaspoon catsup or chili sauce. If electric frypan is used, set at medium temperature, add 1/2 cup water and watch as needed to add more. Be sure water is cooked away before serving.

A Century of Recipes Through the Windows of Time

Pork Tenderloin Thunder Bay

12 slices bacon
2 cans drained mushrooms
1 onion, chopped
2 1/2 pounds pork, cut into
   thin strips

1 egg
Bread crumbs

Fry bacon, chop and drain. In some of the fat, sauté mushrooms and onion and combine with bacon. Dip pork tenderloin in egg and then bread crumbs. Layer into casserole with bacon and mushrooms. Bake at 350° for 45 minutes covered. Serves approximately 6 people.

Note: Use 3 pounds pork, 3 cans mushrooms, 18 slices bacon and 1 1/2 onions for serving 8-10 people.

How to Make A Steamship Float

City Chicken

2 pounds pork (lean pork
  sirloin or pork butt), trimmed,
  cut into 1-inch cubes
2 pounds leg veal, trimmed,
  cut into 1-inch cubes
24-36 wooden skewers
  (4½ - 5-inches)

Salt and pepper to taste
½ cup vegetable shortening
2 cups plain dry bread crumbs
2-4 eggs, beaten, divided
3-4 tablespoons water

Skewer pork and veal on skewers, alternating cubes, 5-6 pieces of meat on each skewer. Season with salt and pepper. Melt shortening in large skillet. Place bread crumbs in a shallow bowl. Set aside. Roll skewered meat in bread crumbs, then in beaten egg. (Add more eggs, if necessary.) Then roll in bread crumbs a second time. Gently press bread crumbs into skewered meat. Place in hot vegetable shortening, turning to brown all sides. Each skewer will take about 5 minutes. Depending on the size of the pan, about 5-8 will fit in the pan at once. Repeat for each skewer. Add water to roasting pan under rack. After each skewer browns, place on rack in roasting pan. Cover tightly with pan cover or foil. Bake at 350° for 45-50 minutes. City Chicken should be steamy and well-cooked. Avoid overbaking as meat will be dry. Makes 24-36 skewers.

Simply Sensational

Company Pork Chops

6 Ida Red apples, peeled,
  thickly sliced
6 pork chops
2 teaspoons butter or
  margarine

6 tablespoons brown sugar
6 tablespoons catsup

Preheat the oven to 375°. Line a large baking dish with enough foil to overlap the casserole and seal. Arrange the apple slices in a single layer in the prepared dish. Brown the pork chops in the butter in a skillet. Arrange over the apples. Sprinkle with the brown sugar and spread with the catsup. Fold the foil over the pork chops, sealing with a double fold. Bake at 375° for one hour or until the pork chops and apples are tender. Serve immediately. Serves 6.

The Dexter Cider Mill Apple Cookbook

Oriental Pork Almandine

1 pound boneless pork chops
  (or cutlets)
1/3 cup all-purpose flour
2 cups chicken broth
3 tablespoons soy sauce
1/2 cup almonds, sliced
2 tablespoons butter (or
  margarine)
1/4 pound mushrooms, sliced

1 medium onion, sliced
  lengthwise
2 cups celery, diagonally
  sliced
Green onions, sliced
  (optional)
Hot cooked rice, chow mein
  noodles or egg noodles

Trim excess fat from pork chops. Cut meat in 3/4-inch cubes. Roll in flour. Put in 3-quart saucepan and sauté over high heat, stirring frequently, until lightly browned. Stir in broth and soy sauce. In small skillet, toast almonds lightly in one tablespoon butter. Remove from skillet and set aside. Melt remaining butter in skillet. Add mushrooms and onion. Sauté until onion is tender. Add mushrooms, onion, and celery to pork. Bring to a boil and simmer, covered, for 30 minutes, or until pork is tender. Stir in almonds. Turn into serving dish. Garnish with green onions, if used. Serve with rice or noodles.

Pleasures from the Good Earth

House of Chan Egg Rolls

1 head cabbage, finely sliced
1 large onion, finely sliced
2 carrots, finely sliced
1 - 1¹/₂ pounds ground pork
15 (or so) fresh mushrooms,
   finely sliced
2 cloves garlic, finely
   sliced/diced

1 tablespoon lemon pepper
1 tablespoon Accent
1 tablespoon salt (or soy
   sauce)
1 egg
2 (25-count) packages spring
   roll skins (egg roll skins)

Blend cabbage, onion, carrots, pork, and mushrooms by hand in large bowl. Add garlic, lemon pepper, Accent, and salt (or soy sauce). Crack egg and place in small bowl. With large spoon dip out mixture and place on corner of egg roll skin. Roll halfway, fold over ends. Dip end in egg to seal roll. Fill wok halfway with vegetable oil and heat to 350°. Deep fry egg rolls until golden brown (1-3 minutes). Lay egg rolls on paper towel to absorb the oil. Let them cool a few minutes and serve hot.

Trendfully Cookin'

Ham and Asparagus Casserole

3-4 tablespoons butter
1 teaspoon grated onion
Dash garlic salt
1 teaspoon paprika
¹/₂ teaspoon salt
¹/₈ teaspoon pepper
2 tablespoons flour

3 cups milk
2 cups grated sharp Cheddar
   cheese
2 (10-ounce) packages frozen
   asparagus
1 cup poultry stuffing crumbs
2 cups sliced cooked ham

Melt 2 tablespoons butter and blend in grated onion and seasonings along with flour. Slowly add milk and heat, stirring constantly until thickened. Add cheese and stir until melted. Cook asparagus according to directions and cut into 1-inch lengths. Preheat oven to 375°. In the bottom of 2-quart buttered casserole, sprinkle a layer of stuffing crumbs. Add layer of ham and one of asparagus. Now pour part of cheese sauce over and repeat layer of ham, asparagus and sauce until ingredients are used. Top with remaining crumbs and butter. Bake 45 minutes or until bubbly and browned.

Recipes & Remembrances II

Apple and Sausage Ring

1 Jonathan apple, peeled,
  finely chopped
2 pounds mild pork sausage
2 eggs, slightly beaten

1/2 cup milk
11/2 cups herb stuffing mix
1/4 cup minced onion

Preheat the oven to 350°. Combine the apple, sausage, eggs, milk, stuffing mix, and onion in a large bowl; mix well. Press into a 10-inch ring mold. Bake at 350° for one hour or until cooked through; drain well. Invert onto a serving platter. Garnish with apple slices and serve immediately. Serves 6-8.

The Dexter Cider Mill Apple Cookbook

Sausage Skillet Dinner

12 ounces fully cooked smoked
  pork link sausage, cut diagonally into 1-inch pieces
2 tablespoons water
1 medium onion
2 small red cooking apples
2 tablespoons butter, divided

12 ounces natural frozen potato
  wedges
1/4 cup cider vinegar
3 tablespoons sugar
1/2 teaspoon caraway seed
2 tablespoons chopped parsley

Place sausage and water in large nonstick frying pan; cover tightly and cook over medium heat 8 minutes, stirring occasionally. Meanwhile cut onion into 12 wedges; core and cut each apple into 8 wedges. Remove sausage to warm platter. Pour off drippings. Cook and stir onion and apples in one tablespoon of the butter in same frying pan 4 minutes or until apples are just tender. Remove to sausage platter.

Heat remaining one tablespoon butter; add potatoes and cook, covered, over medium-high heat 5 minutes or until potatoes are tender and golden brown, stirring occasionally. Combine vinegar, sugar and caraway seed. Reduce heat, return sausage, apple mixture and vinegar mixture to frying pan and cook one minute, or until heated through, stirring gently. Sprinkle with parsley.

Chelsea Cooks

Teriyaki Venison

1 can beef consommé
1/4 cup teriyaki sauce
1/4 cup chopped onion
Dash garlic powder

1 teaspoon seasoned salt
2 pounds of sirloin venison,
  diagonally cut
1 teaspoon vegetable oil

Make a marinade with the consommé, teriyaki sauce, onion, garlic powder, and seasoned salt. Put meat into large bowl and pour marinade over and let stand overnight in refrigerator. Drain meat, heat wok with vegetable oil. Cook meat a little at a time just until tender. Serve with wild rice.

Fish & Game Menu Cookbook

Curried Caribou

4 caribou round steaks
1 tablespoon butter
1 sweet onion, sliced
1 green pepper, sliced
1 pound fresh mushrooms,
  sliced

1/2 teaspoon curry powder
1 can consommé
Seasoning salt and pepper

Brown steaks in butter in large frypan. Place vegetables over steak; mix curry powder with consommé and pour over steak and vegetables. Cover and cook for one hour.

Fish & Game Menu Cookbook

Pete's Best Venison Bar-B-Q

2 pounds venison steak
1 medium onion, diced
2 tablespoons beef base
1/2 (12-ounce) bottle ketchup
1/2 (12-ounce) bottle Bar-B-Q
  sauce

1 teaspoon garlic salt
1 teaspoon pepper
1 - 2 tablespoons vegetable oil
Cornstarch

Cut venison into 1/2-inch strips and place into heated cooking oil; lightly brown both sides. Remove venison from frying pan and place into pressure cooker. Add all of remaining ingredients except cornstarch. With your now empty ketchup and Bar-B-Q bottles, fill both 1/2 full with water and shake well; empty into pressure cooker. Set pressure cooker on 10 pounds for 20 minutes. Thicken with cornstarch to make gravy. Serve over noodles or mashed potatoes. Enjoy!

Home Cookin': Almont Elementary PTA

Down-Home Stir Fry

1/2 pound venison
Milk for soaking
2 tablespoons shortening
1/2 cup green peppers,
  chopped
1/2 cup onions, chopped
1/2 cup mushrooms

1 cup broccoli, chopped
1/2 teaspoon salt, or to taste
1/2 teaspoon garlic salt
1/2 teaspoon seasoning salt
3 tablespoons soy sauce
1 cup tomatoes, chopped

Cut about 1/2 pound venison in strips and soak in milk for one hour. Melt 2 tablespoons shortening in large frying pan. Heat to medium-high. Remove meat strips from milk, drain, and place in frying pan. Stir, and then add peppers, onions, mushrooms, and broccoli. Stir, season with salt, garlic salt, seasoning salt, and soy sauce. Stir, add tomatoes and cook 6 more minutes, stirring often. Serve over rice.

Mrs. Boone's Wild Game Cookbook

Moose Supreme

1 (4-pound) moose roast
$1/4$ cup red wine vinegar
Salt and pepper to taste

Garlic powder to taste
$1/2$ fresh lemon, thinly sliced

BASTING SAUCE:
$1/2$ stick melted butter or
  margarine
2 tablespoons liquid honey
$1/4$ cup red wine vinegar

Juice from remaining lemon
Grated peel from one fresh
  orange
1 teaspoon mixed herbs

Brush roast with red wine vinegar; mix salt, pepper, and garlic powder together and sprinkle over roast. Place lemon slices over roast.
Place in roasting pan, bake in slow (275°) oven for 4 hours. Mix
basting sauce together and baste roast often while baking.

Fish & Game Menu Cookbook

Cakes

"The Tridge" is a unique three-legged footbridge that spans the confluence of the Tittabwassee and Chippewa Rivers. Midland.

Apple Cider Cupcakes
with Cider Cream Cheese Frosting

3 cups unpasteurized apple
  cider
3/4 cup vegetable shortening
1 3/4 cups sugar
2 large eggs

2 cups flour, sifted
1/8 teaspoon ground cloves
1 teaspoon cinnamon
1 teaspoon baking soda
Pinch of salt

In large saucepan boil cider until it is reduced to about 1 1/2 cups and let it cool. In large bowl with mixer, beat shortening and sugar until mixture is fluffy and beat in eggs one at a time. Into bowl, sift together the flour, cloves, cinnamon, baking soda, and pinch of salt. Stir in reduced cider and combine the mixture well.

Divide the batter among 18 paper-lined 1/2-cup muffin tins and bake in the middle of preheated 375° oven for 25 minutes or until tester comes out clean. Transfer cupcakes to a rack. Let cool and remove from tins.

ICING:

2 cups apple cider
6 ounces cream cheese, cut
  into bits and softened

1/2 cup powdered sugar
Pinch of salt

In a saucepan boil the cider until reduced to about 1/4 cup and let cool. In a bowl with mixer beat together the cream cheese, powdered sugar, the reduced cider and pinch of salt until icing is smooth. Frost cupcakes.

Note: Can also reduce cider in glass measuring cup in microwave.

Heavenly Helpings

Apple Torte

CRUST:

2 cups all-purpose flour
1/2 teaspoon salt
3/4 cup brown sugar

3/4 cup shortening
2 cups quick cooking oatmeal

Mix together with pie blender.

FILLING:

6-7 apples, peeled and sliced
8 eggs (beaten)
3 cups sugar
1/2 cup all-purpose flour

Dash of salt
Cinnamon
Butter

Line a 10x14-inch cake pan with all but one cup of the oatmeal mixture, pressing it down firmly. Put apples into the crust. Beat eggs, sugar, flour, and salt together. Pour the filling over the apples and sprinkle the remaining cup of oatmeal mixture over this. Lightly sprinkle the top of torte with cinnamon and dot with dabs of butter. Bake in 350° oven for about one hour or until custard is done when knife comes out clean.

Northcountry Kitchens Cookbook

Raw Apple Walnut Cake

3 eggs, beaten
2 cups sugar
1/2 cup cooking oil
2 teaspoons vanilla
2 cups flour
2 teaspoons soda

2 teaspoons cinnamon
1/2 teaspoon nutmeg
1/4 teaspoon salt
4 cups diced, unpeeled apples
1 cup coarsely chopped
   walnuts

Mix all ingredients. Pour into a greased 9x13-inch baking dish. Bake at 325° for 50 minutes.

FROSTING:

2 (3-ounce) packages cream
   cheese
4 teaspoons margarine

1 1/2 cups powdered sugar
1/2 teaspoon vanilla

Mix and spread on cake.

Recipes & Remembrances II

Apple Pudding Cake with Cinnamon Butter Sauce

1 cup brown sugar, firmly
    packed
1/4 cup margarine, softened
1 egg
1 cup all-purpose flour

1 teaspoon baking soda
1 teaspoon cinnamon
1/2 teaspoon nutmeg
1/2 teaspoon salt
2 cups apples, chopped

Heat oven to 350°. Grease an 8-inch square pan. In large bowl, beat brown sugar and margarine until light and fluffy; beat in egg. Add flour, baking soda, cinnamon, nutmeg, and salt; mix well. Stir in apples. Spread batter in greased pan. Bake for 25-35 minutes or until toothpick comes out clean.

CINNAMON BUTTER SAUCE:
1/3 cup butter
2/3 cup sugar

1/3 cup half-and-half
1/2 teaspoon cinnamon

Combine all ingredients in small saucepan. Heat over medium heat, stirring frequently. Serve warm over warm cake.

Pleasures from the Good Earth

Blackberry Cake

1 quart blackberries
3/4 cup sugar
3 cups marshmallows (about
    20 large marshmallows)
1 (3-ounce) package berry
    flavored gelatin mix

1 (18.5-ounce) package yellow
    or white cake mix, prepared
    according to package
    directions, but unbaked
Ice cream or sweetened,
    whipped cream (optional)

Preheat oven to 350°. Pour berries into buttered 9x13-inch pan. Sprinkle sugar, marshmallows, and gelatin mix over berries. Pour prepared cake batter evenly over berries and marshmallows. Bake at 350° for 50-55 minutes, or until top is browned and a toothpick inserted near center comes out clean. Cool. Invert cake when serving so berries are on top of each slice of cake. If desired, top with ice cream or sweetened, whipped cream.

Good Food From Michigan

Blueberries and Yogurt Cake

A great cake for snack, dessert or breakfast.

1¹/₂ cups margarine,
    softened
3¹/₂ cups sugar, divided
4 eggs, beaten
3 cups flour
3 cups whole wheat flour
1 tablespoon baking soda

1 teaspoon salt
3 cups plain yogurt
1 tablespoon cinnamon
3 teaspoons vanilla
3 cups fresh blueberries
1¹/₂ cups chopped walnuts

Preheat oven to 350°. Spray 2 (9x13-inch) pans with nonstick cooking spray. In a large bowl, cream the margarine with 3 cups of the sugar. Add the beaten eggs. In a medium bowl, combine the flours, baking soda, and salt. Add the dry ingredients alternately with the plain yogurt to the eggs mixture. Reserve one half of this batter. Fill the 2 prepared pans evenly with the remaining batter. Combine the remaining ¹/₂ cup sugar with the cinnamon and vanilla. Reserve one half of this sugar mixture. Spread the remaining sugar mixture on top of the batter in the prepared pans. Sprinkle half of the blueberries and half of the chopped walnuts on top. Repeat the layers. Bake 55-60 minutes.

Nutrition per serving: Cal 425; Fat 18g; Prot 7g; Carb 58g; Chol 39mg; Fiber 1g; Vit A 586IU; Sod 361mg; Iron 1mg; Vit C 3mg.

Smart Snacks

K's Carrot Cake

3 cups raw grated carrots
2 cups flour
2 cups sugar
1¹/₂ cups oil
¹/₂ teaspoon salt
2 teaspoons cinnamon

2 teaspoons soda
4 eggs
1 (10¹/₂-ounce) can crushed
    pineapple, drained
1 cup walnuts, chopped

Mix first 9 ingredients. Add nuts. Bake in a greased 9x13-inch pan at 350° for 45 minutes or until done. Do not overcook. Frost.

CARROT CAKE FROSTING:

1 stick butter
1 (8-ounce) package cream
    cheese

1 pound powdered sugar
1 teaspoon vanilla

Cream butter and cheese together. Add sugar and vanilla. Spread on cake. Enjoy.

Woman's National Farm and Garden Association - Rochester
Cookbook Volume II

Cherry Cake with Sauce

¹/₄ cup shortening
³/₄ cup sugar
1 egg
1¹/₂ cups flour
2 teaspoons baking powder
¹/₂ teaspoon salt

¹/₂ cup milk
¹/₄ teaspoon almond extract
2 cups sour cherries (well
    drained, reserve juice)
¹/₂ cup walnuts

Cream shortening, sugar, and egg. Sift dry ingredients together and add to shortening mixture, alternating with milk. Add flavoring. Fold in cherries and nuts. Bake in greased 9-inch baking dish for 45 minutes at 375°.

SAUCE:

Reserved cherry juice with
    enough water to make 1 cup
³/₄ cup sugar

2 tablespoons cornstarch
Sweetened whipped cream for
    garnish if desired

Mix juice mixture with sugar and cornstarch. Cook slowly until thickened and clear. Stir while sauce cooks. Serve sauce over individual pieces of warm cake. Garnish with whipped cream, if desired.

The Bell Tower Cookbook

Williamsburg Orange Cake

2³/₄ cups cake flour
1¹/₂ cups sugar
1¹/₂ teaspoons baking soda
³/₄ teaspoon salt
1¹/₂ cups buttermilk
¹/₂ cup softened margarine
¹/₄ cup shortening

3 eggs
1¹/₂ teaspoons vanilla
1 cup golden raisins, cut up
¹/₂ cup finely chopped nuts
1 tablespoon grated orange
  peel

Heat oven to 350°. Grease and flour 3 (8-inch) round layer pans. Beat all ingredients in large mixer bowl on low speed, scraping bowl constantly, 30 seconds. Beat on high speed, scraping bowl occasionally, 3 minutes. Pour into pans. Bake until wooden pick inserted in center comes out clean, 30-35 minutes; cool. Frost with Williamsburg Butter Frosting.

WILLIAMSBURG BUTTER FROSTING:

¹/₂ cup softened margarine
4¹/₂ cups powdered sugar

4-5 tablespoons orange juice
1 tablespoon grated orange peel

Mix margarine and powdered sugar. Beat in orange juice and orange peel.

Allen Park Garden Club Recipe Book

Orange Torte

1 tablespoon Knox gelatin
  (unflavored)
¹/₄ cup cold water
¹/₂ cup boiling water
1 cup orange juice (fresh, not
  frozen)

5 tablespoons lemon juice (2
  lemons, fresh squeezed)
1 cup sugar
2 cups fresh whipping cream
  (whipped)
1 angel food cake

Soften gelatine in cold water, add boiling water and stir till dissolved. Add orange juice, lemon juice, and sugar; stir till dissolved. Refrigerate till set (little thicker than honey). Fold in whipped cream. Break cake into bite-size pieces. Fold into above mixture. Put in a 9-inch springform pan or angel food cake pan. Refrigerate until set (overnight or about 5 hours).

Recipes and Memories

Patrick's "A Bit O' Green Cake"

1 package white cake mix
1 small box instant pistachio
   pudding mix
3 eggs
1 cup vegetable oil

1 cup ginger ale
1 teaspoon vanilla
$1/2$ cup chopped almonds or
   walnuts, if desired

In large mixing bowl combine cake mix, pudding, eggs, oil, ginger ale, vanilla, and nuts, if desired. Beat at medium speed 2 minutes. Pour into greased Bundt pan and bake in 350° oven for about 50 minutes or until top springs back when touched with fingertip. Let cool in pan 10 minutes. Invert onto cake platter. Let cool completely.

FROSTING:

1 package instant pistachio
   pudding mix
$1^1/4$ cups milk

1 ($4^1/2$-ounce) container
   whipped topping or
$1^1/2$ cups whipped cream

In mixing bowl combine pudding mix and milk. Beat until smooth and thick. Fold in whipped topping or whipped cream. Frost cool cake.

Simply Sensational

Pecan Bourbon Cake

For those who don't like fruitcakes. This is a favorite at our house.

2 cups finely chopped pecans
1 cup bourbon, divided
$3^1/2$ cups sifted flour
$1^1/2$ teaspoons baking powder
$1/2$ teaspoon nutmeg
$1/2$ teaspoon cinnamon

$1/4$ teaspoon ground cloves
2 cups unsalted butter
$2^1/2$ cups sugar
8 eggs, well beaten
$1^1/2$ teaspoons amaretto
   liqueur

Preheat oven to 350°. Butter 2 (9-inch) loaf pans. Combine pecans and $1/2$ cup bourbon; let stand. Sift together dry ingredients. Cream butter and gradually add sugar, then beaten eggs, and beat very well. Stir in flour mixture and mix just until combined. Stir in pecans and bourbon. Pour into pans and bake for one hour. Cool in pans 15 minutes. Turn out. Soak 2 pieces of cheesecloth in remaining bourbon. Wrap each cake in a piece of cheesecloth, then wrap in foil. Refrigerate for one week before serving.

Historically Delicious

Rouge Rum Cake

1/2 cup chopped nuts (walnuts
  or pecans)
1 package yellow cake mix
1 package Jello instant butter
  pecan pudding and pie filling

4 eggs
1/2 cup water
1/2 cup Wesson oil
1/2 cup cheap dark 80-proof
  rum

Preheat oven to 325°. Grease and flour 10-inch tube pan and sprinkle nuts over bottom. Mix all ingredients together. Pour batter over nuts and bake for one hour. Cool and invert to serving plate. Prick top.

GLAZE:
1/2 stick margarine
2 tablespoons water

1/2 cup granulated sugar
1/4 cup dark rum

Melt margarine in saucepan. Stir in water and sugar. Boil 5 minutes, stirring constantly. Remove from heat and stir in rum. Spoon or brush evenly over top and sides of cake. Allow cake to absorb Glaze and repeat until Glaze is used up.

Note: Cake holds up well if wrapped in foil and stored tightly. Good up to about 4 months stored this way.

How to Mke A Steamship Float

Tutti-Frutti Cake

1/4 cup orange juice
1 tablespoon lemon juice
11/4 cups sugar, divided
1/2 cup butter
3 tablespoons finely grated
  orange peel
1 tablespoon finely grated
  lemon peel

1/2 cup seedless raisins,
  chopped
1 egg, beaten
11/3 cups sifted cake flour
1/2 teaspoon baking powder
1 teaspoon baking soda
1/2 teaspoon salt
1 cup buttermilk

Combine fruit juices and 1/2 cup sugar. Stir until sugar dissolves. Let stand. Cream butter to consistency of mayonnaise. Add remaining sugar gradually while creaming. Beat in grated peels and raisins. Add egg; beat well. Mix and sift flour, baking powder, baking soda, and salt. Sift into butter mixture alternately with buttermilk.

Bake in 9-inch well-greased and floured square cake pan at 350° for about 40 minutes or until cake tests done. Remove from oven, spoon juice/sugar mixture evenly over top. Cool in pan. Cut in squares to serve with whipped cream. Yields: 9 servings.

Ferndale Friends Cook Book

Chop Suey Cake

2 cups flour
2 eggs
1 cup sugar
2 teaspoons baking soda
1 (20-ounce) can crushed
  pineapple, undrained
1 cup walnuts
1/2 cup grated coconut (optional)

1 (8-ounce) package cream
  cheese, softened
1/2 cup butter, softened
2 cups confectioners' sugar
2 tablespoons milk
1 teaspoon vanilla
Chopped nuts, if desired for
  garnish

In large bowl (do not use mixer or processor) combine flour, eggs, sugar, baking soda, pineapple and juice, walnuts, and coconut, if desired. Mix with wooden spoon until thoroughly moistened and combined; pour into greased 9x13-inch baking pan. Bake at 350° for 30-40 minutes until puffed and browned on top. Remove pan from oven and place on wire rack.

In medium bowl, mix cream cheese and butter together until color is uniform. Gradually add confectioners' sugar and milk and stir until smooth. Stir in vanilla. With broad spatula, spread icing generously on cake while cake is still warm. Top may be garnished with chopped nuts, if desired. Cool cake completely and refrigerate until serving time. Leftovers should be stored in refrigerator. Makes about 20 servings.

Ferndale Friends Cook Book

Lemon Verbena Cake

1 (18¹/₄-ounce) yellow cake
    mix
1 (3³/₄-ounce) package
    lemon instant pudding
4 eggs, unbeaten

3 tablespoons dried lemon
    verbena, crushed, or 6
    tablespoons fresh lemon
    verbena, diced

Preheat oven to 350°. Blend all ingredients and beat 8 minutes. Pour mixture into 13x9x2-inch pan lined with brown paper. Bake for 45-50 minutes. Cake is done when skewer comes out clean.

LEMON VERBENA GLAZE:

10-15 fresh lemon verbena
    leaves
3 tablespoons water

³/₄ cup confectioners' sugar
1 tablespoon vanilla

Place fresh lemon verbena leaves in water in a microwave-safe container and microwave at HIGH for 3 minutes. Let steep until cool. Remove leaves. Mix with confectioners' sugar and vanilla.

Herbal Favorites

My Mother's Spice Cake

1 cup sugar
1 cup sour cream
¹/₄ cup butter
2 eggs
1 tablespoon molasses

2 cups flour
1 teaspoon soda
1 teaspoon cinnamon
¹/₄ teaspoon nutmeg
¹/₂ teaspoon cloves

Mix together sugar, cream, butter, eggs, and molasses. Mix well. Add flour, soda, and spices sifted together. Bake in 9x13-inch pan at 350° for 45 minutes.

CARAMEL FROSTING:

1¹/₂ cups light brown sugar
2 tablespoons butter

4 tablespoons cream
1 tablespoon vanilla

Boil for 3 minutes, remove from heat and beat until right consistency to spread.

Halvorson-Johnson Family Reunion Cookbook

Milk Dud Cake

6 egg yolks
1 cup sugar
1 cup Holland Rusk crumbs,
  crushed fine
1/2 cup finely chopped walnuts
1 teaspoon baking powder
1 teaspoon vanilla

6 egg whites, beaten stiff
6 ounces Milk Dud candies
1/2 cup milk
1 cup powdered sugar
2 teaspoon butter or
  margarine
1 pint whipping cream

Beat egg yolks till light yellow; add sugar, beating again. In separate bowl, add crumbs, nuts, baking powder, and vanilla. Add this mixture to the egg yolks. Beat egg whites till stiff and fold into crumb mixture. Spread into a 9x13-inch greased pan and bake for 30 minutes at 350°. Cool cake completely in pan.

Melt Milk Duds, milk, powdered sugar, and butter in pan until smooth; set aside to cool to room temperature. Whip cream and spread on cool cake. Place sauce over whipped cream, cover, and place in refrigerator overnight.

Note: Dip your knife in warm water when cutting cake.

From Our Kitchens with Love

Tofu Cheesecake

CRUST:

3 cups ground granola
2 teaspoons coriander
2-3 tablespoons oil

3-4 tablespoons water
2 tablespoons honey

Blend 2 cups granola on high until fine (2 cups granola = 1 1/2 - 1 2/3 cups when ground). Pour into bowl and repeat. Measure 3 cups ground granola and put in bowl. Add remaining ingredients. Stir together with fork and then mix together well with hands. Add honey only if granola is unsweetened. For baked pie shell, press into bottom and sides of 9x13-inch baking dish. Bake at 350° for 30 minutes.

FILLING:

4 cups mashed tofu
2 tablespoons vanilla
1 1/2 teaspoons salt
2/3 cup honey
1/2 cup oil

1/4 cup pineapple juice
1/2 teaspoon lemon extract or
  1 tablespoon lemon juice
1/2 teaspoon coriander

CONTINUED

Rinse, drain, mash and measure tofu. Put tofu in bowl and add remaining ingredients. Stir together well. Blend half of filling on high until velvety smooth, stopping blender 2-3 times to stir contents. Pour over crust. Repeat procedure with other half. Spread filling evenly over crust. Bake at 350° for 20-30 minutes until edges are lightly browned and middle is firm. Remove from oven. Cool slightly. Cover with 4 cups strawberry or blueberry topping. Yield: 1 (9x13-inch) cheesecake.

Country Life: Vegetarian Cookbook

Apple Cheesecake

Easy to prepare and tastes fabulous, this is a nice fall dessert.

1/2 cup melted butter or margarine	1 egg
1/3 cup sugar	1/2 teaspoon vanilla extract
1 cup flour	3 cups thinly sliced apples
1/4 teaspoon vanilla extract	1/3 cup sugar
1 (8-ounce) package cream cheese, softened	1 teaspoon cinnamon
1/4 cup sugar	Sliced almonds to taste (optional)

Mix the butter, 1/3 cup sugar, flour, and 1/4 teaspoon vanilla in a bowl. Press the mixture over the bottom and one inch up the side of a 9-inch springform pan.

Mix the cream cheese, 1/4 cup sugar, egg, and 1/2 teaspoon vanilla in a bowl. Pour the mixture over the prepared layer.

Toss the apples with 1/3 cup sugar and cinnamon in a bowl. Spoon the apple mixture over the cream cheese mixture. Sprinkle with the almonds. Bake at 450° for 10 minutes. Reduce the oven temperature to 400°. Bake for 25 minutes longer. Cool in the pan. Yield: 16 servings.

Dawn to Dusk

The shape of Michigan is like a mitten. People use their held-up hand to point out where something is geographically. Also they utilize the hand for descriptions like: most of Michigan's sugar beet crop is grown in the "thumb" area.

Cheesecake

CRUST:

1 stick margarine, melted
1/3 cup sugar

1¹/4 cups ground graham crackers

Mix together ingredients in 9x13-inch pan with a fork to cover bottom. Bake at 350° for 8 minutes.

FILLING:

3 (8-ounce) packages cream cheese, softened
2 eggs

³/4 cup sugar
1 teaspoon vanilla
¹/2 teaspoon lemon juice

Beat ingredients on high until whipped. Pour over crust. Bake at 350° for 30 minutes. Cool completely.

TOPPING:

1 pint sour cream
3 tablespoons sugar

1 teaspoon vanilla

Mix ingredients well. Pour on top of cheesecake. Bake at 400° for 5 minutes. Cool 6-8 hours or overnight.

SAUCE:

1 (10-ounce) package frozen strawberries, raspberries, or blueberries, thawed (save juice)

2 tablespoons sugar
1 tablespoon cornstarch
1 teaspoon lemon juice

Add enough water to juice to make ³/4 cup of juice. Combine sugar and cornstarch in a 2-cup measuring cup; mix well. Stir in juice and lemon juice. Microwave on HIGH (3-5 minutes) until thick. Stir occasionally. Stir in fruit; cool completely. Pour over cheesecake and serve.

Home Cookin': Almont Elementary PTA

 Chesterfield is the home of the 95-year-old Lionel company that manufactures miniature diesel engines, cabooses, and train cars, and is home to one of the world's largest miniature train layouts—1,000 feet of track and eight trains.

Cookies and Candies

A steam-powered engine rides the Huckleberry Railroad, Michigan's only authentic narrow-gauge rail line. Crossroads Village, Flint.

Oatmeal Pecan Dreams

With a recipe this simple, anyone can have home-baked cookies anytime!

1 cup (2 sticks) margarine	1¹/₄ teaspoons vanilla
¹/₂ cup sugar	12 pecan halves cut in half,
1 cup flour	lengthwise
¹/₂ cup oatmeal	

Put all ingredients except pecans into food processor or blender. Blend until completely mixed. Drop by teaspoonful (or make into small balls) onto an ungreased cookie sheet. Press one pecan piece into each cookie. Bake at 350° for 10-15 minutes. Yield: 2 dozen cookies.

Just Inn Time for Breakfast

Nature's Candy Kisses

A great way to pop some natural ingredients into their mouths.

1¹/₄ cups peanut butter	1¹/₄ cups quick cooking oats
³/₄ cup honey	¹/₂ cup graham cracker
1¹/₂ teaspoons vanilla	crumbs
1¹/₄ cups instant non-fat dry	¹/₄ cup wheat germ
milk	1 cup powdered sugar

In a large bowl, blend the peanut butter, honey and vanilla. Add the dry milk, oats, graham cracker crumbs and wheat germ; mix well. Refrigerate 1-2 hours. Place the powdered sugar in a small bowl. Roll the peanut butter mixture into balls, using one heaping teaspoon of the mixture per ball. Shape each ball into a "kiss" (a pyramid with a round base). Roll each kiss through the powdered sugar. Refrigerate several hours or overnight.

Nutrition per serving: Cal 191; Fat 7g; Carb 25g; Chol 1mg; Vit A 152IU; Sod 49mg; Iron 1mg; Vit C 0mg.

Smart Snacks

More than 80,000 gallons of syrup are produced in Michigan each year. A tree must have a least a 10-inch diameter (30 to 40 years old) before it can be tapped for the sap to make Michigan maple syrup. It takes about 40 gallons of sap to produce one gallon of maple syrup.

Grandma Howes' Oatmeal Cookies

1 cup sugar
1 cup shortening
2 eggs (unbeaten)
1 cup raisins, cooked
2 tablespoons liquid off
 raisins, dissolved with 1
 teaspoon soda

2 cups flour
1 teaspoon salt
1 teaspoon cinnamon
1/2 teaspoon allspice
1 teaspoon vanilla
2 cups quick oats

Mix sugar and shortening; add eggs, then raisins (cooked) and liquid off raisins, and soda. Mix; add dry ingredients and vanilla. Mix; add quick oats. Bake at 350° until lightly browned.

Country Cookbook

Growling Tummy Cookies

A wholesome way to tame a busy group of cookie monsters.

1 1/4 cups margarine,
 softened
1 cup sugar
1 1/4 cups brown sugar
2 eggs
1 teaspoon vanilla
1/3 cup crunchy peanut butter
1 1/4 cups flour

1 cup whole wheat flour
1 teaspoon baking soda
1/2 teaspoon baking powder
1/2 teaspoon salt
1 1/2 cups quick cooking oats
1 1/4 cups raisin bran cereal
1/8 cup wheat germ
1 cup chocolate chips

Preheat oven to 350°. Spray 2 cookie sheets with nonstick cooking spray. In a large bowl, cream the margarine with sugar and brown sugar. Blend in the eggs, vanilla, and peanut butter. In a medium bowl, mix the flours, baking soda, baking powder and salt. Add these dry ingredients to the creamed mixture. Fold in the oats, raisin bran, wheat germ, and chocolate chips; mix well. Drop by scant 1/8 cupfuls onto the prepared cookie sheets. Bake 11-13 minutes, until the edges turn brown.

Nutrition per serving: Cal 274; Fat 15g; Prot 4g; Carb 32g; Chol 18mg; Fiber 0g; Vit A 501IU; Sod 224mg; Iron 2mg; Vit C 0mg.

Smart Snacks

Chocolate Drop Cookies

1/2 cup shortening
2 (1-ounce) squares
  unsweetened chocolate
1 cup brown sugar
1 egg
1 teaspoon vanilla
1/2 cup buttermilk
11/2 cups sifted all-purpose
  flour

1/2 teaspoon baking powder
1/2 teaspoon soda
1/4 teaspoon salt
1/2 cup chopped walnuts
1 (6-ounce) package
  semi-sweet chocolate morsels

Melt shortening and unsweetened chocolate together in saucepan. Cool
10 minutes. Stir brown sugar and chocolate together. Beat in egg,
vanilla, and buttermilk. Sift together dry ingredients and add to chocolate mix. Stir in nuts and chocolate pieces. Drop from teaspoon on
greased cookie sheet. Top with walnut halves, if desired. Bake at
375° for 10-12 minutes. Makes 31/2 dozen.

Home Cookin': First Congregational United Church of Christ

Devil's Food Drop Cookies

This is a wonderful, old-fashioned cookie. Delicious, especially at holiday time. Great for chocolate freaks!

1/2 cup margarine	2 cups all-purpose flour
1 cup brown sugar	1/2 teaspoon baking soda
1 egg	1/4 teaspoon salt
1 teaspoon vanilla	3/4 cup sour cream
2 (1-ounce) squares unsweetened chocolate (melted and cooled)	1/2 cup finely chopped walnuts

Cream margarine and sugar till fluffy. Beat in egg and vanilla. Stir in chocolate. Sift together all dry ingredients, adding to chocolate mixture alternately with the sour cream. Mix well and stir in walnuts. Drop from teaspoon, 2 inches apart, on foil-covered cookie sheet (dull side up). Bake at 350° for 10 minutes or just until done. Remove and cool. Frost with Mocha Frosting.

MOCHA FROSTING:

1/4 cup softened margarine	Dash of salt
2 teaspoons instant coffee	3 cups confectioners' sugar
2 tablespoons cocoa (regular type, dry)	3 tablespoons milk
	1 teaspoon vanilla

Cream margarine, coffee, cocoa, and salt; slowly cream in one cup of the sugar, then add remaining 2 cups sugar, milk, and vanilla. Beat until smooth. Makes about 41/2 dozen cookies.

Note: Hand mix to attain delicate texture; store in airtight cookie tin.

Recipes and Memories

Marblehead Molasses Cookies

4 cups flour	2 teaspoons ginger
1/2 teaspoon salt	11/2 cups shortening
4 teaspoons soda	2 cups sugar
2 teaspoons cinnamon	1/2 cup molasses
2 teaspoons cloves	2 eggs

Sift together flour, salt, soda, cinnamon, cloves, and ginger and set aside. Cream shortening and sugar. Add molasses and eggs. Beat well. Add sifted dry ingredients and mix well. Refrigerate. Roll into balls and bake at 350° for 20 minutes.

How to Make A Steamship Float

Engelkusse
(Chocolate Angel Kisses)

1 (4-ounce) package sweet
   cooking chocolate
1 tablespoon butter
2 eggs
³/₄ cup sugar
¹/₃ cup unsifted all-purpose
   flour

¹/₄ teaspoon baking powder
¹/₈ teaspoon salt
2 cups flaked coconut
¹/₂ teaspoon cinnamon
1 teaspoon vanilla

Melt chocolate and butter over low heat. Set aside. Beat eggs until foamy and light in color. Add sugar, 2 tablespoons at a time, beating constantly until mixture is thick and light in color (about 5 minutes.) Fold in flour, baking powder, and salt. Stir in chocolate, coconut, cinnamon, and vanilla. Drop dough on well greased and lightly floured baking sheet. Bake 15 minutes at 325°. Remove from oven and let stand a few minutes. Yield: 3 dozen.

Cookies and Bars

"I Need a Hug" Peanut Butter Cookies

1 cup unsalted butter,
   softened
1 cup crunchy peanut butter
1 cup granulated sugar
1 cup firmly packed light
   brown sugar

2 eggs
2¹/₂ cups flour
1 teaspoon baking powder
1¹/₂ teaspoons baking soda
¹/₂ teaspoon salt

Preheat oven to 375°. In a large bowl, cream butter, peanut butter, sugar, and brown sugar. Beat in eggs. Sift together flour, baking powder, baking soda and salt. Stir into the batter. Cover bowl and refrigerate batter for one hour. Roll into 1-inch balls and place on ungreased baking sheets. Flatten balls with a fork, making a crisscross pattern. Bake on middle level of preheated oven about 10 minutes or until cookies begin to brown. Do not overbake. Remove immediately to cooling racks.

Note: For a softer cookie, substitute ¹/₃ of the 2 sugars with granulated fructose, a natural fruit sugar sold in supermarkets or health food stores.

Blissfield Preschool Cookbook

Chewy Applesauce and PB Cookies

The 5-dozen cookies from this recipe will disappear fast!

3¹/₂ cups all-purpose flour
¹/₂ teaspoon salt
1¹/₂ teaspoons baking soda
1 cup unsweetened Michigan
    applesauce

1 cup peanut butter
2¹/₂ cups brown sugar
2 egg whites
2 teaspoons vanilla extract

In a small bowl combine flour, salt, and baking soda. In a large bowl, thoroughly mix together remaining ingredients. Add the dry ingredients, mixing until combined. Drop by rounded measuring tablespoonful onto cookie sheets coated with nonstick soy oil cooking spray. Bake in 375° oven about 10 minutes or until light golden brown. Cool on wire racks.

Per serving: Cal 89; Cal from Fat 22%; Sod 64mg; Chol 0mg.

Michigan Gourmet Cookbook

Applesauce Cookies

1 cup sugar
¹/₂ cup shortening
1 egg, beatem
1 cup applesauce
3 cups flour
1 teaspoon soda

¹/₂ teaspoon nutmeg
¹/₂ teaspoon cinnamon
¹/₂ teaspoon salt
1 cup nutmeats
1 cup butterscotch bits or
    chocolate chips

Cream sugar and shortening. Add beaten egg and applesauce. Sift all dry ingredients together and add to mixture. Add nuts and butterscotch bits. Drop by teaspoon on greased cookie sheet. Bake at 350° for 12-15 minutes. This is a soft cookie which stays moist. Makes about 4 dozen.

Come and Dine

Kalamazoo was known as "Paper City" for its many paper and cardboard mills, most of which are now closed; and the "Celery City" after the crop once grown in muck fields south and east of town. Celery was first commercially grown in the US in the Kalamazoo area.

Apple Blondies

"I like apples best when they are turned into cookies," said a three-year old.

1 (3-ounce) package light
   cream cheese, softened
1 cup margarine, softened
3¹/₂ cups brown sugar
3 eggs
2 teaspoons vanilla
2 cups flour

2 cups whole wheat flour
1 tablespoon baking powder
¹/₂ teaspoon salt
2 cups apples, peeled and
   chopped
1 cup raisins

Preheat oven to 350°. Spray 2 (9x13-inch) pans with nonstick cooking spray. In a large bowl, cream the light cream cheese with the margarine and brown sugar. Beat in the eggs and vanilla. In a medium bowl, combine the flours with the baking powder and salt. Add these dry ingredients to the creamed mixture. Fold in the chopped apples and raisins. Spread the batter evenly in the 2 prepared pans. Bake 25-30 minutes. Cool before cutting.

Nutrition per serving: Cal 257; Fat 9g; Prot 4g; Carb 39g; Chol 29mg; Fiber 0g; Vit A 398IU; Sod 211mg; Iron 1mg; Vit C 1mg.

Smart Snacks

Apple Spice Cookies

1/2 cup butter, softened	1 teaspoon salt
1 1/3 cups brown sugar	1 teaspoon cinnamon
1 egg	1 teaspoon cloves
1/4 cup milk	1 teaspoon nutmeg
2 cups sifted flour	1 cup chopped apples
1 teaspoon baking soda	1 cup chopped nuts

FROSTING:

1 tablespoon soft butter	3 tablespoons milk
1 1/2 cups confectioners' sugar	1/4 teaspoon vanilla

Cream butter and sugar until light. Add egg and milk, beating until smooth. Sift dry ingredients together and stir into butter mixture with the apples and nuts. Drop by teaspoonfuls on greased cookie sheet. Bake at 375° for 10 minutes. Cool and frost. Yield: 4 dozen.

The Junior League of Grand Rapids Cookbook I

Lemon Thyme Cookies

An unusual and tasty cookie from an herb lady in Northern Michigan.

2 1/2 cups unbleached flour	1 1/2 cups sugar
1 teaspoon cream of tartar	2 eggs
1 cup unsalted butter, softened	3 tablespoons fresh lemon thyme, finely chopped

Sift together flour and cream of tartar. Cream butter with sugar; add eggs and mix well. Work in flour mixture until well blended. Stir in lemon thyme. Chill for several hours. Roll into balls the size of small walnuts. Bake on greased cookie sheet 10 minutes in a preheated 350° oven.

Historically Delicious

Sugar & Spice Cookies

A flavorful spice cookie with a delicious aftertaste.

³/₄ cup shortening	1 teaspoon cinnamon
1 cup brown sugar	¹/₂ teaspoon ground ginger
1 egg	¹/₄ teaspoon ground cloves
¹/₄ cup molasses	¹/₄ teaspoon salt
2¹/₄ cups sifted flour	2 tablespoons sugar
2 teaspoons baking soda	3 dozen red cinnamon candies

Cream together shortening and sugar until fluffy. Add egg and molasses; blend well. Sift together next 6 ingredients. Stir into creamed mixture. Form balls using one teaspoon dough. Roll in sugar and place about 2 inches apart on a greased baking sheet. Bake at 375° for 10 minutes or until golden brown. Place a red cinnamon candy in middle of each cookie. Yield: 3 dozen.

Cookies and Bars

Grandma Sloan's Christmas Cookies

2³/₄ cups flour	1 cup sugar
2 teaspoons baking powder	³/₄ cup butter or margarine,
2 eggs	softened
1 teaspoon vanilla	

Mix flour and baking powder well. Set aside. Mix eggs, vanilla, sugar, and softened butter well. Add dry ingredients slowly. Chill one hour. Lightly flour work area and rolling pin. Cut out cookies and bake on ungreased cookie sheets until edges are light golden at 375°. Sprinkle with sugar before baking, or frost.

Hint: Keep dough cold and covered; chill rolling pin for easier handling; thin cookies are crisp, thicker cookies are soft.

Blissfield Preschool Cookbook

With the closing of Burdick Street to auto traffic in 1959. Kalamazoo Mall became the first outdoor pedestrian shopping mall in the United States.

Butter Dreams
(Snow Balls)

This is an attractive Christmas cookie.

1 pound butter
1 cup sugar
4 1/2 cups flour
4 teaspoons vanilla

2 regular-size jars maraschino cherries, cut in halves and drained

Cream butter and sugar; add flour and vanilla. Roll into small balls. Place 1/2 cherry on top and press down. Bake at 350° for 12-15 minutes. Tops will be white and bottoms slightly browned; cool.

ICING:

1/2 pound margarine
Dash of lemon juice
1/2 teaspoon vanilla

1/2 cup evaporated milk
1 box powdered sugar
Angel Flake coconut

Mix all but coconut. Spread icing around cookie, leaving cherry uncovered. Cover icing with coconut.

From Our Kitchens with Love

Cinnamon Tea Cookies

Not only are these good at "tea-time," but a favorite on the Christmas tray.

1 cup butter, softened
3/4 cup sugar
1 egg, separated
1 teaspoon vanilla

2 cups flour
4 teaspoons cinnamon
1/2 cup ground pecans or walnuts

Preheat oven to 350°. In a large mixing bowl, cream together butter and sugar. Beat in egg yolk and vanilla. Combine flour and cinnamon, then blend in with a wooden spoon. Form into balls, using a 1/2 teaspoon as a measure.

Beat the egg white only until frothy. Dip 1/2 of each ball in egg white then ground nuts. Place, dipped-side up, on ungreased cookie sheet, one inch apart. Bake 12 minutes. Yield: 8 dozen.

Hollyhocks & Radishes

Pepparkakor Cookies

3³/₄ cups flour
1 tablespoon ginger
1 tablespoon cinnamon
2 teaspoons cloves
1 teaspoon baking soda

1 cup oleo
1 cup sugar
1 egg
¹/₂ cup molasses

Sift flour, ginger, cinnamon, cloves, and baking soda together. Cream oleo, gradually add sugar, beating until fluffy. Add egg and molasses, beat well. Add flour mixture gradually; beat until well blended. Wrap in wax paper; chill overnight. Heat oven to 350°. Roll out part of dough at a time on floured board. Cut out with floured fancy cutters. Transfer to lightly greased cookie sheet. Bake 8-10 minutes or until lightly brown. Drizzle with frosting (powdered sugar and water). Makes 6 dozen.

Halvorson-Johnson Family Reunion Cookbook

Blow Out Cookies

2 cups flour
1 teaspoon baking powder
¹/₄ teaspoon salt
¹/₂ cup chunky peanut butter
¹/₂ cup soft butter
¹/₂ cup brown sugar
¹/₂ cup granulated sugar
1 egg

1 teaspoon vanilla
¹/₄ cup milk
³/₄ cup chocolate chips
³/₄ cup honey roasted peanuts
³/₄ cup coarsely chopped
    frozen miniature peanut
    butter cups candy

Combine flour, baking powder, and salt. Beat peanut butter and butter until fluffy. Add both sugars; beat until light. Add egg. Beat 3 minutes. Add vanilla. Stir in dry ingredients, add milk. Beat thoroughly. Fold in chips, nuts, then candy. Drop by 2-tablespoon clumps on ungreased baking sheet. Bake at 375° for 10-12 minutes.

Recipes & Remembrances II

Sour Cream Sugar Cookies

1 cup margarine
1¹/₂ cups sugar
3 eggs
1 cup sour cream
4 cups flour
1 teaspoon baking soda

2 teaspoons baking powder
¹/₂ teaspoon salt
¹/₂ teaspoon nutmeg (or 1
   teaspoon vanilla or lemon
   extract)

Cream margarine; add sugar gradually. Add eggs and mix well. Stir in sour cream and dry ingredients which have been measured together. Chill thoroughly. Roll out. Bake at 350° for 8-10 minutes. Do not overbake. Cookies should not be brown.

Note: Dough is very soft and hard to handle unless it is kept cold. Take only small amounts of dough out of refrigerator at a time.

Chelsea Cooks

Lemon Pie Cookies

1¹/₂ cups flour
¹/₂ cup powdered sugar
³/₄ cup margarine
3 eggs

1¹/₂ cups sugar
3 tablespoons flour
3 tablespoons lemon juice

Mix first 3 ingredients and pat into 13x9x2-inch pan. Bake at 350° for 20 minutes. Mix remaining ingredients and pour into baked crust. Bake ¹/₂ hour longer. Cool and cut into squares. Sprinkle with powdered sugar.

Home Cookin': First Congregational United Church of Christ

You can relive a piece of history and even learn to dance the so-cool steps of the Temptations, Smokey Robinson and the Miracles, Diana Ross and the Supremes, Marvin Gaye, and other Motown greats at Motown Historical Museum's Hitsville U.S.A. in Detroit and at the Henry Ford Museum & Greenfield Village in Dearborn. The saga of how Berry Gordy churned out hit after hit to move a generation, is said to be so big it takes two museums to tell it.

Almond Apricot Delights

1 1/2 cups dried apricots,
  coarsely chopped
2 tablespoons cognac
1/2 cup almond paste
1/2 cup powdered sugar

2 teaspoons instant coffee
2 teaspoons cocoa
1/4 cup powdered sugar
1 teaspoon cocoa

Combine the first 6 ingredients in food processor or blender, and purée. Combine 1/4 cup powdered sugar and cocoa. Roll apricot mixture into marble-size balls and shake in the powdered sugar mixture. Store in an airtight container with the leftover powdered sugar mixture to prevent them from sticking. Best kept in the freezer. Makes 50 balls.

Note: A quick way to roll out the balls is to do it assembly-line-fashion a dozen at a time. Scoop out about a dozen little spoonfuls on waxed paper, roll them one after the other, drop them into the bag and shake them all together.

Per serving (each): Cal 29; Prot 0g; Fat 0.7g; (trace saturated fat); Carb 5g; Dietary fiber 0g; Chol 0mg; Sod 3mg; Cal 9mg; Iron 0.3mg. Exchanges: fruit 13; fat trace (not recommended for diabetics).

High Fit - Low Fat

Coconut Pecan Squares

1/2 cup butter
1/2 cup brown sugar
1 cup + 2 tablespoons flour,
  sifted
1 cup chopped nuts

1 1/2 cups coconut
1/2 teaspoon salt
2 eggs, well beaten
1 cup brown sugar
1 teaspoon vanilla

Cream butter, 1/2 cup brown sugar, and one cup flour. Pat into 7x11-inch pan. Bake in 375° oven for 10 minutes. Combine nuts, coconut, 2 tablespoons flour, and salt. Put aside.

    Combine beaten eggs, 1 cup brown sugar, and vanilla. Slowly add coconut/nut mixture to egg mixture and spread on top of partially baked crust. Bake 20 minutes longer. Cool and cut into squares.

Chelsea Cooks

Walnut Dreams

1 cup butter, room
   temperature
$1/2$ cup sugar
2 cups flour
1 pound brown sugar
2 cups chopped walnuts

$1/4$ cup flour
4 eggs
1 teaspoon salt
1 teaspoon baking powder
1 teaspoon vanilla

Cream butter and sugar. Gradually add flour. Spread evenly in greased jelly-roll pan. Bake 15 minutes in 350° oven. Combine brown sugar, nuts, flour, eggs, salt, baking powder, and vanilla. Pour over crust. Continue baking until set, about 15-17 minutes. Cool completely.

FROSTING:

2 cups powdered sugar
3 tablespoons milk

$1/4$ stick butter, melted

Combine powdered sugar, milk and butter. Blend until smooth. Spread evenly on pastry. Cut into squares.

Cookies and Bars

Crunchy Caramel Chocolate Chews

$1/2$ cup margarine
$1/2$ cup molasses
4 cups Rice Chex
80 Kraft caramels

6 tablespoons milk
1 (12-ounce) bag of chocolate
  chips
2 cups walnuts or pecans

Melt margarine with molasses over low heat. Stir in Rice Chex; press into 13x9-inch pan. Bake at 350° for 10 minutes. Melt caramels with milk in heavy saucepan over low heat. Pour over crust, sprinkle with chocolate chips and nuts; press into pan. Cool and cut into squares.

Seasoned Cooks II

Skillet Cookies

Great to make on a hot day.

$1/2$ cup oleo
2 eggs (slightly beaten)
1 (8-ounce) package dates,
  chopped

1 cup sugar
1 cup nuts, chopped
2 cups Rice Krispies
Coconut

Melt oleo in heavy skillet. Add eggs, dates, and sugar. Stir vigorously for 10 minutes, or until mixture is thick and brown. Turn off heat. Add nuts and Rice Krispies. Drop by teaspoonful into a small bowl containing coconut. Roll into balls.

Cookies and Bars

Chocolate-Cherry Squares

1¹/₄ cups chocolate wafer
  cookie crumbs
2 tablespoons sugar
¹/₄ cup oleo, melted
3 squares semi-sweet
  chocolate

¹/₄ cup water
4 ounces cream cheese,
  softened
2 cups chocolate Cool Whip
1 (21-ounce) can cherry pie
  filling

Mix crumbs, sugar, and oleo in 9-inch square pan. Press firmly into bottom of pan. Refrigerate 10 minutes. Microwave chocolate and water 1-2 minutes or until chocolate is almost melted, stirring halfway through heating time. Stir until chocolate is completely melted. Beat cream cheese until smooth and fluffy. Gradually beat in chocolate mixture. Gently stir in 2 cups of Cool Whip. Spread evenly over crumb crust. Spoon pie filling over chocolate layer. Refrigerate 3 hours or until set. Garnish with remaining whipped topping and chocolate curls, if desired. Cut into squares. Store leftovers in refrigerator.

Trendfully Cookin'

Pumpkin Cheesecake Bars

1 (16-ounce) package pound
  cake mix
3 eggs
2 tablespoons butter or
  margarine, melted
1 (8-ounce) package cream
  cheese, softened

1 (14-ounce) can sweetened
  condensed milk
1 (18-ounce) can pumpkin pie
  filling
¹/₂ cup chopped nuts

Preheat oven to 350°. In large mixer bowl, on low speed, combine cake mix, one egg, and melted margarine until crumbly. Press onto bottom of 15x10x1-inch jelly roll pan. Set aside. In larger mixer bowl, beat cream cheese until smooth. Gradually beat in sweetened condensed milk, 2 eggs, and pumpkin; mix well. Pour over crust, sprinkle nuts on top. Bake for 30-35 minutes or until set. Cool. Chill, cut into bars. Store in refrigerator. Makes 48 bars.

Just Inn Time for Breakfast

Buttery Apple Squares

Great lunch box or picnic treats.

2 cups all-purpose flour
1 teaspoon salt
²/₃ cup butter or margarine,
   chilled
1 egg yolk
¹/₂ cup milk
5 medium Rome Beauty
   apples, peeled, thinly sliced,
   (or 5 cups)

2 tablespoons flour
³/₄ cup sugar
1 teaspoon cinnamon
1 tablespoon butter or
   margarine
1 egg white, slightly beaten

Preheat the oven to 375°. Sift 2 cups flour and salt into a bowl. Cut in ²/₃ cup butter until the mixture resembles large peas. Add a mixture of the egg yolk and milk, mixing just until moistened. Divide the dough into 2 equal portions and pat one of the portions over the bottom of a greased 7x10-inch baking pan. Spread the apples in the prepared pan.

Mix 2 tablespoons flour, sugar, and cinnamon in a small bowl. Sprinkle over the apples and dot with one tablespoon butter. Roll the remaining dough on a lightly floured surface. Place it over the apples; seal the edges and cut vents. Brush lightly with the egg white. Bake at 375° for one hour or until the crust is light brown and the apples are tender.

FROSTING:

¹/₂ cup confectioners' sugar
2 tablespoons light cream or
   milk

¹/₂ teaspoon vanilla extract

Combine the confectioners' sugar, cream, and vanilla in a bowl and mix well. Spread over the warm apple dessert. Cut into squares to serve.

The Dexter Cider Mill Apple Cookbook

 Rockford is the home of Hush Puppies shoes, which was founded in 1883.

Iced Spice Bars

1¹/₂ cups all-purpose flour
1 cup sugar
¹/₂ cup milk
¹/₂ cup vegetable oil
2 eggs
1 teaspoon salt

1 teaspoon baking soda
1 teaspoon cinnamon
1 teaspoon cloves
¹/₂ cup chopped pecans or
    walnuts
¹/₂ cup raisins

Preheat oven to 375°. Grease jelly roll pan. Combine first 9 ingredients in large bowl and mix well. Stir in nuts and raisins. Turn batter into prepared 10x15-inch jelly roll pan spreading evenly. Bake until golden brown, about 20 minutes. Cool bars in pan on rack 10 minutes, then frost. Yield: 4 dozen bars.

FROSTING:
1 cup powdered sugar   ¹/₂ cup hot water

Blend powdered sugar and water in small bowl until smooth. Cover bars evenly with icing. Cool completely before slicing. Store in airtight container.

Cookies and Bars

Baby Ruth Bars

Oh boy, are these good!

¹/₂ cup white sugar
¹/₂ cup brown sugar
1 cup corn syrup
1 cup peanut butter

6 cups corn flakes
1 cup salted peanuts
1 (8-ounce) Hershey
    chocolate bar, melted

Place sugars and syrup in saucepan and bring to a boil. Add the peanut butter, corn flakes, and nuts. Press firmly into greased 9-inch square or 13x9x2-inch pan. Melt chocolate and spread over top.

Cookies and Bars

Chocolate Revel Bars

1 cup butter or margarine
2 cups brown sugar
2 eggs
2 teaspoons vanilla
2¹/₂ cups sifted all-purpose
   flour

1 teaspoon baking soda
1 teaspoon salt
3 cups quick-cooking rolled
   oats

In large mixer bowl, cream together the butter or margarine and the brown sugar. Beat in eggs and vanilla. Sift together flour, soda, and salt. Stir in oats. Stir dry ingredients into cream mixture till blended; set aside.

FILLING:

1 (15-ounce) can sweetened
   condensed milk
1 (12-ounce) package (2 cups)
   semi-sweet chocolate pieces

2 tablespoons butter or margarine
¹/₂ teaspoon salt
2 teaspoons vanilla
1 cup chopped walnuts

In heavy saucepan over low heat, melt together sweetened condensed milk, chocolate pieces, butter or margarine, and salt, stirring till smooth. Stir in vanilla and nuts.

Pat ²/₃ of oat mixture in bottom of 15¹/₂x10¹/₂x1-inch pan. Spread chocolate mixture over dough. Dot with remaining oat mixture. Bake 25-30 minutes at 350°. Cool; cut into 2x1-inch bars. Yield: about 75.

Cookies and Bars

Crème De Menthe Bars

BOTTOM LAYER:

3 squares chocolate, melted
2 cups firmly packed brown
  sugar
3 eggs

1¹/₄ cups flour
¹/₂ teaspoon salt
¹/₄ teaspoon baking soda
1 teaspoon vanilla

Mix all ingredients together and spread on greased cookie sheet (9x12-inch). Pop into 350° oven for 30 minutes. When toothpick comes out clean, cool.

MIDDLE LAYER:

4 cups powdered sugar
2 tablespoons coffee cream
2 sticks butter or oleo

3 shots of crème de menthe
¹/₂ teaspoon peppermint
  extract

Mix all ingredients together and spread over cooled bottom layer. Refrigerate until firm.

TOP LAYER:

12 ounces chocolate chips

3 tablespoons oil

Melt chocolate chips in oil. Spread over top of middle layer; refrigerate. Serves 24-36.

From Our Kitchens with Love

Nut Fudge

2¹/₄ cups sugar
¹/₄ cup margarine
1 cup evaporated milk
16 large marshmallows

1 teaspoon vanilla
1 cup (6 ounces) chocolate
  chips
1 cup nuts

Mix sugar, margarine, evaporated milk and marshmallows in large glass bowl. Microwave 5 minutes on HIGH. Stir and microwave until bubbly on top, about 3 minutes on HIGH. Stir in vanilla, chocolate chips and nuts. Set in cold water and stir until it starts to set. Spread in an 8x9-inch buttered pan. May also be cooked over medium heat, stirring constantly, until boiling. Boil and stir 5 minutes. Continue with directions. Fudge should cook to soft ball stage.

Centennial Cookbook

Raspberry Chocolate Buttercreams

Well worth the effort.

BASE:

4 ounces unsweetened
  chocolate
$1/2$ cup butter or margarine
2 cups sugar

$1/4$ teaspoon salt
1 teaspoon vanilla
4 eggs
1 cup flour

In a small saucepan over low heat, melt unsweetened chocolate and butter, stirring constantly. Remove from heat. Cool. In a large bowl, beat sugar, salt, vanilla, and eggs. Stir in melted chocolate and flour. Spread mixture evenly in pan. Bake at 350° for 25-30 minutes. Cool.

FILLING:

1 cup seedless raspberry
  preserves
2 ounces semi-sweet
  chocolate
1 ounce unsweetened
  chocolate

$1/3$ cup sugar
$1/4$ cup water
2 eggs
1 cup unsalted butter or
  margarine, softened

Spread raspberry preserves over base. In small saucepan over low heat, melt semi-sweet chocolate and unsweetened chocolate, stirring constantly. Remove from heat. In another saucepan, bring sugar and water to a boil. Boil one minute. In large bowl, beat eggs until frothy. Gradually add sugar-water mixture and beat on highest speed for 5 minutes or until thick and lemon colored. Gradually add butter, a small piece at a time, beating well after each addition. Add melted chocolate and beat until smooth. Spread filling carefully over preserves.

GLAZE:

1 ounce unsweetened
  chocolate

1 tablespoon butter or
  margarine

Melt over low heat, chocolate and butter, stirring constantly. Drizzle over filling. Refrigerate one hour; cut into bars. Store in refrigerator. Yields 36 bars.

Some Enchanted Eating

Peanut Butter Logs

2 cups peanut butter
1/2 cup butter
16 ounces (41/2 cups) sifted
    powdered sugar

3 cups Rice Krispies
1 (6-ounce) package
    semi-sweet chocolate chips

In saucepan, melt peanut butter and butter. In large bowl, combine powdered sugar and cereal. Pour peanut butter mixture over cereal mixture. Blend with hands. Roll into 1/2-inch balls. Chill till firm. Melt chocolate in double boiler. Dip candies in this and swirl top with back of spoon. Place on wax paper in cookie sheet. Chill. Makes 100 candies.

From Our Home to Yours

Gingerbread House Dough

This does taste good, though it's a bit hard on the teeth.

1 cup butter, melted	1 teaspoon salt
1 cup sugar	1 teaspoon nutmeg
1¹/₃ cups molasses	1 tablespoon ginger
1 teaspoon baking soda	5 cups flour

Add the sugar and molasses to the butter. Mix soda, salt, nutmeg, ginger, and 4 cups of the flour and add to the other mix. Knead in the last cup of flour. Roll out to ¹/₄-inch thick and cut into shapes. Bake 350° for 12-15 minutes.

For a finished house that would fit on a cookie sheet, make 1¹/₂ recipes. It's easiest to roll the dough right on the baking sheet so pieces don't get distorted. Cut out any windows or holes for ornaments before baking. The best glue is a simple frosting of water and powdered sugar, made thick. Stored in a dry place, these houses can keep for years.

Tasteful Art

Michigan's Little Bavaria, Frankenmuth, rolls out the *willkommen* mat for all visitors to their charming town. It's alpine-style buildings, covered bridges, and peak-roofed cottages give it a storybook atmosphere.

Pies and Desserts

The Glockenspiel Clock Tower's 35-bell carillon plays seven times each day. Storybook characters pop out from behind a bronze door at the top. Frankenmuth.

Michigan Four Seasons Pie

Versatile.

CRUST:

1/2 cup butter	1 tablespoon water
1 1/2 cups flour	

Melt the butter in a 9-inch pie pan. Add the flour and water. Mix with a fork and press into the bottom and sides of the pan. Bake at 425° for 15 minutes.

SYRUP:

1 cup sugar	4 cups sliced fresh Michigan
1 tablespoon cornstarch	fruit
1 cup water	
1/4 cup dry flavored gelatin	
powder	

Combine sugar, cornstarch and water. Boil one minute or until clear. Stir the gelatin into the syrup and cool. Pour mixture over the fresh fruit which has been placed in the baked pastry shell. Serves 6-8.

Variations: Use strawberry gelatin for strawberry pie, peach for peach pie, lemon for blueberry pie, raspberry for raspberry pie.

Some Enchanted Eating

Deep-Dish Cherry Pie

A deep-dish cherry pie with a new way with the crust and a meringue-type cake topping.

1 cup flour	1/2 cup margarine
1 tablespoon powdered sugar	1 can cherry pie mix

Sift flour and powdered sugar together; cut in butter. Pat evely over bottom and sides of 10-inch deep-dish pie pan. Bake in moderate oven (350°) for 15 minutes until lightly browned. Spread cherry pie mix over partially-baked crust; top with Meringue Cake Topping.

CONTINUED

MERINGUE CAKE TOPPING:

2 egg whites
1 cup sugar
3/4 cup flour
1/2 teaspoon baking powder
3 tablespoons coffee cream or
   half-and-half

1 teaspoon vanilla
3/4 cup coarsely chopped
   pecans
1/2 cup flaked coconut

Beat egg whites until very frothy, gradually add sugar a little at a time; beat until stiff peaks form. Sift flour and baking powder together; fold in meringue mixture alternately with cream. Fold in vanilla, nuts, and coconut; do not beat. Turn out over top of cherries. If desired, arrange a crown of candied cherries and chopped pecans over meringue. Bake in moderate oven (350°) for 30 minutes; do not overbake.

Great Lakes Cookery

Traverse City Cherry Berry Pie

Traverse City is the capital of Michigan's fabulous cherry-producing region.

2 unbaked 9-inch pie crusts
10 ounces frozen raspberries,
   thawed
3 tablespoons cornstarch
1/2 teaspoon salt
3/4 cup sugar

2 cups pitted fresh red tart
   cherries
1/2 teaspoon ground
   cinnamon
1 quart vanilla or cinnamon
   ice cream

Preheat oven to 425°. Line a pie plate with one of the pie crusts. Drain raspberries, reserving syrup. Add water to syrup to make one cup. In a saucepan, combine the cup of liquid with the cornstarch, salt, and sugar. When cornstarch is dissolved, add the cherries. Cook over low heat, stirring, until mixture is thick and clear. Stir in raspberries and cinnamon. Pour filling into pastry shell. Top with second crust, crimping the edge and venting the top. Bake for 30 minutes or until the filling is hot and the crust is golden. Cool and serve with a scoop of ice cream. Serves 6-8.

Cranbrook Reflections

Easy Pear Pie

This pie recipe is a little different from most pie recipes, but it is my favorite kind of recipe - easy and delicious!

3 or 4 fresh, ripe pears
1 unbaked 9-inch pie crust
1 cup sugar
1 cup all-purpose flour
1/4 cup melted butter or
   margarine

2 eggs
1 teaspoon lemon juice
1/2 teaspoon vanilla
1/2 teaspoon ground ginger

Prreheat oven to 400°. Wash and drain pears. Cut pears lengthwise into halves; remove core and stem ends with paring knife. Arrange pears cut-side-down in pie shell, with wide ends of pears near outside edge of shell. Set aside. Beat sugar, flour, melted butter, eggs, lemon juice, vanilla, and ginger with electric mixer until smooth and blended. Pour into pear-lined shell.

Bake for 40-45 minutes, or until golden brown and top springs back when lightly pressed with finger. Serve warm. Refrigerate any left-overs. Yield: 1 (9-inch) pie.

Good Food From Michigan

Raspberry and Cream Pie

1 (9-inch) pie shell

Preheat oven to 400°. Prepare an unbaked 9-inch pie shell.

FILLING:
1/2 cup flour
3/4 - 1 cup sugar
1 1/4 cup heavy cream (whipping)

Dash of cinnamon
4 cups fresh raspberries

Blend the flour, sugar, cream, and cinnamon with a wire whisk or fork. Put the raspberries in a large bowl and pour the cream mixture over them. Stir gently to coat the raspberries. Pour the raspberry-cream mixture into the unbaked pie shell. Bake at 400° about 40 minutes or until set. Serve at room temperature or slightly chilled.

Note: Leftover pie needs to be refrigerated.

Come and Dine

Blueberry Sour Cream Pie

1 ready-made pie crust

Follow one-crust pie directions on package. Place in 9-inch glass pie plate. Fold edge under, crimp, freeze 10 minutes. Line crust with foil, fill with dried beans or pie weights. Bake until sides are set, about 12 minutes. Remove foil and beans.

FILLING:

1 cup sour cream	$3/4$ teaspoon almond extract
$3/4$ cup sugar	$1/4$ teaspoon salt
$2^1/2$ tablespoons flour	$2^1/2$ cups fresh blueberries
1 egg, beaten to blend	

Mix first 6 ingredients in medium bowl to blend. Mix in blueberries. Spoon into crust. Bake at 350° until filling is just set, about 25 minutes.

TOPPING:

6 tablespoons flour	$1/3$ cup chopped pecans
$1/4$ cup ($1/2$ stick) chilled unsalted butter, cut into pieces	2 tablespoons sugar

Using fingertips, mix flour and butter in medium bowl until small clumps form. Mix in pecans and sugar. Spoon topping over pie. Bake until topping browns lightly, about 12 minutes. Cool pie at room temperature.

Blissfield Preschool Cookbook

Peaches and Cream Pie

CRUST:

1/2 cup lard
1 1/2 cups flour
1/4 teaspoon baking powder
1/4 teaspoon salt

1/2 egg, beaten
2 1/2 tablespoons water
1/2 tablespoon vinegar

Prepare pie crust first by blending lard into flour, baking powder, and salt. Mix together egg, water, and vinegar; add to lard mixture. Press into bottom of pie pan.

FILLING:

4 cups peaches
1/2 cup sugar
1/2 teaspoon cinnamon

2 eggs
4 tablespoons cream

Mix together peaches, sugar, and cinnamon. Beat eggs with the cream and pour over peaches. Pour peach mixture on top of crust.

CRUMB TOPPING:

1/4 cup + 2 tablespoons butter
3/4 cup brown sugar

3/4 cup flour

Mix butter and brown sugar. Cut in flour and sprinkle over pie. Bake at 425° for 35-45 minutes.

From Our Home to Yours

Visitors from all over the country come to marvel at the millions of tulips that line the city streets in Holland at their annual Tulip Time Festival in May. Dutch Dancers dressed in traditional Dutch costumes and the gorgeous tulips highlight the 10-day festival, among the top five festivals in the US.

Peach Sunburst Pie

Peeled, raw peach halves
1 unbaked crust
1/2 cup butter

1 cup sugar
2 tablespoons flour
1 egg, slightly beaten

Place peach halves, cut-side-down, in crust. Cream the soft butter with the sugar to which the flour has been added. Combine with beaten egg. Pour this over the peaches. Bake at 350° for 55 minutes.

Note: A drop or two of almond extract, a few grains of salt, as well as nutmeg will add to this pie.

Sharing Our Best Volume II

Real Lemon Pie

Lemon lovers claim that this is the ultimate dessert...that lemon meringue pie cannot compare.

Pastry for a 2-crust, 8-9-inch
  pie
1 1/2 tablespoons sugar
1 teaspoon cinnamon or
  nutmeg
3 lemons

1 1/2 cups sugar
3 tablespoons flour
6 tablespoons butter, softened
3 eggs
1/2 cup water

Preheat oven to 400°. Roll out 1/2 of pastry. Cut out a 9-inch circle of dough, using the base of a 9-inch, deep pie plate as a guide, and place on an ungreased cookie sheet. Cut into 8 wedges. Combine sugar and spice, and sprinkle over wedges. Bake 5 minutes. Cool. Roll out remaining pastry and line pie plate, crimping edge.

    Grate yellow part of lemons' rinds. Peel, then slice lemons as thinly as possible, discarding seeds and any coarse pith. In a mixing bowl, cream together sugar, flour, and butter. Beat in eggs, then water. Stir in lemon slices and grated rind. Pour into prepared pie shell. Bake 25 minutes, then remove pie from oven. Using a metal spatula, quickly arrange baked pastry wedges on top of filling. Return to oven, then bake another 5-10 minutes for filling to set. Cool on rack, and serve at room temperature. Serves 8.

Hollyhocks & Radishes

Oatmeal Pie

1¹/₂ sticks butter
1¹/₂ cups sugar
4 eggs, beaten
2 teaspoons salt

1¹/₂ cups corn syrup
1¹/₂ cups quick oats
1 cup coconut
2 pie shells, unbaked

Cream together the butter and sugar. Add the beaten eggs. Mix together salt, corn syrup, oats, and coconut. Add to first mixture and pour into 2 unbaked pie shells. Bake at 350° for 35-40 minutes. Very rich. Flavor similar to pecan pie. Makes 2 pies.

Renaissance Cuisine

Glazed Fruit Pie

BUTTER CRUST:
¹/₄ pound oleo, melted
2 tablespoons water

1¹/₄ cups flour

Melt butter in water until melted; add flour. Press in pan and bake at 325° only until very lightly browned.

GLAZE:
1 cup water
1 cup sugar
2 tablespoons cornstarch

4 tablespoons Jello
Fresh fruit

Boil water, sugar, and cornstarch until glossy; add dry Jello (use strawberry Jello for strawberries, etc.). Pour over fresh fruit in cold shell.

Country Cookbook

Citrus Ice Cream Pie

1 pint ice cream (flavor of
   choice
1 (6-ounce) can concentrated
   orange juice, undiluted

1 (8-ounce) carton Cool Whip
   (lowfat, if desired)
1 graham cracker pie crust

Soften ice cream. Mix together with juice and Cool Whip. Pour into graham cracker pie crust. Cover and place in freezer at least one hour. Makes one 9-inch pie.

Sharing Our Best Vol. II

Harvest Time Pizza

2 cups all-purpose flour	1 egg, beaten
1 tablespoon sugar	1/4 cup ice water
1 teaspoon salt	1 teaspoon white vinegar
3/4 cup vegetable shortening	

Mix the flour, sugar, and salt in a bowl. Cut in the shortening until the mixture resembles large peas. Combine the egg, ice water, and vinegar in a bowl and mix well. Add to the crumb mixture and stir with a fork to form a dough. Chill, wrapped, for 2 hours or longer. Press into an ungreased 15-inch pizza pan and flute the edge.

3-4 large Royal Gala or McIntosh apples, peeled, thinly sliced	11/2 cups sour cream
	1 tablespoon all-purpose flour
	1/2 cup firmly packed brown
1/2 cup sugar	sugar
1 teaspoon cinnamon	1/2 cup slivered blanched
Salt to taste	almonds (optional)

Preheat the oven to 400°. Arrange the apple slices in overlapping circles over the pastry, beginning at the edge and working toward the center. Mix the sugar, 1/2 teaspoon of the cinnamon and salt in a small bowl. Sprinkle over the apples. Combine the sour cream, flour, brown sugar, and the remaining 1/2 teaspoon cinnamon in a bowl and mix well. Spread evenly over the apples and sprinkle with the almonds. Bake at 400° for 10 minutes. Reduce the oven temperature to 350° and bake for 20-30 minutes longer or until the apples are tender. Cut into wedges and serve warm or at room temperature. Serves 8.

The Dexter Cider Mill Apple Cookbook

Apple - Pecan Pie

2 tablespoons butter
1 teaspoon vanilla extract
1 cup light brown sugar
3 eggs
1 cup coarsely chopped
   pecans

$^3/_4$ cup dark corn syrup
$^1/_2$ cup thick applesauce
$^1/_2$ teaspoon cinnamon
1 unbaked 9-inch pie shell

Cream butter with extract until softened. Gradually add brown sugar, beat thoroughly. Add eggs, beat thoroughly. Blend in the pecans, corn syrup, applesauce, and cinnamon. Turn filling into unbaked pie shell. Bake at 450° 10 minutes, reduce heat to 350°, and bake 40 minutes longer. Cool pie.

Cook Book: The Best of Michigan

Mom Miller's Old Fashioned Pumpkin Pie

3 tablespoons butter or
   margarine
$^1/_3$ cup firmly packed brown
   sugar
$^1/_3$ cup chopped pecans
1 unbaked pie shell
2 cups pumpkin, no spices
   added

1 cup sugar
$^1/_2$ teaspoon salt
1 teaspoon cinnamon
$^1/_2$ teaspoon ginger
$^1/_4$ teaspoon nutmeg
1 cup undiluted evaporated
   milk

Mix together butter, brown sugar, and pecans. Smooth into bottom of unbaked pie shell and bake at 450° for 10 minutes. Cool on wire rack for 10 minutes. While hot, prick any bubbles with a fork tine. Reduce heat to 350° for pumpkin pie. Beat remaining ingredients smooth and pour into shell over pecan bottom. Bake for 45-50 minutes.

From Our Home to Yours

 Michigan is the second largest producer of plums in the nation. The state has approximately 415,000 plum trees.

Killer Peanut Butter and Fudge Ripple Pie

1 (8-ounce) package cream
  cheese, softened
3/4 cup powdered sugar
1/4 cup peanut butter
1 teaspoon vanilla
2 eggs

1 pre-made chocolate crumb
  pie crust
1 cup whipping cream,
  whipped
1/2 cup semi-sweet chocolate
  chips, melted

In a bowl combine cream cheese, powdered sugar, peanut butter, and vanilla; beat at medium speed until smooth and well blended. Add eggs, one at a time, beating well after each addition. Fold in whipped cream. Spoon into crust. Spoon melted chocolate randomly over the filling. Gently pull knife through the chocolate to marble. Freeze. When ready to serve, let stand at room temperature about 15 minutes before serving. Serves 8-10.

What's Cookin'

Green Tomato Pie

1 cup sugar
1 teaspoon salt
1/2 teaspoon cinnamon
2 tablespoons flour
1/2 teaspoon nutmeg
6-8 green tomatoes, cored,
  quartered and thinly sliced

1 teaspoon grated lemon rind
  or 1/2 teaspoon lemon extract
  or 3 tablespoons lemon juice
1/2 cup raisins
2 layer pie crust
1 tablespoon butter or
  margarine

Combine the first 5 ingredients. Add the tomatoes. Stir in the lemon rind and raisins. Turn into pastry-lined pie pan and dot with butter or margarine. Place top crust on pie. Seal and flute edges. Cut slits in top. Bake in hot oven at 425° for 40-45 minutes or until tomatoes are tender. Serve slightly warm.

Sharing Our Best Volume II

 A 300-year-old Monarch pine soars to 155 feet in Hartwick Pines State Park near Grayling.

Ricotta Raspberry Tart

An excellent brunch dessert.

2 cups ricotta cheese
Zest of 1 orange
3 eggs

$^1/_2$ cup granulated sugar
4 cups raspberries

Preheat oven to 350°. Grease well a 12-inch spring-form pan. In a large bowl, mix together the ricotta and orange zest. Lightly beat eggs and add them and the granulated sugar to the ricotta; mix well. Pour the mixture into the prepared pan and top with the raspberries; set aside.

TOPPING:

$^3/_4$ cup unsalted butter
$^1/_2$ cup confectioners' sugar
1 egg

$^1/_2$ cup toasted almonds
$^1/_2$ teaspoon almond extract
$^1/_2$ teaspoon salt

1$^1/_2$ cups all-purpose flour

In a medium bowl, mix well the butter and confectioners' sugar. Add one egg and mix again. Add the flour, almonds, almond extract, and salt; mix well. Crumble this topping over raspberries and bake for 35-45 minutes or until a tester inserted in the center of the cheese custard comes out clean. Allow to cool completely before chilling for an hour before serving. Serve chilled.

Home Cookin': Almont Elementary PTA

Lazy Cherry Cobbler

Sure to be a family favorite.

2 (20-ounce) cans cherry pie
   filling
1/2 (20-ounce) can water
1/2 teaspoon almond extract

1 1/2 cups self-rising flour
1 cup sugar
1 cup skim milk

Preheat oven to 375°. Combine cherries, water, and almond extract. Mix well. Place in ungreased 9x13-inch baking pan. In a mixing bowl, combine dry ingredients and mix well. Add milk and stir until well mixed. Pour evenly over cherries. Then run a knife through the mixture as if marbelizing. Bake 25-40 minutes until golden brown. Serves 12.

Options: Use reduced-sugar pie filling. Use other fruits such as blueberries. To make an 8x8-inch pan, use one can of fruit and 1/4 cup water, one cup self-rising flour, 2/3 cup sugar and 2/3 cup milk.

Nutrition: (per serving): Cal 242; Sat Fat 0g; Total Fat 0g; Prot 3g; Carb 57g; Chol 0mg; Fiber 0g; Vit A 118 IU; Sod 188mg; Iron 1mg; Vit C 0mg.

"Life Tastes Better Than Steak" Cookbook

Zehndeer's Rhubarb Crunch

3 eggs, slightly beaten
1 1/2 cups sugar
1/4 cup flour

4 cups sliced rhubarb (discard
   leaves; use only stems)

TOPPING:
1 cup brown sugar
1 cup flour
1 cup uncooked oatmeal (not
   instant)

1/2 cup soft butter
Whipped topping

In a large bowl, mix eggs, sugar, flour. Add rhubarb, pour into a 9x13-inch baking pan, and spread evenly. In another bowl, mix topping ingredients (except whipped topping). Spread this over the rhubarb mixture. Bake at 375° about 45 minutes. Remove from oven. Cut into squares and serve with whipped topping.

Cook Book: The Best of Michigan

Hemingway's Fresh Fruit Cobbler

1 cup flour	1 tablespoon butter
1 cup sugar	1/4 cup cinnamon sugar
1 teaspoon baking soda	1 1/2 cups fresh chopped fruit
1 egg	to include favorite fruits on
2/3 cup milk	hand like pears, pineapple,
2 teaspoons lemon juice	strawberries, blueberries,
1 teaspoon vanilla	raspberries and bananas

Mix flour, sugar, and baking soda together in medium bowl. Mix egg, milk, vanilla, and lemon juice in another bowl; pour into flour mixture. Mix until blended.

Chop fruit into raspberry-size pieces. Grease small glass casserole or 9-inch smooth pie pan with one tablespoon butter; add cinnamon sugar to pan—swirl out excess butter. Add chopped fruit except bananas; cover fruit with batter. Put sliced bananas on top of batter; sprinkle with cinnamon sugar.

Bake in 325° oven 20-25 minutes or until done. Use toothpick to test for doneness in center. Let rest 5 minutes before serving. Makes 4 generous servings.

Note: The fruit can be chopped and mixed ahead of time, though do not mix strawberries, raspberries, or blueberries until the last minute.

Four Seasons Cookbook

Michigan produces about three-fourths of the world's tart cherries. Brought over by European settlers, the cherry trees only have a productive life of about 5 years. Traverse City, one of the state's most popular vacation areas, is known as the "Cherry Capital of the World."

Spicy Cranberry-Pear Crisp

FILLING:

4 medium ripe pears such as Scarlet Bartlets (you can substitute apples)

2¹/₂ cups fresh or frozen cranberries

³/₄ cup brown sugar

¹/₄ cup barley flour (or oat bran)

¹/₄ teaspoon ground allspice*

¹/₄ teaspoon ground cardamom*

2 tablespoons frozen concentrated orange juice

TOPPING:

¹/₄ cup brown sugar

¹/₂ cup oat bran

¹/₂ cup oatmeal

1 tablespoon Canola oil

¹/₄ cup sliced almonds

Preheat oven to 400° and lightly oil (using one of the vegetable cooking sprays) a 12-inch-diameter pie dish. Wash, core and thinly slice the pears. Wash and sort the cranberries. Combine fruit with the rest of the filling ingredients, mixing well, then arrange in the baking dish. Combine the topping ingredients and sprinkle evenly over the fruit. Bake in the middle of the preheated oven for 35-45 minutes or until lightly browned on top and the fruit is bubbly. If the top begins to brown too soon, tent with foil or parchment. Best served slightly warm or at room temperature. Makes 11 servings.

*Buy whole spices and grind in a mortar and pestle just before using for optimum flavor.

Note: Vary the fruit according to what's in season; dried cranberries may be substituted for fresh ones; increase the orange juice to ¹/₃ cup.

Per serving: Cal 186; Prot 2g; Fat 3g; (trace Sat); Carb 39g; Dietary fiber 3g; Chol 0mg; Sod 7mg; Cal 34mg; Iron 1mg. Exchanges: Bread ¹/₂; Fruit 2; Fat ¹/₂ (Not recommended for diabetics).

High Fit - Low Fat

In the brrrrr cold of February, sled-dog racers and their canine teams glide through snowy forests and across frozen lakes on a 240-mile round-trip for the annual UP Sled Dog 200. The frigid route bisects the Upper Peninsula from Marquette south to Escanaba and back.

Bread Pudding with Lemon Sauce

4 cups scalded milk
2¹/₂ cups bread cubes
³/₄ cup sugar
2 tablespoons butter

¹/₄ teaspoon salt
4 eggs, slightly beaten
1 teaspoon vanilla
Raisins as desired

Soak bread in milk for 5 minutes. Add sugar, butter, and salt; pour slowly over beaten eggs. Add raisins (if desired) and vanilla, and mix well. Pour into greased baking dish. Bake in pan of hot water at 350° until firm—about 50 minutes. Serve warm with Lemon Sauce (optional).

LEMON SAUCE:
1 tablespoon cornstarch
¹/₂ cup sugar
¹/₂ teaspoon salt
1 cup boiling water

2 tablespoons butter
1¹/₂ tablespoons lemon juice
A little nutmeg

Mix cornstarch, sugar, and salt; gradually add boiling water and cook over low heat until thick and clear. Add butter, lemon juice, and small amount of nutmeg; blend.

Home Cookin': First Congregational United Church of Christ

Pineapple Bread Pudding

1/4 cup butter or oleo
1 small package instant
   vanilla pudding
1 teaspoon cinnamon
3 eggs
3 cups milk
1 (8-ounce) can crushed
   pineapple (do not drain)

1/2 cup coconut
1/2 cup raisins
1 teaspoon vanilla
8 slices day-old bread (cut
   into cubes

Cream together the butter, pudding, cinnamon; mix until fluffy, then add eggs, one at a time; set aside.

In another bowl, combine milk, undrained pineapple, coconut, raisins, and vanilla. Blend into creamed mixture, fold in bread crumbs. Pour into 2-quart casserole baking dish. Place in large baking pan of hot water and bake. Bake 1 1/4 hours at 325°.

Ferndale Friends Cook Book

Banana Date Pudding

2 cups water
3/4 cup cashew pieces
1 cup pitted dates
1 teaspoon vanilla

1/8 teaspoon salt
2 tablespoons cornstarch
1 1/4 cups thinly sliced
  bananas (2 medium)

Blend first 6 ingredients 1-3 minutes on high speed until creamy. Pour into saucepan and bring to a boil, stirring constantly. Cook until thick. Slightly cool. Add sliced bananas. Chill. May serve hot or cold. Yield: 3 cups.

Country Life: Vegetarian Cookbook

Swedish Rice Pudding

6 eggs, beaten
1/2 cup white sugar
1 cup brown sugar (not
  packed)
Pinch salt
1/2 teaspoon cinnamon
1/4 teaspoon nutmeg
4 1/2 cups mixture whole milk
  and half-and-half (scalded)

2 tablespoons butter, melted
  in hot milk
2 tablespoons vanilla, less if
  desired
2 cups rice, cooked the day
  before
Raisins, optional

Beat eggs; add sugars, salt, cinnamon, and nutmeg. Mix well. Slowly add heated milk and melted butter. Mix. Add vanilla and rice; mix. Add raisins if desired. Put into a buttered large casserole. Sprinkle a little brown sugar and cinnamon over top. Place casserole into a pie pan with hot water. Bake 1 - 1 1/2 hours at 325° or until knife inserted into center comes out clean. Let cool.

Halvorson-Johnson Family Reunion Cookbook

Golf is great in the Great Lakes State. The historic Oakland Hills Country Club in Bloomfield Hills has hosted the game's most prestigious tournament, the U.S Open Championship six times. Great "designer" courses throughout the state drive home Michigan's growing reputation as America's summer golf capital.

Apple Pudding

1 cup white sugar
1/4 cup oleo
1 beaten egg
3 chopped, unpeeled medium
 apples
1 cup plus 1 tablespoon flour

1 teaspoon soda
1/2 teaspoon cinnamon
1/2 teaspoon nutmeg
Pinch salt
1 cup chopped nuts

Cream sugar and oleo together. Add egg and apples. Sift together dry ingredients, then add to creamed mixture. Add nuts. Pour into greased and lightly floured 9x13-inch pan. Bake at 325° for one hour. Serve with hot Rich Sauce or Vanilla Sauce.

RICH SAUCE:

1/2 cup butter
1/2 cup white sugar
1/2 cup brown sugar
1/2 cup evaporated milk

2 tablespoons white Karo
 syrup
1 teaspoon vanilla

Heat butter and sugars in double boiler. When melted, add milk, syrup and vanilla. Stir until hot.

VANILLA SAUCE:

2 tablespoons cornstarch
3/4 cup sugar
2 cups boiling water

Pinch salt
3/4 teaspoon vanilla
2 tablespoons butter

Mix together cornstarch and sugar; add boiling water. Stir well. Boil 5 minutes. Remove from heat. Add salt, vanilla, and butter.

Note: Vanilla sauce is good on Brown Betty, Peach Cobbler, etc.

Halvorson-Johnson Family Reunion Cookbook

Sweet Potato Pudding with a Twist

2^1/$_2$ cups milk
6 cups grated raw sweet
  potatoes
3 eggs
1 cup sugar

2 teaspoons cinnamon
^{1}/$_2$ cup slivered almonds
2 tablespoon butter
^{1}/$_2$ cup bourbon or rum,
  optional

Butter a 2-quart casserole dish. Pour milk into a large mixing bowl. Grate sweet potatoes into milk to prevent darkening. In a medium mixing bowl, beat eggs and sugar until thick. Add cinnamon and almonds. Add egg mixture to sweet potatoes and milk; mix well. Turn into buttered casserole and dot with butter. Bake at 300° for about 1^1/$_2$ hours or until pudding is set. Just before serving, pour bourbon or rum over the top. Yield: 6-8 servings.

Something Special

Pineapple Kugel
(Nonfat)

1 (12-ounce) package
  Yolk-Less noodles
^{1}/$_2$ cup applesauce
1 (8-ounce) carton nonfat sour
  cream or nonfat yogurt
1 (12-ounce) carton nonfat
  cottage chees
1 teaspoon vanilla

8 ounces crushed pineapple
^{1}/$_2$ cup sugar
^{1}/$_2$ cup dried cherries
Cinnamon to taste
3 egg whites
Crushed cornflake crumbs
  with cinnamon (optional
  topping)

Cook and drain noodles; set aside. In a large bowl, mix together everything, except egg whites and crumbs. Beat egg whites and fold into mixture; add cooked noodles. Spray Pam on 9x13-inch pan. Pour in mixture. Add topping if desired. Bake at 350° for 35-45 minutes.

The Fruit of Her Hands

Date Roll

1 small package chopped dates, chopped	1 cup chopped nuts (English walnuts)
1 cup miniature marshmallows	1/2 cup milk or half-and-half
1/3 box Honey Maid Nabisco graham crackers (rolled into crumbs)	1 teaspoon vanilla

Mix all ingredients together well. Form into roll (about 3 inches in diameter). Wrap securely in aluminum foil and refrigerate. Will keep several days. When ready to serve, slice and top with whipped cream or Cool Whip. Serves 8.

Allen Park Garden Club Recipe Book

Plymouth has the Ice Sculpture Spectacular in January, a competition resulting in incredibly beautiful icy scenes and frozen figures. Wielding chisels, chain saws, picks and axes, international teams of ice artists and chefs transform 200 tons of ice into more than 200 shimmering sculptures. After dark the frozen masterpieces sparkle in the glow of hundreds of colored lights.

Frangelico White and Dark Chocolate Mousse

A chocolate lover's dream.

CRUST:

2/3 cup crushed chocolate
  wafer cookies
1/3 cup crushed graham crackers

1/4 cup butter, melted

Preheat oven to 350°. Combine cookies, graham crackers, and butter. Press into a springform pan. Bake for 8 minutes. Cool crust on rack.

BOTTOM LAYER:

1 1/2 cups heavy whipping
  cream, chilled
4 ounces semi-sweet
  chocolate, melted
6 egg yolks

3/4 cup sugar
1/2 cup hazelnut liqueur
  (Frangelico)
2 ounces unsweetened
  chocolate, melted

Whip cream until soft peaks form and set aside. Melt chocolate over double boiler. Beat egg yolks and gradually add sugar until mixture is pale yellow and batter falls in ribbons. Beat in liqueur, then add melted chocolates. Gradually fold in whipped cream, 1/3 at a time. Pour chocolate mousse onto crust and freeze 30 minutes or until set.

TOP LAYER:

1 1/3 cups heavy whipping
  cream, chilled
10 ounces good quality white
  chocolate

3/4 cup heavy whipping
  cream, chilled
3 tablespoons hazelnut
  liqueur (Frangelico)

Whip 1 1/3 cups cream until soft peaks form and set aside. Chop white chocolate into tiny pieces. In a large saucepan, bring 3/4 cup cream to a boil, simmer for 2 minutes. Add white chocolate to cream, blend until smooth. Add liqueur. Gradually fold in whipped cream, 1/3 at a time. Pour white chocolate mousse on top of chocolate mousse layer. Freeze for at least 8 hours. Remove from freezer 10-15 minutes before serving. Separate from edges with warm knife.

CHOCOLATE TOPPING:

2 ounces semi-sweet
  chocolate

1 tablespoon butter

After mousse is set; melt chocolate with butter. Drizzle on top for decoration. Serve immediately. Serves 10-12.

The Bountiful Arbor

Pistachio Pineapple Dessert

Good for St. Patrick's Day.

2 cups shortbread cookie
 crumbs (about 14) or vanilla
 wafer crumbs (about 50)
1/2 cup plus 3 tablespoons
 chopped pistachio nuts or
 pecans
1/4 cup butter or margarine,
 melted
1 (8-ounce) package cream
 cheese, softened
1 (14-ounce) can sweetened
 condensed milk (not
 evaporated milk)

1/4 cup lime juice from
 concentrate
1 (4-serving) package instant
 pistachio pudding and pie
 filling mix
1 (8-ounce) can crushed
 pineapple, undrained
1 cup (1/2 pint) whipping
 cream, whipped

Preheat oven to 350°. Combine cookie crumbs, 3 tablespoons nuts and margarine; press firmly on bottom of 9-inch springform pan or 9x13-inch pan. Bake 8-10 minutes. Cool. Meanwhile, in large bowl, beat cheese until fluffy. Gradually beat in condensed milk, then lime juice and pudding mix until smooth. Stir in 1/2 cup nuts and pineapple. Fold in whipped cream. Pour in pan. Chill 6 hours. Garnish as desired.

Recipes & Remembrances II

Swiss Chocolate Truffle

1 Duncan Hines Brownie Mix
 or 1 chocolate cake mix
3 bananas
2 large instant mousse or
 chocolate pudding mixes,
 prepared

2 (8-ounce) containers Cool
 Whip
Chopped nuts
Cherries

Prepare brownies or cake according to package directions; cool and cut into cubes. In 9x13-inch pan, layer 1/2 of cake or brownie cubes then top with 1/2 of bananas, 1/2 of pudding, and 1/2 of Cool Whip. Sprinkle nuts on top. Repeat layers and top with cherries.

Crystal Clear Cooking

Diabetic Cream Puff Desserts

CRUST:

1 cup water

1 cup flour

1/2 cup margarine (1 stick)

4 eggs

Bring water and margarine to a boil. Remove from heat and add flour, stirring until dough forms a ball. Beat in thoroughly, one egg at a time. Continue beating mixture until smooth and velvety. Spread in a greased 9x13-inch pan. Bake at 400° for 30 minutes. Push down bumps after baking.

FILLING:

2 1/2 cups milk

2 small packages instant
   pudding (sugar-free variety,
   any flavor)

1 (8-ounce) package cream
   cheese, softened

1 (12-ounce) carton lite
   whipped topping

Combine milk and pudding; add softened cream cheese and whip together. Pour over cooled crust. Top with lite whipped topping. Drizzle chocolate (or any flavor of choice) ice cream topping over top of whipped topping, if desired.

Note: Eggbeaters can be used in place of eggs.

Centennial Cookbook

Heavenly Cherry Angel Food Trifle

5 cups angel food cake cubes
1/4 cup cherry liqueur,
  optional
1 cup powdered sugar
1 (3-ounce) package cream
  cheese, softened
1 (8-ounce) package frozen
  non-dairy whipped topping,
  thawed and divided

1/2 cup toasted chopped
  pecans
1 (21-ounce) can cherry filling
  or topping

Place cake cubes in large bowl. Sprinkle with liqueur, if desired; let stand 30 minutes. In medium bowl, combine powdered sugar and cream cheese; beat until blended. Reserve 2 tablespoons whipped topping; fold remaining topping into cheese mixture. Stir topping mixture and pecans into cake cubes; mix well.

Spoon cake mixture into a pretty glass or crystal bowl. Spread cherry filling evenly on top. (Or if desired layer 1/2 cake mixture and cherry filling. Repeat layers.) Cover and refrigerate at least 3 hours. Garnish servings with reserved whipped topping. Yield: 8-10 servings.

Good Food From Michigan

Parking Lot Pear Sorbet

This refreshing sorbet got its name because we picked the pears from trees that grow in our parking lot at the University of Michigan Medical Center's Preventive Cardiology clinic which is located in the Domino's Pizza World Headquarters in Ann Arbor, Michigan.

8 ripe pears, peeled and cored
2 tablespoons fresh lemon
  juice
1/2 cup frozen apple juice
  concentrate, thawed

1 tablespoon crystalized
  ginger, finely chopped
1/2 pint fresh strawberries or
  raspberries (optional garnish)

Place all ingredients in the bowl of a food processor fitted with a steel "S" blade and purée until smooth. Place in an airtight container in the freezer, break up and return to the food processor. Purée until smooth and light. Return to the freezer until ready to serve. Scoop into chilled bowls and serve, garnished with fresh berries in season, if desired. Makes 12 servings. Yields 6 cups.

Nutrient calculations per 1/2 cup serving: Cal 95; Total Fat 0.5g (Sat 0g); Chol 0mg; Carb 24g; Dietary Fiber 2.9g; Prot 1g; Sod 5mg; Cal 19mg; Iron 0.7mg. Exchanges 1 1/2 fruit.

High Fit - Low Fat Vegetarian

French Preserved Raspberries and Liqueur

After preserving, this berry flavored liqueur can be given as a gift or kept to preserve the raspberries for year-long use in desserts, sauces, or as a garnish.

4 cups fresh unblemished
  raspberries
18 ounces good quality brandy
1/2 cup sugar or superfine
  sugar

1/2 cup crème de cassis
  liqueur (French black currant
  liqueur)

Use only select raspberries. Rinse carefully and spoon into a sterilized 1-liter glass jar, preferably with a rubber ring and spring lid. In a ceramic bowl, mix sugar and brandy until dissolved. Pour over berries. Add 1/2 cup liqueur. Cover tightly. Refrigerate 2-3 weeks. To use or give liqueur as a gift, carefully strain into small glass bottles and seal. Store remaining berries in refrigerator, covered with liqueur. Makes 1 liter.

Cranbrook Reflections

Puzzled Apples

A fun way to eat a favorite fruit.

24 apples	¹/₈ cup quick cooking oats
1¹/₂ cups peanut butter	¹/₈ cup wheat germ
¹/₄ cup raisins	¹/₄ cup lemon juice

Core each apple. In a large bowl, combine the remaining ingredients. Fill each cored apple with this mixture. Wrap each filled apple tightly in plastic wrap or foil and refrigerate one hour. Unwrap and slice each apple crosswise into ¹/₂-inch slices. Brush each slice lightly with lemon juice. Reconstruct each apple, rewrap and refrigerate. Allow the children to unwrap and take apart the apples themselves.

Nutrition per serving: Cal 241; Fat 9g; Prot 5g; Carb 36g; Chol 0mg; Fiber 2g; Vit A 107IU; Sod 3mg; Iron 1mg; Vit C 11mg.

Smart Snacks

Index

The Gerald R. Ford Museum in Grand Rapids includes a full-scale reproduction of the Oval Office decorated as it was during Ford's presidency.

INDEX

INDEX

INDEX

INDEX

Catalog
of
Contributing
Cookbooks

Grand Traverse Light warned passing schooners and steamers of the rocky shore at Grand Traverse Bay's west side. The restored lighthouse is now a museum.

CATALOG
of
CONTRIBUTING COOKBOOKS

All recipes in this book have been selected from the Michigan cookbooks shown on the following pages. Individuals who wish to obtain a copy of any particular book may do so by sending a check or money order to the address listed. Prices are subject to change. Please note the postage and handling charges that are required. State residents add tax only when requested. Retailers are invited to call or write to same address for discount information. Quail Ridge Press is proud to preserve America's food heritage by keeping many of their recipes in print.

ALLEN PARK GARDEN CLUB RECIPE BOOK
c/o Ann Sansalone
4050 Wall
Allen Park, MI 48101-3073   313-928-9506

Our 350 recipes come from members, including 2 recipe contest winners, 2 home economic teachers, and a food and kitchen equipment specialist. We are nonprofit, and garden for community facilities. We also sponsor a tree distribution program and a children's garden club. We are better cooks than gardeners—and some of us are very good gardeners!

$ 5.00 Retail price
$ 2.00 Postage and handling
Make check payable to Allen Park Garden Club

THE BELL TOWER COOKBOOK
Catholic Community of St. Andrew Church
Rochester, MI

Nearly 500 tried and true recipes from parishioners and popular restaurants. Besides mealtime recipes, there is a special section on Culinary Gifts and edible wildflowers/plants. Proceeds go to charitable agencies who help feed those in crisis. Throughout the ages people have made mealtime an art, enhanced only by good conversation and blessed by God. Currently out of print.

BLISSFIELD PRESCHOOL COOKBOOK

Blissfield Preschool Co-op
P. O. Box 2
Blissfield, MI 49228

The Blissfield Preschool Cookbook contains about 165 recipes and has 72 pages. The recipes are a collection of family favorites from past and present members. The parents' contributions to the book were part of their responsibility as co-op members of our preschool. Everyone's involvement is what makes our school successful.

$ 5.00 Retail price
$ 2.50 Postage and handling
Make check payable to Blissfield Preschool

THE BOUNTIFUL ARBOR

The Junior League of Ann Arbor
P. O. Box 7704
Ann Arbor, MI 48107-7704   734-996-8818

The Junior League of Ann Arbor presents this choice collection of unique and delicious recipes inspired by the diversity and charisma of Ann Arbor, Michigan. From savory appetizers to scrumptious desserts, with fresh ideas for every meal in between, *The Bountiful Arbor* truly offers something for everyone.

$19.95 Retail price
$ 1.20 Tax for Michigan residents
$ 2.50 Postage and handling
Make check payable to The Junior League of Ann Arbor
ISBN 0-9641313-07

BRINGING GRAND TASTES TO GRAND TRAVERSE

Newcomers Club of Grand Traverse
c/o Nancy E. Byron
8827 Dawn Circle
Traverse City, MI 49686   231-922-5048

A blending of 480 favorite recipes from all over the country to share with new friends, our book incorporates landmarks and trivia common to the Grand Traverse area, plus cherry recipes from the cherry-growing capital of the world, and home of the National Cherry Festival. Three-ring hardcover binder.

$15.00 Retail price
$ .90 Tax for Michigan residents
$ 3.50 Postage and handling
Make check payable to Newcomers Club of Grand Traverse

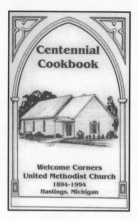

CENTENNIAL COOKBOOK

Welcome Corners United Methodist Church
c/o Darlene Pickard
3680 Fighter Road
Hastings, MI   49058   616-945-5974

Our book is dedicated to all cooks. In our homes today, as always, life is centered around the kitchen. It is with this in mind that we have compiled these recipes. Some treasured family keepsakes that have been passed down for generations, some new, but all reflect the love of good cooking and family traditions. Ringbound, 235 pages, over 600 recipes.

$12.00 Retail price
$ 1.50 Postage and handling
Make check payable to Welcome Corners United Methodist Church

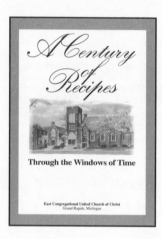

A CENTURY OF RECIPES
THROUGH THE WINDOWS OF TIME

East Congregational United Church of Christ
1005 Giddings SE
Grand Rapids, MI   49506   616-245-0578

A Century of Recipes Through the Windows of Time contains 238 pages of recipes from members and friends of East Church. It was compiled in recognition of the church's 100-year celebration of service. Along with the recipes, the book contains a brief history of the church and its ministers, and highlights the church's beautiful Chartres (France) Glass Windows.

$ 8.00 Retail price
$ .60 Tax for Michigan residents
$ 3.00 Postage and handling
Make check payable to East Congregational United Church of Christ

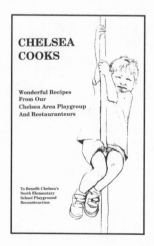

CHELSEA COOKS

Chelsea Area Playgroup
13720 Rustic Drive
Gregory, MI   48137   734-475-8814

Our Chelsea Area Playgroup began to gather in March, 1991, with lunch buffets, picnics at the beach, and Christmas parties. This cookbook includes the most requested recipes from our gatherings and meals delivered to families of new babies, tried-and-true family favorites, as well as recipes from our local restaurants.

$ 7.00 Retail price
$ 2.00 Postage and handling
Make check payable to Chelsea Cooks

COME AND DINE

St. Paul's United Methodist Church
Attn: Lynn Hodgkin
P. O. Box 80307
Rochester, MI 48308-0307   248-656-5168

Cooking has never been easier than with this "heavenly" collection of 835 tried-and-true favorites. This 1995 cookbook was compiled by the United Methodist Women of St. Paul's Church (founded in Rochester in 1858) with the proceeds supporting mission projects. Included with the recipes are various photographs of stained glass windows from the Church.

$12.00 Retail price
$ 3.00 Postage and handling
Make check payable to St. Paul's United Methodist Women

COOK BOOK: THE BEST OF MICHIGAN

June Harding
Ferndale, MI

Sometimes the best things come in small packages. This mini-cookbook has 63 recipes in 57 pages, but they are all treasured Michigan favorite recipes. The book includes a brief history of Michigan and six Michigan poems. Currently out of print.

COOKIES AND BARS

Dorothy Zehnder/Bavarian Inn Restaurant
1055 South Main Street
Frankenmuth, MI 48734   517-652-6155

Dorothy Zehnder, at 74 years of age and married 53 years, works six days a week as Kitchen Manager of Bavarian Inn Restaurant in Frankenmuth. She truly loves every minute she spends in the kitchen. Dorothy and her daughters worked together to produce this cookbook. Roxie, a dietitian, tested the recipes gathered by her sister, Judith, from Dorothy's vast supply. 107 pages. 70 recipes.

$ 6.95 Retail price
$ .41 Tax for Michigan residents
$ 2.50 Postage and handling
Make check payable to Promotions Plus, Inc.

COUNTRY COOKBOOK

Marilla Historical Society
20281 Bigge Road
Copemish, MI 49625   231-362-3745

The Marilla *Country Cookbook* has 232 pages and includes over 700 recipes. Many of the recipes date back to the early 1900's when the German Brethren people settled this community. Good food was a part of every celebration and Marilla was noted for fat women and good cooks! This area is known for good fruit—strawberries and cherries are the best!

$12.00 Retail price
$ 2.00 Postage and handling
Make check payable to Marilla Historical Society

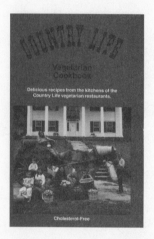

COUNTRY LIFE VEGETARIAN COOKBOOK

Edited by Diana Fleming
Family Health Publications
Hope, MI

Delicious recipes from the kitchens of the Country Life vegetarian restaurants worldwide. Recipes are cholesterol free and vegan. ". . . If anyone can put a dent in the 'Golden Arches,' it's going to be the friendly folks at Country Life."—Whole Life Times Report. Currently out of print.

CRANBROOK REFLECTIONS: A CULINARY COLLECTION

Cranbrook House and Gardens Auxiliary
P. O. Box 801
Bloomfield Hills, MI 48303-0801   248-645-3149

Cranbrook Reflections has 205 pages which includes 256 tested recipes featuring Michigan produce. There are contributions by notable metropolitan Detroit area restaurant chefs, as well as by members of the Cranbrook House and Gardens Auxiliary.

$20.00 Retail price, includes tax
$ 3.50 Postage and handling
Make check payable to Cranbrook Reflections
ISBN 0-9628714-0-0

CRYSTAL CLEAR COOKING

by Judy Brouwer
3600 Crystal Drive   Fax 231-882-5658
Beulah, MI   49617   231-882-5298 or 231-866-7788

Crystal Clear Cooking is an encyclopedia of over 1,000 simple, clear, easy-to-read and easy-to-prepare favorite recipes with "common" household ingredients with that wonderful homemade taste from family, friends, and great cooks. There are 22 categories to choose from such as appetizers, desserts, meats, salads, soups, sugarless foods and much more.

$19.95 Retail price
$ 1.20 Tax for Michigan residents
$ 3.25 Postage and handling
Make check payable to Judy Brouwer

DAD'S COOK BOOK

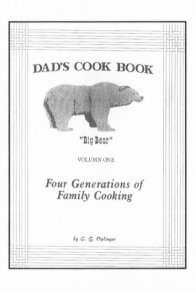

by C. G. Oplinger
Sliverwood, MI   48760

Four generations of family cooking. Most recipes have been revised to lower sodium and fat content, plus adding a considerable amount of vegetables. Easy to read, 14-point type, easy to follow. Contents include main dishes, soups, baking, salads, poultry, casserole, canning, sportsman section, meat cutting, wine charts, herbs, spices, and aromatic seeds. Currently out of print.

DAWN TO DUSK

Holland Junior Welfare League
P. O. Box 1633
Holland, MI   49422

As its name suggests, this cookbook's eight chapters will take you through the day starting with "Breakfast in Bed" and concluding with "Midnight Snacks." The over 250 triple-tested recipes are elegant, yet easy. Additionally you'll find breathtaking photos, interesting history, wine selection tips and traditional Dutch recipes. Hard bound, 238 pages. All proceeds benefit Holland area children.

$19.95 Retail price
$ 1.20 Tax for Michigan residents
$ 2.50 Postage and handling
Make check payable to Holland Junior Welfare League
ISBN 0-9612710-0-0

THE DEXTER CIDER MILL
APPLE COOKBOOK

Katherine Merkel Koziski
P. O. Box 217
Chelsea, MI 48118   313-475-1126 or 426-8531

Endorsed by the Michigan Apple Committee, apple lovers around the world will enjoy this cookbook. 44 taste-tempting apple recipes, stunning photographs of all recipes and the cider-making process, and a history of the Mill. Interesting to read, satisfying to use, this beautiful book won the Mid-America Publisher's Association '96 Book Award.

$16.95 Retail price
$ 3.00 Postage and handling
Make check payable to Dexter Cider Mill, Inc.
ISBN 0-87197-427-4

FERNDALE FRIENDS COOK BOOK

June Harding
Ferndale, MI

Ferndale friends contributed their favorite recipes to this collection. Michigan has a bumper crop of apples, and we love to bake apple cakes. We have many fine Polish and Italian cooks who pass their favorites on to each generation. 350 recipes in 167 pages. Currently out of print.

FISH & GAME MENU COOKBOOK:
MEAL PLANNING FOR SPORTSMEN

by Kay L. Richey
P. O. Box 192
Grawn, MI 49637   FAX 231-263-7898

This cookbook is designed for those people who fish and hunt but want a quick and easy meal with a minimum of kitchen time. Spiral bound and contains 140 recipes which will produce the finest table fare from fish and game found on the North American continent. Enjoy the finest eating nature can provide.

$10.00 Retail price
$ .60 Tax for Michigan residents
$ 3.00 Postage and handling
Make check payable to S.O.E., Inc.

FOUR SEASONS COOKBOOK

by Bea Smith
Avery Color Studios
511 D. Avenue
Gwinn, MI 49841
800-722-9925

Bea Smith of Boyne City has collaborated with Avery Color Studios to produce an anthology of her favorite seasonal recipes. A contemporary collector's cookbook with 144 pages of down-home, tasty, seasonal recipes to delight the work-a-day cook and satisfy the most discerning palate. 196 recipes.

$12.95 Retail price
$ .72 Tax for Michigan residents
$ 4.50 Postage and handling
Make check payable to Avery Color Studios
ISBN 0-932212-79-4

FROM OUR HOME TO YOURS

United Home Health Services, Inc.
Canton, MI

From Our Home To Yours features over 350 recipes from over 200 contributors. This "not necessarily low-fat" cookbook has a laminated cover. Recipes are presented in large print and one to a page. Dietitian tips are included. Proceeds go to Patient Support Fund. Currently out of print.

FROM OUR KITCHENS WITH LOVE

St. Mark Orthodox Church
400 West Hamlin Road
Rochester Hills, MI 48307   734-656-1630

From the simple to the unique, there's something for everyone's taste in our 186-page cookbook, with 435 family, traditional, and ethnic favorite recipes.

$10.00 Retail price
$ 2.00 Postage and handling
Make check payable to St. Mark Orthodox Church

THE FRUIT OF HER HANDS

Temple Israel Sisterhood
Attn: Gift Shop
5725 Walnut Lake Road
West Bloomfield, MI 48323   248-661-5700

The Fruit of Her Hands offers recipes from the families and
friends of Temple Israel Sisterhood. Some are traditional;
others have been updated to be more "heart-smart." It is
approximately 230 pages, and is a loose-leaf style reference
book of Jewish holidays, festivals, ceremonials, benedictions,
recipes and menus.

$20.00 Retail price
$ 5.00 Postage and handling
Make check payable to Temple Israel Sisterhood

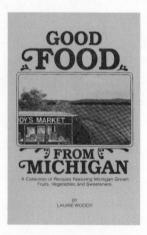

GOOD FOOD FROM MICHIGAN

by Laurie Woody
5706 Wentworth
Johnston, IA 50131   515-278-8792

The book features 24 different fruits, vegetables and sweeten-
ers grown commercially in Michigan. Find out how to pick
the best peaches, how to store cherries at home, and how to
ripen pears. Each chapter in the book has hints on selecting
and storing the food featured in that chapter, as well as recipes
using that food.

$12.95 Retail price
$ 3.50 Postage and handling
Make check payable to Laurie Woody

GREAT LAKES COOKERY

by Bea Smith
Avery Color Studios
511 D. Avenue
Gwinn, MI 49841   800-722-9925

A great cook and writer, Bea believes in preserving the best of
the past to insure a better life for the future. A real treasure, set
up in a four-season format, this book offers many recipes for
each season. 170 pages. 179 recipes with illustrations and
helpful hints.

$13.95 Retail price
$ .78 Tax for Michigan residents
$ 4.50 Postage and handling
Make check payable to Avery Color Studios
ISBN 0-932212-68-9

HALVORSON-JOHNSON FAMILY REUNION COOKBOOK

c/o Betty Hilliard
10165 Horseshoe Creek Road
Kaleva, MI 49645

Favorite family recipes are shared by descendents of the original family reunion first held in 1930. Rich in Scandinavian heritage, these dishes range from classic Swedish meatballs, rice pudding and desserts to modern potluck favorites including tamale pie and Texas sheet cake. Includes a brief family hisotry and anecdotes.

$10.00 Retail price, includes postage
Make check payable to Halvorson-Johnson Family Reunion

HEAVENLY HELPINGS

Friends of Hospice
1480 North M-52
Owosso, MI 48867   517-725-2299

Heavenly Helpings is a compliation of favorite family recipes from Doctors, Nurses, Home Health Aides, Clergy, Social Workers and Volunteers. These dedicated people are among the best cooks in Shiawassee County. The delicious recipes in this edition are uncomplicated and have simple ingredients. *Heavenly Helpings* is perfect for any gift-giving occasion.

$6.95   Retail price, includes postage
Make check payable to Friends of Hospice

HERBAL FAVORITES

Gennessee County Herb Society
c/o Ulrika Vanover
12219 Jennings Road
Linden, MI 48451   810-629-8763

Compiled by members of the Genessee County Herb Society using the herbs that are grown in their home gardens. It includes a section on Herb seasonings, condiments, and making herbal household products, and features recipes from Bible Soup to Scripture Cake. This cokbook answers the most asked question about herbs. . . "Now that they're growing, what do I do with them!"

$ 8.00 Retail price
$ .40 Tax for Michigan residents
$ 4.00 Postage and handling
Make check payable to Genessee County Herb Society

HIGH FIT - LOW FAT

The University of Michigan Medical Center
24 Frank Lloyd Wright Drive
Ann Arbor, MI 48106   734-998-7645

Incorporates delicious food with healthy eating, yet the' textures, flavors, and presentation of the food are exquisite. Each recipe includes nutritional calculations and diabetic exchanges. The text offers invaluable information to the cardiac rehabilitation patient, the athlete, and the general public. So, if you think healthy recipes are boring—this book will change your mind.

$14.95 Retail price
$ .90 Tax for Michigan residents
$ 4.00 Postage and handling ($1.00 each additional)
Make check payable to The University of Michigan
ISBN 0-87197-260-3

HIGH FIT - LOW FAT VEGETARIAN

The University of Michigan Medical Center
24 Frank Lloyd Wright Drive
Ann Arbor, MI 48106   734-998-7645

Introducing vegetarian meals into your daily plan is a healthy alternative, consistent with national guidelines to reduce the risk of obesity, cancer and heart disease. Easy-to-follow recipes feature fresh, whole ingredients. Nutrient calculations, diabetic exchanges and menues are included. This is a manual for integrating luscious, wholesome meals into busy life-styles.

$14.95 Retail price
$ .90 Tax for Michigan residents
$ 4.00 Postage and handling ($1.00 each additional)
Make check payable to The University of Michigan
ISBN 0-9649656-1-5

HISTORICALLY DELICIOUS

Tri-Cities Historical Society
1 North Harbor
Grand Haven, MI 49417   616-842-0700

The *Historically Delicious* cookbook and almanac was produced by the Tri-Cities Historical Society to raise funds for the museum's many preservation and education activities. The 200-page book contains recipes from local families—many handed down through generations with stories attached—and some more recent innovations.

$ 5.00 Retail price
$ 3.00 Postage and handling
Make check payable to Tri-Cities Museum

HOLLYHOCKS & RADISHES

by Bonnie Stewart Mickelson
Pickle Point Publishing
P. O. Box 4107
Bellevue, WA 98009   800-462-6105

A remarkably touching storybook-cookbook about a delightful farm woman and her celebrated garden stand in Michigan's beautiful Upper Peninsula. Jam-packed with top-notch recipes, it has won four national awards and is truly a classic. 280 recipes; 320 pages. It's a wonderful gift.

$19.95 Retail price (softcover) $26.95 (hardcover)
$ 1.20 Tax for Michigan residents $ 1.70 Tax
$ 3.50 Postage and handling
Make check payable to Pickle Point, Inc.
ISBN 0-9622412-0-2 (softcover)   0-9622412-1-0 (hardcover)

HOME COOKIN'

Almont Elementary PTA
Almont, MI

Home Cookin': Treasured Recipes is a cookbook of 80 pages consisting of 227 recipes. Each delicious, home-tested recipe was submitted by parents, teachers and students of Almont Elementary School. Currently out of print.

HOME COOKIN'

First Congregational United Church of Christ
104 West Locust Street
Morenci, MI 49256   517-458-6142

In a small town of 2,100 people and six churches, our UCC women have a superlative culinary reputation. Sometimes the best things come in small packages; though our book is small (60+ pages of recipes), we think it's the best!

$ 5.00 Retail price
$ 2.00 Postage and handling
Make check payable to Women's Covenant of FCUCC

The famous Great Lakes cookbook
prepared by American Steamship Company

HOW TO MAKE A STEAMSHIP FLOAT AND OTHER GREAT LAKES RECIPES

Harbor House Publishers
221 Water Street
Boyne City, MI 49712   231-582-2814

From the chefs and the staff of one of the largest Great Lakes fleets, here are more than 200 of the best, never-before-published recipes. An authentic bit of Great Lakes memorabilia, the book contains the favorite recipes of the Great Lakes maritime industry as prepared by and for American Steamship Company. Spiral bound, 135 pages, softcover.

$10.95 Retail price / Visa/MC accepted
$ 2.50 Postage and handling
Make check payable to Harbor House Publishers, Inc.
ISBN 0-937360-05-8

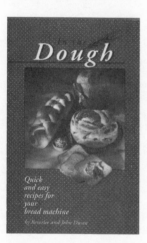

Quick
and easy
recipes for
your
bread machine

by Beverlee and John Dusso

IN THE DOUGH

The J. B. Dough Company
P. O. Box 557
St. Joseph, MI 49085   800-528-6222

Simple, yet creative ways to bake exceptional bread using J. B. Dough's gourmet premixes, an automatic bread maker, and a few additional ingredients. Recipes for everyting from Country Apple Coffee Cake to Rosemary-Garlic Focaccia. About the only thing we've left out of this book is the time and effort that's usually required to make bread this good.

$12.95 Retail price
$ .77 Tax for Michigan residents
$ 2.95 Postage and handling
Make check payable to The J. B. Dough Co.

THE JUNIOR LEAGUE OF GRAND RAPIDS COOKBOOK I

25 Sheldon SE Suite 240
Grand Rapids, MI 49503   616-451-0452

The Grand Rapids Junior League Cookbook I is 430 pages of recipes, unique party ideas, and "wardrobe" ideas. There is no need for entertaining to be expensive. Learn how to get everything together from the theme, to the recipes, to enjoying your guests. Over 800 recipes included.

$15.95 Retail price
$ .64 Tax for Michigan residents
$ 2.00 Postage and handling
Make check payable to Junior League of Grand Rapids

Tracy & Phyllis Winters

JUST INN TIME FOR BREAKFAST

Tracy and Phyllis Winters
P. O. Box 501
Greensburg, IN   47240   800-457-3230

Continuing the tradition of providing exceptional hospitality, Michigan B & B Innkeepers share their recips in this 128-page book. Chock-full of 93 tantalizing recipes from Bubble Bread Coffee Cake to Potato/Sausage Casserole, Italian Crab Meat Dip to Pumpkin Cheesecake Bars, everything from breakfast favorites to snack-time treats.

$10.95 Retail price
$ 2.00 Postage and handling
Make check payable to Winters Publishing
ISBN 0-9625329-4-0

"LIFE TASTES BETTER THAN STEAK" COOKBOOK

by Gerry Krag, R.D.
Avery Color Studios
511 D. Avenue
Gwinn, MI   49841   800-722-9925

A collection of 185 heart-healthy reversal recipes developed by patients of a successful heart disease reversal program who have decided that "Life Tastes Better Than Steak." These delicious dishes prove that food can taste great while still being extrememly low-fat and vegetarian. Nutrional information supplied with each recipe.

$17.95 Retail price
$ 1.08 Tax for Michigan residents
$ 4.50 Postage and handling
Make check payable to Avery Color Studios
ISBN 0-932212-90-5

MICHIGAN GOURMET COOKBOOK

Michigan Gourmet Television
Lansing, MI

The Michigan Gourmet Cookbook contains more than 100 recipes from the award-winning Michigan PBS television series. Currently out of print.

MRS. BOONE'S WILD GAME COOKBOOK

Momentum Books
1174 E. Big Beaver Road
Troy, MI 48083   248-689-0936

Mrs. Boone shares her favorite recipes for every type of game—venison, waterfowl, small game and fish. The tried-and-true techniques help both the novice and the experienced cook to capture the special flavors of perfectly prepared game.

$12.95 Retail price
$ .78 Tax for Michigan residents
$ 3.95 Postage and handling
Make check payable to Momentum Books
ISBN 1-879094-08-8

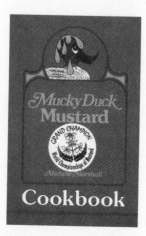

MUCKY DUCK MUSTARD COOKBOOK

by Michele Marshall
Mucky Duck Mustard Co.
P. O. Box 8338
Bloomfield Hills, MI 48302   248-681-8200

Award-winning Mucky Duck (1996 Grand Champion, International Mustard Celebration, Napa Valley, California) is an English pub-style gourmet mustard. Mucky Duck adds piquancy and interest to almost all foods. It's great versatility is demonstrated in this original and unusual softcover cookbook of approximately 175 recipes and 125 pages.

$12.95 Retail price
$ .78 Tax for Michigan residents
$ 1.22 Postage and handling
Make check payable to Mucky Duck Mustard Co.
ISBN 0-87197-317-0

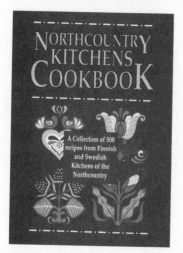

NORTHCOUNTRY KITCHENS COOKBOOK

Avery Color Studios
511 D. Avenue
Gwinn, MI 49841   800-722-9925

A collection of more than 500 recipes from the Northcountry's finest cooks. Many unusual Finnish and Swedish recipes featuring breads and sweet rolls, desserts, salads and dressings, casseroles and main dishes, soups and vegetables, sandwiches, candies and wild game. Every homemaker will enjoy using this attractive guide to delicious taste-tempting foods. 176 pages. 500 recipes.

$13.95 Retail price
$ .84 Tax for Michigan residents
$ 4.50 Postage and handling
Make check payable to Avery Color Studios
ISBN 0-932212-21-2

OF THESE YE MAY FREELY EAT

by JoAnn Rachor
Family Health Publications
Hope, MI

"JoAnn has become a real expert in developing imaginative and delicious recipes . . . I highly recommend [it] for those who really care about their health and vitality."—Dr. Mary Ruth Swope. 5½ x 8½, paperback, 90 pages, over 250 recipes—cholesterol free, high fiber, low fat, economical, easy to prepare, vegan recipes. Currently out of print.

OPAA! GREEK COOKING DETROIT STYLE

by George Gekas
Bonus Books
160 E. Illinois Street
Chicago, IL 60611   312-467-0580

In just about every major city in the US, the neighborhood that's called Greektown means great food, good drink, and fun. In this easy-to-use cookbook, you'll find recipes for delicious, authentic Greek dishes from baklava to bread salad, from saganaki to stuffed grape leaves. 173 pages; lay-flat binding.

$14.95 Retail price
$ 4.00 Postage and handling
Make check payable to Bonus Books
ISBN 0-929387-93-7

OUR BEST HOME COOKING

Keep Michigan Beautiful, Inc.
P. O. Box 664
Farmington, MI 48332   248-477-6647

Michigan's abundance of food and changing seasons provide spice and variety to "our best home cooking," a 172-page collection whose proceeds benefit "Keep Michigan Beautiful, Inc." Three hundred recipes reflect cooking from farms and cities to the shores of the Great Lakes. It has a laminated cover and is spiral bound.

$ 5.00 Retail price (3 for $10.00)
$ 1.50 Postage and handling ($2.00 for 2 or 3 books)
Make check payable to Keep Michigan Beautiful, Inc.

PLEASURES FROM THE GOOD EARTH

Heritage Circle of RLDS Church
c/o Gloria Bigelow
1377 West Hyde Road
St. John, MI 48879   517-224-1736

Much more than a cookbook was harvested during the making of this book. This 148-page book with over 350 recipes is a reflection of our history and our heritage. From potluck favorites to sipping lemonade in the shade, there's a pleasure for every pallet.

$ 8.00 Retail price
$ 3.00 Postage and handling
Make check payable to RLDS Church, Heritage Circle

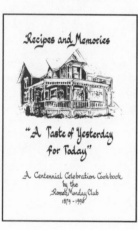

RECIPES AND MEMORIES
A TASTE OF YESTERDAY FOR TODAY

Romeo Monday Club
P. O. Box 32
Romeo, MI 48065   810-752-5263

These old family recipes are more than just yummy—they are a link between generations. This beautiful, hardcover book contains 327 recipes both old and new, plus lovely illustrations of historic homes within the Village of Romeo. It will hold special appeal for sentimental cooks with an affinity for that which is deliciously old-fashioned. 156 pages, ringbound, illustrated.

$12.00 Retail price
$ 4.00 Postage and handling
Make check payable to Romeo Monday Club

RECIPES AND REMEMBRANCES II

Rockwood Area Historical Society
P. O. Box 68
Rockwood, MI 48173   734-379-3521

There are 450 recipes on 158 pages in our hard cover book, *Recipes and Remembrances II.* The Heritage section includes many old recipes that have been handed down from Mothers and Grandmothers. It also contains many health-conscience, ethnic and wild game recipes. We wanted this book to be not only useful, but fun to read.

$ 8.00 Retail price
$ 2.00 Postage and handling
Make check payable to Rockwood Area Historical Society

RENAISSANCE CUISINE

Fontbonne Auxiliary of St. John Hospital & Medical Center
22101 Moross Road
Detroit, MI 48236   313-343-7586

The *Renaissance Cuisine* cookbook, 391 pages in length, is a representation of our Fontbonne Auxiliary members' favorite recipes. The Fontbonne Auxiliary represents over one thousand members, the majority of whom are from the wealthier suburbs of the metropolitan Detroit area. This is our fourth printing of this book, as demand for it continues.

$12.95 Retail price
$ .78 Tax for Michigan residents
$ 3.00 Postage and handling
Make check payable to Fontbonne Auxiliary
ISBN 0-9069656

SEASONED COOKS II

Isabella County Commission on Aging
3480 S. Isabella Road   Fax 517-773-0514
Mt. Pleasant, MI 48858   517-772-0748

Seasoned Cooks II brings together the efforts of both young and old alike. Our older adult citizens furnished the recipes, and children from area schools provided the art work for our category pages. All proceeds are used for the services and programs made available through the Isabella County Commission on Aging. 320 pages; over 500 excellent recipes.

$ 3.00 Retail price
$ 2.00 Postage and handling
Make check payable to Isabella County Commission on Aging

SHARING OUR BEST VOLUME II

Harrietta Area Civic Club
Harrietta, MI

Our comb-bound book contains 300 pages, 600 recipes, witty sayings, helpful hints, and includes recipes from our small group in the "peaceful little village" in the "valley of the beautiful," as well as from government figures and area residents. Currently out of print.

THE SIMPLY GREAT II COOKBOOK

Momentum Books
1174 E. Big Beaver Road
Troy, MI 48083   248-689-0936

Chefs and staff of the great Chuck Muer restaurants have compiled an entirely new collection of simply great recipes that faithful diners have enjoyed for years. Each recipe is new and different and has been carefully reviewed and scaled down to portions appropriate for the home cook. 165 pages, 92 recipes.

$19.95 Retail price
$ 1.20 Tax for Michigan residents
$ 3.50 Postage and handling
Make check payable to Momentum Books, Ltd.
ISBN 1-879094-38-X

SIMPLY SENSATIONAL

Our Lady Queen of Apostles Parish
Hamtramck, MI

Simply Sensational is a wonderful collection of 550 treasured recipes. Included in this 230-page, hard-cover, comb-bound edition are many excellent Polish recipes—culinary delights sure to become favorites for many. Queen of Apostles Parish is located in Hamtramck, a charming ethnic city, described as "A Touch of Europe in America." Currently out of print.

SMART SNACKS

By Betsy Rhein and Sandy Drummond
TBM Publications
977 Butternut Drive Suite 212
Holland, MI 49424   616-786-9515

Smart Snacks is a must for parents who face the challenge of preparing wholesome snacks for groups of children. Each recipe is uniquely tailored to serve twenty-four hungry snackers. This 121-page book has been reviewed by dietitians and contains over 140 kid-pleasing recipes. Each recipe includes a nutritional analysis.

$ 9.95 Retail price
$ .55 Tax for Michigan residents
$ 1.50 Postage and handling
Make check payable to TBM Publications.
ISBN 0-9647229-0-1

SOME ENCHANTED EATING
Friends of the Symphony Publications
P. O. Box 1603
Muskegon, MI 49443   231-726-3231

Some Enchanted Eating is a collection of recipes from Friends of the West Shore Symphony. Over 400 kitchen-tested recipes using fresh wholesome ingredients. Elegant art and illustrations throughout. Readable, sensible instructions embellished with helpful hints. Laminated hard cover, specially designed to lie flat when opened.

$23.95 Retail price
$ 1.44 Tax for Michigan residents
$ 3.50 Postage and handling
Make check payable to Friends of the Symphony Publications
ISBN 0-9617142-0-4

SOMETHING SPECIAL
Sharon Zubosky Breyer
4524 Brunson Place
Traverse City, MI   49684   231-929-9751

Simple but elegant—those were the guidelines for the 544 recipes in this beautiful book. Most selections can be prepared partially or completely in advance using easily obtainable ingredients. With the brief, easy-to-follow directions, even novice cooks can amaze their family and friends with their culinary accomplishments.

$14.00 Retail price
$ 2.50 Postage and handling
Make check payable to O.P.S. Enterprises

TASTEFUL ART
Working Women Artists
BH/WWA Cook
3422 Ridgefield Road
Lansing, MI 48906   517-321-2917

Here's an eclectic collection ranging from traditional to exotic. Many dishes are original creations of the artists in our organization. The 100 pages and 89 recipes are dotted with illustrations done by members. Many recipes have personal comments, making this a friendly gift-type book from the heart. Note: Cover image varies.

$14.95 Retail price
$ 1.50 Postage and handling
Make check payable to Working Women Artists

TRENDFULLY COOKIN'

Trendway Corporation
Holland, MI

A collection of 250 favorite recipes gathered from the many people of Trendway. This book holds more than marvelous recipes, it represents the spirit of the company, a demonstration of the camaraderie and creativity that we bring to our work. For those who helped produce the 142-page book, it is proof of our perseverance and commitment to quality. Currently out of print.

WHAT'S COOKIN

by Jeanne E. Briggs
7339 Orlin Court Northeast
Rockford, MI 49341   231-874-7816 ro 874-6730

I have been writing a food column for the Rockford Squire Newspaper for many years. My readers requested a collection of my favorite recipes in book form, my oldest son Jason kept me on task to complete it. Cooking for my husband and 3 sons has been a wonderful challenge and brought me a great deal of satisfaction and the desire to share with others what I love—good food.

$10.00 Retail price
$ 2.00 Postage and handling
Make check payable to Jeanne E. Briggs

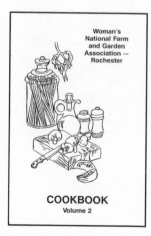

WOMAN'S NATIONAL FARM AND GARDEN ASSOCIATION ROCHESTER COOKBOOK VOLUME II

c/o Shirley Schneider
Troy, MI 48098   248-879-2218

Our members have shared and enjoyed the over 500 recipes in this 205-page book. It is easy to read and fun to prepare the many appetizers, beverages, salads, soups, meats, fish, fowl and all manner of desserts. Includes a handy herb and spice guide, pages for notes, kitchen hints, and alphabetically listed foods with their caloric count. *Volume I* is also available.

$ 9.00 Retail price
$ .54 Tax for Michigan residents
$ 1.75 Postage and handling
Make check payable to Rochester Branch WNF&G Association

Preserving America's Food Heritage

Best of the Best State Cookbook Series

Best of the Best from **ALABAMA** 288 pages, $16.95	Best of the Best from **INDIANA** 288 pages, $16.95	Best of the Best from **MISSOURI** 304 pages, $16.95	Best of the Best from **SO. CAROLINA** 288 pages, $16.95
Best of the Best from **ARIZONA** 288 pages, $16.95	Best of the Best from **IOWA** 288 pages, $16.95	Best of the Best from **NEW ENGLAND** 368 pages, $16.95	Best of the Best from **TENNESSEE** 288 pages, $16.95
Best of the Best from **ARKANSAS** 288 pages, $16.95	Best of the Best from **KENTUCKY** 288 pages, $16.95	Best of the Best from **NEW MEXICO** 288 pages, $16.95	Best of the Best from **TEXAS** 352 pages, $16.95
Best of the Best from **CALIFORNIA** 384 pages, $16.95	Best of the Best from **LOUISIANA** 288 pages, $16.95	Best of the Best from **NEW YORK** 288 pages, $16.95	Best of the Best from **TEXAS II** 352 pages, $16.95
Best of the Best from **COLORADO** 288 pages, $16.95	Best of the Best from **LOUISIANA II** 288 pages, $16.95	Best of the Best from **NO. CAROLINA** 288 pages, $16.95	Best of the Best from **VIRGINIA** 320 pages, $16.95
Best of the Best from **FLORIDA** 288 pages, $16.95	Best of the Best from **MICHIGAN** 288 pages, $16.95	Best of the Best from **OHIO** 352 pages, $16.95	Best of the Best from **WASHINGTON** 288 pages, $16.95
Best of the Best from **GEORGIA** 336 pages, $16.95	Best of the Best from the **MID-ATLANTIC** 288 pages, $16.95	Best of the Best from **OKLAHOMA** 288 pages, $16.95	Best of the Best from **WEST VIRGINIA** 288 pages, $16.95
Best of the Best from the **GREAT PLAINS** 288 pages, $16.95	Best of the Best from **MINNESOTA** 288 pages, $16.95	Best of the Best from **OREGON** 288 pages, $16.95	Best of the Best from **WISCONSIN** 288 pages, $16.95
Best of the Best from **ILLINOIS** 288 pages, $16.95	Best of the Best from **MISSISSIPPI** 288 pages, $16.95	Best of the Best from **PENNSYLVANIA** 320 pages, $16.95	

Cookbooks listed above have been completed as of December 31, 2002. All cookbooks are ringbound except California, which is paperbound. Note: Great Plains consists of North Dakota, South Dakota, Nebraska, and Kansas; Mid-Atlantic includes Maryland, Delaware, New Jersey, and Washington, D.C.; New England is comprised of Rhode Island, Connecticut, Massachusetts, Vermont, New Hampshire, and Maine.

Special discount offers available!

(See previous page for details.)

To order by credit card, call toll-free **1-800-343-1583** or visit our website at **www.quailridge.com** to order online. Use the form below to send check or money order.

- -

Order form

Use this form for sending check or money order to:
QUAIL RIDGE PRESS • P. O. Box 123 • Brandon, MS 39043

❏ Check enclosed

Charge to: ❏ Visa ❏ MC ❏ AmEx ❏ Disc

Card # _____

Expiration Date _____

Signature _____

Name _____

Address _____

City/State/Zip _____

Phone # _____

Email Address _____

Qty.	Title of Book (State) or Set	Total

Subtotal _____

7% Tax for MS residents _____

Postage ($4.00 any number of books) + 4.00

Total _____